# Commentaries and C
# Business Organizatio

*2005-2006 Supplement*

2005-2006 Supplement

# Commentaries and Cases on the Law of Business Organization

**William T. Allen**
*Jack Nusbaum Professor of Law & Business*
*New York University*
*Of Counsel, Wachtell, Lipton, Rosen and Katz*

*and*

**Reinier Kraakman**
*Ezra Ripley Thayer Professor of Law*
*Harvard Law School*

111 Eighth Avenue, New York, NY 10011
www.aspenpublishers.com

© 2005 Aspen Publishers, Inc.
a Wolters Kluwer business
*www.aspenpublishers.com*

>   Aspen Publishers
>   Attn: Permissions Department
>   111 Eighth Avenue, 7th Floor
>   New York, NY 10011-5201

Printed in the United States of America

2 3 4 5 6 7 8 9 0

ISBN 0-7355-5934-1

**Library of Congress Cataloging-in-Publication Data**

Allen, William T.
 Commentaries and cases on the law of business organization / William T. Allen,
Reinier Kraakman.
  p. cm.
 Includes bibliographical references and index.
 ISBN 0-7355-3384-9 (casebook)
 ISBN 0-7355-5934-1 (supplement)
  1. Corporation law — United States — Cases.  2. Business enterprises — Law
and legislation — United States — Cases.  I. Kraakman, Reinier H.  II. Title.
KF1413.A435  2003
346.73'065 — dc21

                                                    2002034496

# About Aspen Publishers

Aspen Publishers, headquartered in New York City, is a leading information provider for attorneys, business professionals, and law students. Written by preeminent authorities, our products consist of analytical and practical information covering both U.S. and international topics. We publish in the full range of formats, including updated manuals, books, periodicals, CDs, and online products.

Our proprietary content is complemented by 2,500 legal databases, containing over 11 million documents, available through our Loislaw division. Aspen Publishers also offers a wide range of topical legal and business databases linked to Loislaw's primary material. Our mission is to provide accurate, timely, and authoritative content in easily accessible formats, supported by unmatched customer care.

To order any Aspen Publishers title, go to *www.aspenpublishers.com* or call 1-800-638-8437.

To reinstate your manual update service, call 1-800-638-8437.

For more information on Loislaw products, go to *www.loislaw.com* or call 1-800-364-2512.

For Customer Care issues, e-mail *CustomerCare@aspenpublishers.com*; call 1-800-234-1660; or fax 1-800-901-9075.

### Aspen Publishers
#### a Wolters Kluwer business

# Contents

**Chapter 3: The Problems of Joint Ownership: The Law of Partnership**                                1

3.5. Termination (Dissolution and Disassociation)                         1
    3.5.1. Accounting for Partnership's Financial Status and
    Performance                                                          1
        Note on Restated Income                                    1


**Chapter 5: Debt, Equity, and Economic Value**                            3

5.3. Estimating the Firm's Cost of Capital                                 3
    5.3.2. Estimating the Firm's Cost of Equity                         3
        Note on *In re Emerging Communications,*
        *Inc. Shareholders Litigation*                             3


**Chapter 7: Normal Governance: The Voting System**                        5

7.9. The Federal Proxy Rules                                               5
    7.9.2. Rule 14a-8: Shareholder Proposals                            5
        Note on the Proposed Rule 14a-11, the
        "Shareholder Proxy Access Rule"                            5


**Chapter 8: Normal Governance: The Duty of Care**                         7

8.6. The Board's Duty to Monitor: Losses "Caused"
by Board Passivity                                                         7
        In the Matter of Michael Marchese                          7
        Note on *Beam v. Martha Stewart*                          12
        BEAM v. MARTHA STEWART                                    12


**Chapter 9: Conflict Transactions: The Duty of Loyalty**                 17

9.4. Director and Management Compensation                                 17
    9.4.2. Option Grants and the Law of Director and
    Officer Compensation                                              17

Excessive Compensation and Further
Erosion in the Business Judgment Rule?        17
IN RE THE WALT DISNEY COMPANY
DERIVATIVE LITIGATION                         18
Questions on *Disney*                          28
Note on the Formal Structure of Director
Liability for Inattention                     28
Note: A Duty of Good Faith and
Section 102(b)(7)                              29
Prefatory Note on Disney Post-Trial Opinion    31
Background Note                               32
IN RE WALT DISNEY COMPANY
DERIVATIVE LITIGATION (2005)                  33
9.5. Corporate Opportunity Doctrine                   74
9.5.1.  Determining Which Opportunities
"Belong" to the Corporation                   74
IN RE EBAY, INC. SHAREHOLDERS
LITIGATION                                    74
BEAM v. MARTHA STEWART                         78
Note on Presenting Possible Corporate
Opportunities to the Board of Directors        82


**Chapter 10:  Shareholder Lawsuits**                               **83**

10.1. Distinguishing Between Direct and Derivative Claims    83
Note on *Tooley v. Donaldson, Lufkin &*
*Jenrette, Inc.*                               83
10.4. Balancing the Rights of Boards to Manage the
Corporation and Shareholders' Rights to Obtain
Judicial Review                               84
10.4.2.  Special Litigation Committees         84
IN RE ORACLE CORP. DERIVATIVE
LITIGATION                                    84
More on Independent Directors                 100
BEAM v. MARTHA STEWART                         100


**Chapter 12:  Fundamental Transactions**                           **109**

12.8. The Appraisal Remedy                                  109
12.8.4.  The Nature of "Fair Value"           109
Note on *In re Emerging Communications,*
*Inc., Shareholders Litigation*               109

12.10. Controlling Shareholder Fiduciary Duty on the First Step
of a Two-Step Tender Offer                                                        109
  12.10.3. Special Committees of Independent Directors in
    Controlled Mergers                                                              109
      IN RE EMERGING COMMUNICATIONS,
      INC. SHAREHOLDERS LITIGATION                           110
      A Further Note on the Delaware Law of
      Going-private Mergers                                               125
      IN RE COX COMMUNICATIONS, INC.,
      SHAREHOLDER LITIGATION                                       126
      Questions                                                                        130
      Note: More on Going-private Mergers                          130


**Chapter 13: Public Contests for Corporate Control**                **141**

13.1. Introduction                                                                       141
      Note on the European Union Takeover
      Directive                                                                           141
13.5. Pulling Together *Unocal* and *Revlon*                                142
      Note: Developments in Lock-Ups and
      Fiduciary Outs                                                                 142
      OMNICARE, INC. v. NCS
      HEALTHCARE, INC.                                                         142
      Questions                                                                        164
13.7. Proxy Contests for Corporate Control                                166
  13.7.2. Manipulation of the Proxy Contest                           166
      IN RE THE MONY GROUP INC.
      SHAREHOLDER LITIGATION                                       166
13.8. The Takeover Arms Race Continues                                176
  13.8.2. Mandatory Pill Redemption Bylaws                        176
      Note on *Hollinger Int'l, Inc.*                                        176
      Questions                                                                        177
      Further Note on *Hollinger International*                     178

# Commentaries and Cases on the Law of Business Organization

*2005-2006 Supplement*

# Chapter 3
# The Problems of Joint Ownership: The Law of Partnership

## 3.5 Termination (Dissolution and Disassociation)

### 3.5.1 Accounting for Partnership's Financial Status and Performance

*§3.5.1, page 62: Insert the following material before the questions:*

**NOTE ON RESTATED INCOME**

**PRESS RELEASE 9/10/03**

NEW YORK.

Pleading "innocent oversight," the partners of Washington Square Pharmacia admitted today that the financial statements of the partnership, in the words of New York Attorney General Eliot Spitzer, "don't add-up." Spitzer who has zealously sought to purge the financial markets of misrepresentation and manipulation claimed today that "[n]o level of funny business is too small to provide a safe harbor against vigilant law enforcement."

Restated financial statements were issued by Washington Square today shortly after more than one astute student noticed that the net profit stated for the firm, whose financial statements were used as model for a soon-to-be widely used law school text book on the law of business organization, was massively overstated.

"I guess we were rushing a bit at the end," lamented William Allen. "We neglected to closely review the income statement. But honest, we had almost no *scienter*, and I very much doubt that the contra can be proven by a preponderance of the evidence." Professor Reinier Kraakman could not be reached for comment, but a spokesperson directed all questions to Allen.

As a result of neglecting to deduct the total of all Administrative Expenses from the firm's Gross Profits, the firm Income Statement identified Net Profit as $254,000 rather than the correct number $67,550. The corrected Income Statement then mandated a correction of the partners' capital account — there was a lot less profit to add in. Once the Capital account was corrected, it showed less retained capital, and thus the Balance Sheet at the end of the period had to be restated also. (It was made to balance by adjusting the value of real estate.) Three class action lawsuits were filed by students by the end of the day.

The corrected financial statements of Washington Square Pharmacia follow. Allen who issued the corrected statements today said, "Well I am more of a conceptual thinker, really. Yeah, that's the ticket."

| Washington Square Pharmacia *Restated* Income Statement As of December 31, 2002 | |
| --- | --- |
| Gross Sales | $632,550 |
| Cost of Goods Sold | 311,000 |
| GROSS PROFIT | 321,550 |
| General Administrative Expense | |
| Advertising | 48,000 |
| Mortgage (or rent) | 38,000 |
| Salaries | 168,000 |
| Total General and Administrative Expense | 254,000 |
| **NET PROFIT** | **$67,550** |

| | Opening Balance 1/1/02 | Income FY 2002 | Withdrawals FY 2002 | Closing Balance 12/3/02 |
| --- | --- | --- | --- | --- |
| Allen | $140,000 | $22,517 | $64,666 | $97,851 |
| Kraakman | 140,000 | 22,517 | 74,666 | 87,851 |
| Feelgood | 30,000 | 22,517 | 64,266 (11,749) | |

Washington Square Pharmacia *Restated* Capital Account As of December 31, 2002

| Assets | Liabilities | | |
| --- | --- | --- | --- |
| Cash | $ 5,400 | Accounts Payable | $ 74,000 |
| Accts Receivable | 76,000 | Notes Payable | 136,000 |
| Inventory | 189,000 | Mortgage Note | 350,000 |
| | | | $560,000 |
| Real Estate | 463,553 | Partners Capital | $173,953 |
| **TOTAL ASSETS** | $733,953 | **TOTAL LIABILITIES & CAPITAL** | $733,953 |

Washington Square Pharmacia *Restated* Balance Sheet As of December 31, 2002

# Chapter 5
## Debt, Equity, and Economic Value

### 5.3 Estimating the Firm's Cost of Capital

#### 5.3.2 Estimating the Firm's Cost of Equity

*§5.3.2, page 126: Insert* In re Emerging Communications, Inc., Shareholder Litigation, infra, *at the end of the section:*

### NOTE ON *IN RE EMERGING COMMUNICATIONS, INC. SHAREHOLDERS LITIGATION*

*In re Emerging Communications, Inc. Shareholders Litigation* is an appraisal and freeze-out merger case with a particularly clear valuation discussion that addresses the problems of estimating the corporation's costs of debt and equity.

# Chapter 7

# Normal Governance: The Voting System

## 7.9 The Federal Proxy Rules

### 7.9.2 Rule 14a-8: Shareholder Proposals

*§7.9.2, page 225: Insert the following material before the heading* Corporate Social Responsibilities:

## NOTE ON THE PROPOSED RULE 14A-11, THE "SHAREHOLDER PROXY ACCESS RULE"

In a release entitled "Security Holder Director Nominations," issued in October 2003, the SEC proposed a new Rule 14a-11, which would allow long-term shareholders the power to place their own nominees on a public company's proxy materials under certain limited circumstances. As currently drafted, the Proposed Rule would permit a 5 percent or more shareholder or group of shareholders who have held their stock for at least two years to nominate one, two, or three directors[1] upon the occurrence of one of two triggering circumstances. One trigger is a withhold vote of 35 percent or more for a director nominee on the board's slate during the prior year. The second trigger is passage of a shareholder resolution during the prior year requesting shareholder resolutions, proposed by a shareholder or group of shareholders holding 1 percent or more of the company's stock.

This so-called Shareholder Access Rule has elicited more comment letters than any other in the recent history of the SEC. If newspaper articles are to be believed, the Commission is extremely unlikely to adopt it as a final rule in its current form, and may not adopt it in any form.

Nevertheless, the fierce controversy generated by the Proposed Rule is worth considering. On the one hand, opponents of the Rule argue that it is likely to shift a dangerous amount of power into the hands of institutional shareholders and other institutions that do not necessarily have the best interests of the corporation at heart. Union pension funds, public pension funds with political agendas, and

---

1. According to whether the company board had less than nine, between nine and twenty, or more than twenty directors, respectively.

Institutional Shareholder Services — a for-profit company that advises institutional shareholders on voting policy — are frequently mentioned as institutions with questionable motives that would gain in influence if the Rule were adopted. On the other hand, proponents of the Rule maintain that no shareholder directors can be elected without a majority shareholder vote and that shareholder nominees could only survive the arduous triggering conditions, year-long wait, and subsequent shareholder vote if corporate performance were truly terrible and in strong need of shareholder intervention. Certainly, the Proposed Rule appears only mildly reformist from the standpoint of foreign jurisdictions, such as the U.K., where corporate law has traditionally accorded shareholders a much stronger legal role in the governance of the company.

So which is it? Is the Proposed Rule a dangerous break with board-centric U.S. corporate law that risks a raft of new intrashareholder intra-agency problems? Or is the Proposed Rule a much-needed boost to the ability of shareholders to shake up boards of poorly performing companies? Or, lastly, is the Proposed Rule neither of these, but instead a largely symbolic affirmation of the role of shareholders in corporate governance, with little effect on actual practice or on the real balance of power between the shareholders and the board?

# Chapter 8
# Normal Governance: The Duty of Care

## 8.6 The Board's Duty to Monitor: Losses "Caused" by Board Passivity

*§8.6, Page 271: Insert the following material:*

As a practical matter, state corporate law is not the only legal source of a director's duty of care. Securities law and the SEC also impose negligence-based duties on directors in a variety of contexts. *In the Matter of Michael Marchese*, below, is an especially aggressive assertion of a breach in an outside director's duty to monitor a firm's financial statements. Query whether this case triggers the concerns articulated in *Gagliardi*. The conventional wisdom has it that in the present regulatory environment, outside directors are at least as concerned about SEC enforcement actions as they are about shareholder suits under state law.

### IN THE MATTER OF MICHAEL MARCHESE
Release Nos. 34-47732; AAER-1764;
Administrative Proceeding File No. 3-11092
(April 24, 2003)

ORDER INSTITUTING CEASE-AND-DESIST PROCEEDINGS PURSUANT TO SECTION 21C OF THE SECURITIES EXCHANGE ACT OF 1934, MAKING FINDINGS AND IMPOSING A CEASE-AND-DESIST ORDER

The Securities and Exchange Commission ("Commission") deems it appropriate that cease-and-desist proceedings be, and hereby are, instituted pursuant to Section 21C of the Securities Exchange Act of 1934 ("Exchange Act") against Michael Marchese ("Marchese")("Respondent").

In anticipation of the institution of these proceedings, the Respondent has submitted an Offer of Settlement (the "Offer") which the Commission has determined to accept....

On the basis of this Order and the Respondent's Offer of Settlement, the Commission finds that:

*Michael Marchese,* 52, of Trumbull, Connecticut, was a director of Chancellor Corporation ("Chancellor") from December 1996 to June 1999. He has had no affiliation with Chancellor since 1999 and currently works as a bank loan officer.

*Chancellor Corp.* (File No. 0-11663), incorporated in Massachusetts, maintained its principal place of business in Boston, Massachusetts. From 1983 to 2001, Chancellor's common stock was registered with the Commission pursuant to Section 12(b) of the Exchange Act. On March 9, 2001, Chancellor filed a Form 15 terminating its Commission registration because it had fewer than 300 shareholders....

BACKGROUND

Respondent Marchese became an outside director of Chancellor in December 1996. He was an acquaintance of Brian Adley, who was Chancellor's controlling shareholder, chairman and chief executive officer. Chancellor reported in public filings that Marchese was a member of the company's audit committee from 1996 to May 1999. Marchese never reviewed Chancellor's accounting procedures or internal controls. He generally deferred to Adley when board action was required.

1.  CHANCELLOR PREMATURELY CONSOLIDATED AN
    ACQUIRED SUBSIDIARY'S REVENUE

On August 10, 1998, Chancellor entered into a letter of intent to acquire MRB, a seller of used trucks. A final closing took place on January 29, 1999. When preparing its financial reports for 1998, Chancellor improperly designated August 1, 1998, as the MRB acquisition date for accounting purposes. Chancellor designated that date based on its claim that a preexisting written agreement between Chancellor and MRB gave Chancellor effective control of MRB's operations as of August 1, 1998. When Chancellor's auditors began the audit of Chancellor's year-end 1998 financial statements, they reviewed the agreement and informed Chancellor's management that it did not give Chancellor sufficient control of MRB during 1998 to justify consolidating the two companies' financial statements for accounting purposes. The auditors sent a memorandum to Adley and Marchese in February 1999 setting forth their position that GAAP required a 1999 consolidation date.

During February 1999, Adley directed Chancellor's acting CFO to create and backdate to August 1998 a purported amended management agreement with MRB to provide additional support to justify an August 1, 1998 acquisition date for accounting purposes. This document, however, did not cause the auditors to change their position with respect to the correct acquisition date.

On February 25, 1999, Adley dismissed Chancellor's auditors. Adley did not identify the difference of opinion about the accounting date for the MRB acquisition as a reason for the dismissal. As a director, Respondent Marchese approved the decision to dismiss Chancellor's auditors. He was aware of the disagreement between Chancellor's management and the auditors regarding the appropriate MRB acquisition date for accounting purposes. He knew that the disagreement formed part of the reason for the auditors' dismissal.

After dismissing its prior auditors, Chancellor engaged Metcalf, Rice, Fricke and Davis (now BKR Metcalf Davis)("Metcalf Davis") to conduct the independent audit of its 1998 financial statements. Respondent Marchese approved the engagement. During spring 1999, in connection with the Metcalf Davis audit, Chancellor's CEO Adley caused Chancellor's president and acting CFO to fabricate documents in order to support the 1998 acquisition date. The fabricated documents included letters and memoranda designed to demonstrate Chancellor's control of MRB during 1998. These documents were provided to Metcalf Davis.

In April 1999, after conducting its audit, Metcalf Davis personnel met with Marchese, another outside director, and Chancellor's top management. In the meeting, Metcalf Davis indicated that it would provide an unqualified audit report for Chancellor's 1998 year-end financial statements. For accounting purposes, Metcalf Davis approved an August 1998 acquisition date for MRB.

Marchese knew that Chancellor's prior auditors had disagreed with Chancellor's management and had stated that a 1998 acquisition date did not comport with GAAP. Marchese, however, made no inquiry into the reasons for Metcalf Davis's contrary view. Nor did he determine whether there was any factual support for the 1998 acquisition date.

### 2. CHANCELLOR IMPROPERLY RECORDED A $3.3 MILLION FEE

In connection with Chancellor's acquisition of MRB, Adley caused Chancellor to record $3.3 million in fees to Vestex Capital Corporation ("Vestex"), a private entity he owned. The fees were purportedly for consulting services including identifying, negotiating and closing the MRB acquisition. In fact, no significant consulting services were rendered to Chancellor by Vestex in connection with the acquisition. In order to substantiate the fees to Vestex, Adley directed Chancellor personnel to fabricate numerous documents and provide them to Metcalf Davis while the firm was conducting its audit of Chancellor's 1998 financial results. In addition, at Adley's direction, Chancellor recorded as an asset on its balance sheet the $3.3 million in unsupported Vestex fees rather than recording them as an expense on its income statement. This was inconsistent with GAAP, which provides that costs payable to an outside consultant in business combinations may be capitalized only if the consultant has no affiliation with the companies involved in the acquisition.

The year before, in connection with the preparation of Chancellor's year-end results for 1997, Chancellor's auditors had required the company to write off $1.14 million in related party payments to Adley-controlled entities because there was no substantiation for the payments. Although Marchese knew of the

1997 write-off of payments to Adley's entities, he took no steps to determine whether the $3.3 million MRB acquisition fee to Vestex recorded in 1998 was substantiated. He did not ask Metcalf Davis or Adley any questions about related party transactions.

### 3.   MARCHESE SIGNED A MISLEADING FORM 10-KSB FILED BY CHANCELLOR

On April 16, 1999, Chancellor filed a Form 10-KSB for the year ended December 31, 1998. Adley, Chancellor's president, Chancellor's controller, Marchese and another outside director signed the Form 10-KSB. The Form 10-KSB was materially misleading in several respects.

First, in the financial statements included in its 1998 Form 10-KSB, Chancellor accounted for its acquisition of MRB as of August 1, 1998, and consolidated its financial results with those of MRB. As a result, Chancellor reported annual revenues of $29,639,000, 177% higher than the $10,708,000 revenue figure for Chancellor without the MRB consolidation. It also reported assets of $29,569,000 rather than $8,186,000 (261% higher). The accounting treatment did not comply with GAAP because during 1998 Chancellor did not have the effective control of MRB needed to justify accounting for MRB's acquisition.

Chancellor's Form 10-KSB also falsely represented that Adley's Vestex entity had handled the acquisition of MRB and provided consulting, financing and other services in connection with the acquisition, earning a fee payable of $3.3 million. The fee, for which no significant services in fact had been rendered, was improperly capitalized rather than reported as an expense. As a result, Chancellor reported net income of $850,000 rather than the $2.45 million loss which would have been reported had the fee been expensed, and its assets were overstated by 12%.

Marchese did not seek re-election as a director in 1999. He ceased to be a director of Chancellor on June 25, 1999. In August 1999, Marchese wrote a letter to the Commission staff expressing concern about Chancellor's financial reporting.

## D.   VIOLATIONS

### 1.   MARCHESE VIOLATED AND CAUSED CHANCELLOR'S VIOLATION OF SECTION 10(B) OF THE EXCHANGE ACT AND RULE 10B-5 THEREUNDER

Marchese violated and caused Chancellor's violation of Section 10(b) of the Exchange Act and Rule 10b-5 thereunder when he signed Chancellor's 1998 Form 10-KSB. He was reckless in not knowing that it contained materially misleading statements. Marchese knew that the Form 10-KSB reflected a 1998 MRB acquisition date. He also knew that Chancellor's original audit firm had been fired, with his approval, due in part to its disagreement with the 1998 date.

Nevertheless, he recklessly failed to make any inquiry into the circumstances leading to the new audit firm's approval of a 1998 MRB acquisition date, or whether it was correct. In addition, Marchese knew that in the previous year Chancellor had written off $1.14 million in related-party fees to Adley entities. However, he recklessly failed to make any inquiry into the basis for the reported $3.3 million in fees payable to an entity owned by Chancellor's CEO which were included in Chancellor's 1998 Firm [*sic*] 10-KSB. Marchese failed to make any inquiry into the existence of documents substantiating the services for which the fees were purportedly due.

2.  MARCHESE CAUSED CHANCELLOR'S VIOLATIONS OF SECTIONS 13(A), 13(B)(2)(A) AND 13(B)(2)(B) OF THE EXCHANGE ACT AND RULES 12B-20 AND 13A-1 THEREUNDER

Marchese caused Chancellor's violations of Sections 13(a), 13(b)(2)(A) and 13(b)(2)(B) of the Exchange Act and Rules 12b-20 and 13a-1 thereunder. Section 13(a) of the Exchange Act and Rule 13a-1 require issuers of registered securities to file annual reports with the Commission. The information provided in those reports must be accurate. ...

Section 13(b)(2)(A) of the Exchange Act requires every reporting company to make and keep books, records and accounts that accurately and fairly reflect the issuer's transactions. Section 13(b)(2)(B) requires a company to devise and maintain a system of internal controls sufficient to provide reasonable assurances that transactions are recorded as necessary to permit the preparation of financial statements in conformity with GAAP. These provisions require an issuer to employ and supervise reliable personnel, to maintain reasonable assurances that transactions are executed as authorized and to properly record transactions on an issuer's books. *SEC v. World-Wide Coin Investments, Ltd.*, 567 F. Supp. 724, 750 (N.D.Ga. 1983). A violation of Section 13(b)(2)(A) or 13(b)(2)(B) does not require a showing of scienter. *Id.* at 751.

Marchese's conduct caused Chancellor's violations of Sections 13(a) and 13(b)(2)(A) and Rules 12b-20 and 13a-1. He was reckless in not knowing that Chancellor's Form 10-KSB for 1998 contained materially misleading statements. Further, he signed Chancellor's Form 10-KSB for 1998 without making any inquiry into the basis for the reported fees payable to Adley's company or the basis for the new audit firm's approval of a 1998 MRB acquisition date.

Marchese also caused Chancellor's violations of Section 13(b)(2)(B) of the Exchange Act. He never attempted to determine the reason for Chancellor's varying accounting treatments of the MRB acquisition and related fees to Vestex, and whether these demonstrated a lack of internal controls to ensure accurate financial reporting and prevent improper transfers to related parties. Marchese never reviewed Chancellor's accounting procedures or determined whether in fact there were any internal controls. ...

ACCORDINGLY, IT IS ORDERED:

Pursuant to Section 21C of the Exchange Act, that Respondent Marchese shall cease and desist from committing or causing any violations and any future violations of Section 10(b) of the Exchange Act and Rule 10b-5 promulgated thereunder, and from causing any violations and any future violations of Sections 13(a), 13(b)(2)(A) and 13(B)(2)(B) of the Exchange Act and Rules 12b-20 and 13a-1 promulgated thereunder.

By the Commission.
Jonathan G. Katz
Secretary

§8.6, page 281: Insert the following material after *Carmark*:

## NOTE ON *BEAM v. MARTHA STEWART*

The value of Martha Stewart Omnimedia, Inc. was and is largely tied up in the skill, energy, and public acceptance of the image of its founder and former CEO, Martha Stewart. In one of the most highly publicized trials of recent times, Ms. Stewart was tried and convicted for matters arising out of certain trading of the stock of another corporation, ImClone Systems, Inc. Announcement of Martha's indictment caused the stock of her company to take a severe beating, since the market was concerned that her image as the master homemaker would suffer a severe blemish that would affect the business. The business itself also suffered declines in sales.

Were these losses somehow the responsibility of the Omnimedia board? Given Martha's extraordinary business importance to the welfare of the firm, should the board have taken steps to protect against this sort of risk? Should Ms. Stewart herself be held to have violated a fiduciary duty in engaging in behavior that ultimately caused large stock value losses to the public shareholders of the corporation?

The Delaware Court of Chancery deals with this issue on a motion to dismiss a derivative suit brought by an Omnimedia shareholder in the following excerpt.

## BEAM v. MARTHA STEWART
### 833 A.2d 961 (Del. Ch. 2003)

CHANDLER, Chancellor

Monica A. Beam, a shareholder of Martha Stewart Living Omnimedia, Inc. ("MSO"), brings this derivative action against the defendants, all current directors and a former director of MSO, and against MSO as a nominal defendant. The defendants have filed three separate motions seeking (1) to dismiss Counts II, III, and IV under Court of Chancery Rule 12(b)(6) for failure to state claims upon which relief may be granted; (2) to dismiss the amended complaint under Court of Chancery Rule 23.1 for failure to comply with the demand requirement and for failure adequately to plead demand excusal; or alternatively (3) to stay this action in favor of litigation currently pending in the U.S. District Court for the Southern District of New York. This is the Court's ruling on these motions.

Plaintiff Monica A. Beam is a shareholder of MSO and has been since August 2001. Derivative plaintiff and nominal defendant MSO is a Delaware corporation that operates in the publishing, television, merchandising, and internet industries marketing products bearing the "Martha Stewart" brand name.

Defendant Martha Stewart ("Stewart") is a director of the company and its founder, chairman, chief executive officer, and by far its majority shareholder. MSO's common stock is comprised of Class A and Class B shares. Class A shares are traded on the New York Stock Exchange and are entitled to cast one vote per share on matters voted upon by common stockholders. Class B shares are not publicly traded and are entitled to cast ten votes per share on all matters voted upon by common stockholders. Stewart owns or beneficially holds 100% of the B shares in conjunction with a sufficient number of A shares that she controls roughly 94.4% of the shareholder vote. Stewart, a former stockbroker, has in the past twenty years become a household icon, known for her advice and expertise on virtually all aspects of cooking, decorating, entertaining, and household affairs generally....

The plaintiff seeks relief in relation to three distinct types of activities. The first involves the well-publicized matters surrounding Stewart's alleged improper trading of shares of ImClone Systems, Inc. ("ImClone") and her public statements in the wake of those allegations. The second relates to the private sale of sizeable blocks of MSO stock by both Stewart and Doerr in early 2002. The third challenges the board's decisions with regard to the provision of "split-dollar" insurance for Stewart.

A. STEWART'S IMCLONE TRADING

The market for MSO products is uniquely tied to the personal image and reputation of its founder, Stewart. MSO retains "an exclusive, worldwide, perpetual royalty-free license to use [Stewart's] name, likeness, image, voice and signature for its products and services." In its initial public offering prospectus, MSO recognized that impairment of Stewart's services to the company, including the tarnishing of her public reputation, would have a material adverse effect on its business. The prospectus distinguished Stewart's importance to MSO's business success from that of other executives of the company noting that, "Martha Stewart remains the personification of our brands as well as our senior executive and primary creative force." In fact, under the terms of her employment agreement, Stewart may be terminated for gross misconduct or felony conviction that results in harm to MSO's business or reputation but is permitted discretion over the management of her personal, financial, and legal affairs to the extent that Stewart's management of her own life does not compromise her ability to serve the company.

Stewart's alleged misadventures with ImClone arise in part out of a longstanding personal friendship with Samuel D. Waksal ("Waksal"). Waksal is the former chief executive officer of ImClone as well as a former suiitor [*sic*] of Stewart's daughter. . . . The speculative value of ImClone stock was tied quite directly to the likely success of its application for FDA approval to market the cancer treatment drug Erbitux. On December 26, Waksal received information that the FDA was rejecting the application to market Erbitux. The following day, December 27, he tried to sell his own shares and tipped his father and daughter to do the same. Stewart also sold her shares on December 27. . . . After the close of trading on December 28, ImClone publicly announced the rejection of its application to market Erbitux. The following day the trading price closed slightly more than 20% lower than the closing price on the date that Stewart had sold her shares. By mid-2002, this convergence of events had attracted the interest of the *New York Times* and other news agencies, federal prosecutors, and a committee of the United States House of Representatives. Stewart's publicized attempts to quell any suspicion were ineffective at best because they were undermined by additional information as it came to light and by the other parties' accounts of the events. Ultimately Stewart's prompt efforts to turn away unwanted media and investigative attention failed. Stewart eventually had to discontinue her regular guest appearances on CBS' *The Early Show* because of questioning during the show about her sale of ImClone shares. After barely two months of such adverse publicity, MSO's stock price had declined by slightly more than 65%. In August 2002, James Follo, MSO's chief financial officer, cited uncertainty stemming from the investigation of Stewart in response to questions about earnings prospects in the future. . . .

## A. MOTIONS TO DISMISS COUNTS II, III, AND IV — COURT OF CHANCERY RULE 12(B)(6)

In ruling on a motion to dismiss under Rule 12(b)(6), the Court considers only the allegations in the amended complaint, and any documents incorporated by reference therein. . . .

### 1. COUNT II — FAILURE TO MONITOR STEWART'S PERSONAL ACTIVITIES

Count II of the amended complaint alleges that the director defendants and defendant Patrick breached their fiduciary duties by failing to ensure that Stewart would not conduct her personal, financial, and legal affairs in a manner that would harm the Company, its intellectual property, or its business.

The "duty to monitor" has been litigated in other circumstances, generally where directors were alleged to have been negligent in monitoring the activities of the corporation, activities that led to corporate liability. Plaintiff's allegation, however, that the Board has a duty to monitor the personal affairs of an officer or director is quite novel. That the Company is "closely identified" with Stewart is conceded, but it does not necessarily follow that the Board is required to monitor, much less control, the way Stewart handles her *personal* financial and legal affairs.

In *Graham v. Allis-Chalmers Manufacturing Co.*, the Delaware Supreme Court held that "absent cause for suspicion there is no duty upon the directors to install and operate a corporate system of espionage to ferret out wrongdoing which they have no reason to suspect exists." Despite this statement's implication that a duty to monitor may arise when the board has reason to suspect wrongdoing, it does not burden MSO's Board with a duty to monitor Stewart's *personal* affairs.

First, plaintiff does not allege facts that would give MSO's Board any reason to monitor Stewart's activities before mid-2002 when the allegations regarding her divestment of ImClone stock became public. Second, the quoted statement from *Graham* refers to wrongdoing *by the corporation*. Regardless of Stewart's importance to MSO, she is not the corporation. And it is unreasonable to impose a duty upon the Board to monitor Stewart's personal affairs because such a requirement is neither legitimate nor feasible. Monitoring Stewart by, for example, hiring a private detective to monitor her behavior is more likely to generate liability *to* Stewart under some tort theory than to protect the Company from a decline in its stock price as a result of harm to Stewart's public image.

Even if I accept that the board knew that Stewart's personal actions could result in harm to MSO, it seems patently unreasonable to expect the Board, as an exercise of its supervision *of the Company*, to preemptively thwart a personal call from Stewart to her stockbroker or to fully control her handling of the media attention that followed as a result of her *personal* actions, especially where her statements touched on matters that could subject Stewart to criminal charges. Plaintiff has not cited any case to support this new "duty" to monitor personal affairs. Since the defendant directors had no duty to monitor Stewart's personal actions, plaintiff's allegation that the directors breached their duty ... by failing to monitor Stewart because they were "beholden" to her is irrelevant. Count II is dismissed for failure to state a claim.

# Chapter 9
# Conflict Transactions: The Duty of Loyalty

## 9.4 Director and Management Compensation

### 9.4.2 Option Grants and the Law of Director and Officer Compensation

*§9.4.2, page 325: Add the following material at the end of the section:*

#### EXCESSIVE COMPENSATION AND FURTHER EROSION IN THE BUSINESS JUDGMENT RULE?

No doctrine has been more deeply embedded in American corporation law than that of the business judgment rule. Reduced to its simplest terms, this rule has said to courts "no second guessing board decisions where there is no financial conflict of interest." The benefits of this rule are substantial. But as we have seen in the note to *Smith v. Van Gorkom, supra,* by the mid-1980s, as the hostile takeover movement got rolling, the Delaware Supreme Court began to grow impatient with the extreme deference that the traditional business judgment rule prescribed. In its 1984 *Van Gorkom* decision, that court began the process of crafting a new, less deferential approach to judicial review of corporate transactions that constitute a change in corporate control. (The story is reviewed in the chapters on merger and acquisition transactions). This more intrusive standard of review, however, remained confined to these large and important changes in control transactions. With respect to other, more ordinary board decisions, courts continued to respect the policy reflected in the business judgment rule. As the *Voglestein* excerpt suggests, this remained true of actions attacking board compensation decisions.

In the aftermath of the collapse of the Enron Corporation and the resulting public focus on perceived deficiencies in corporate controls, the judicial urge to correct perceived governance excesses became irresistible. Few areas of corporate governance had drawn more attention during the booming '90s than executive compensation. Therefore, it is perhaps not surprising that the next area of corporate governance to witness erosion of the business judgment rule was executive compensation. The case in which this development burst forth arose from astonishing facts involving a payment of compensation valued at approximately $140 million to Michael Ovitz upon his termination by the Walt Disney Company after a bit more than one year of service. The shareholder suit brought on behalf of the corporation itself claimed, among other things that such a payment constituted a waste (that is, a benefit to the corporation that no reasonable person could conclude represented a fair trade). First time around, the Court of Chancery dismissed the complaint on the ground that the board was made up of a majority of independent directors who had no interest in the transaction. The business judgment rule holds that the business judgment of such a board should not be subject to judicial second-guessing.

On appeal, the Supreme Court of Delaware reversed in part and directed that plaintiff be given an opportunity to replead. *Brehm v. Eisner*, 746 A.2d 244 (Del 2000). When reviewing the re-pleaded complaint on remand, the Chancellor sustained the complaint in the following opinion.

### IN RE THE WALT DISNEY COMPANY DERIVATIVE LITIGATION
Court of Chancery of the State of Delaware
May 28, 2003

*MEMORANDUM OPINION*

CHANDLER, Chancellor.

In this derivative action . . . plaintiffs allege that the defendant directors breached their fiduciary duties when they blindly approved an employment agreement with defendant Michael Ovitz and then, again without any review or deliberation, ignored defendant Michael Eisner's dealings with Ovitz regarding his non-fault termination. Plaintiffs seek rescission and/or money damages from defendants and Ovitz, or compensation for damages allegedly sustained by Disney and disgorgement of Ovitz's unjust enrichment.

The matter is now before the Court [on a motion to dismiss the complaint]. . . .

A.  THE DECISION TO HIRE OVITZ

Michael Eisner is the chief executive officer ("CEO") of the Walt Disney Company. In 1994, Eisner's second-in-command, Frank Wells, died in a helicopter crash. Two other key executives — Jeffrey Katzenberg and Richard Frank — left Disney shortly thereafter, allegedly because of Eisner's management style. Eisner began looking for a new president for Disney and chose Michael Ovitz. Ovitz was founder and head of CAA, a talent agency; he had never been an executive for a publicly owned entertainment company. He had, however, been Eisner's close friend for over twenty-five years.

Eisner decided unilaterally to hire Ovitz. On August 13, 1995, he informed three Old Board members, Stephen Bollenbach, Sanford Litvack, and Irwin

Russell (Eisner's personal attorney), of that fact. All three protested. . . . Nevertheless, Eisner persisted, sending Ovitz a letter on August 14, 1995, that set forth certain material terms of his prospective employment. Before this, neither the Old Board nor the compensation committee had ever discussed hiring Ovitz as president of Disney. No discussions or presentations were made to the compensation committee or to the Old Board regarding Ovitz's hiring as president of Walt Disney until September 26, 1995.

Before informing Bollenbach, Litvack, and Russell on August 13, 1995, Eisner collected information on his own, through his position as the Disney CEO, on the potential hiring of Ovitz. In an internal document created around July 7, 1995, concerns were raised about the number of stock options to be granted to Ovitz. The document warned that the number was far beyond the normal standards of both Disney and corporate America and would receive significant public criticism. Additionally, Graef Crystal, an executive compensation expert, informed board member Russell, via a letter dated August 12, 1995, that, generally speaking, a large signing bonus is hazardous because the full cost is borne immediately and completely even if the executive fails to serve the full term of employment. Neither of these documents, however, were submitted to either the compensation committee or the Old Board before hiring Ovitz. Disney prepared a draft employment agreement on September 23, 1995. A copy of the draft was sent to Ovitz's lawyers, but was not provided to members of the compensation committee.

The compensation committee, consisting of defendants Ignacio Lozano, Jr., Sidney Poitier, Russell, and Raymond Watson, met on September 26, 1995, for just under an hour. Three subjects were discussed at the meeting, one of which was Ovitz's employment. According to the minutes, the committee spent the least amount of time during the meeting discussing Ovitz's hiring. In fact, it appears that more time was spent on discussions of paying $250,000 to Russell for his role in securing Ovitz's employment than was actually spent on discussions of Ovitz's employment. . . . All that occurred during the meeting regarding Ovitz's employment was that Russell reviewed the employment terms with the committee and answered a few questions. Immediately thereafter, the committee adopted a resolution of approval.

No copy of the September 23, 1995 draft employment agreement was actually given to the committee. Instead, the committee members received, at the meeting itself, a rough summary of the agreement. The summary, however, was incomplete. It stated that Ovitz was to receive options to purchase five million shares of stock, but did not state the exercise price. The committee also did not receive any of the materials already produced by Disney regarding Ovitz's possible employment. No spreadsheet or similar type of analytical document showing the potential payout to Ovitz throughout the contract, or the possible cost of his severance package upon a non-fault termination, was created or presented. Nor did the committee request or receive any information as to how the draft agreement compared with similar agreements throughout the entertainment industry, or information regarding other similarly situated executives in the same industry.

The committee also lacked the benefit of an expert to guide them through the process. Graef Crystal, an executive compensation expert, had been hired to provide advice to Disney on Eisner's new employment contract. Even though he had earlier told Russell that large signing bonuses, generally speaking, can be hazardous, neither he nor any other expert had been retained to assist Disney regarding Ovitz's hiring. Thus, no presentations, spreadsheets, written analyses, or opinions were given by any expert for the compensation committee to rely upon in reaching its decision. . . .

The compensation committee was informed that further negotiations would occur and that the stock option grant would be delayed until the final contract was worked out. The committee approved the general terms and conditions of the employment agreement, but did not condition their approval on being able to review the final agreement. Instead, the committee granted Eisner the authority to approve the final terms and conditions of the contract as long as they were within the framework of the draft agreement.

Immediately after the compensation committee met on September 26, the Old Board met. Again, no expert was present to advise the board. Nor were any documents produced to the board for it to review before the meeting regarding the Ovitz contract. The board did not ask for additional information to be collected or presented regarding Ovitz's hiring. According to the minutes, the compensation committee did not make any recommendation or report to the board concerning its resolution to hire Ovitz. Nor did Russell, who allegedly secured Ovitz's employment, make a presentation to the board. The minutes of the meeting were fifteen pages long, but only a page and a half covered Ovitz's possible employment. . . . According to the minutes, the Old Board did not ask any questions about the details of Ovitz's salary, stock options, or possible termination. The Old Board also did not consider the consequences of a termination, or the various payout scenarios that existed. Nevertheless, at that same meeting, the Old Board decided to appoint Ovitz president of Disney. Final negotiation of the employment agreement was left to Eisner, Ovitz's close friend for over twenty-five years.

## B. NEGOTIATION OF THE EMPLOYMENT AGREEMENT

Ovitz was officially hired on October 1, 1995, and began serving as Disney's president, although he did not yet have an executed employment agreement with Disney. . . .

Negotiations continued among Ovitz, Eisner, and their attorneys. The lawyers circulated drafts on October 3, October 10, October 16, October 20, October 23, and December 12, 1995. The employment agreement was physically executed . . . on December 12, 1995. [It] however, was backdated to October 1, 1995, the day Ovitz began working as Disney's president. Additionally, the stock option agreement associated with the employment agreement was executed by Eisner (for Disney) on April 2, 1996. Ovitz did not countersign the stock option agreement until November 15, 1996, when he was already discussing his plans to leave Disney's employ. Neither the Old Board nor the compensation committee reviewed or approved the final employment agreement before it was executed and made binding upon Disney.

## C. THE FINAL VERSION OF OVITZ'S EMPLOYMENT AGREEMENT

The final version of Ovitz's employment agreement differed significantly from the drafts summarized to the compensation committee on September 26, 1995, and October 16, 1995. First, the final version caused Ovitz's stock options to be "in the money" when granted. The September 23rd draft agreement set the exercise price at the stock price on October 2, 1995, the day after Ovitz began as president. On October 16, 1995, the compensation committee agreed to change the exercise price to the price on that date (October 16, 1995), a price similar to that on October 2nd. The agreement was not signed until December 12, 1995, however, at which point the value of Disney stock had increased by eight percent-from $56.875 per share on October 16th to $61.50 per share on December 12th. The overall stock market, according to the Dow Jones Industrial Average, had also increased by about eight percent at the same time. By waiting to sign the agreement until December, but not changing the date of the exercise price, Ovitz had stock options that instantly were "in the money." This allowed Ovitz to play a "win-win" game at Disney's expense — if the market price of Disney stock had fallen between October 16 and December 12, Ovitz could have demanded a downward adjustment to the option exercise price; if the price had risen (as in fact it had) Ovitz would receive "in the money" options.

Another difference in the final version of Ovitz's employment agreement concerned the circumstances surrounding a non-fault termination. The September 23rd draft agreement stated that non-fault termination benefits would only be provided if Disney wrongfully terminated Ovitz, or Ovitz died or became disabled. The October 16th draft contained a very similar definition. These were the only two drafts of which the compensation committee was made aware. The final version of the agreement, however, offered Ovitz a non-fault termination as long as Ovitz did not act with gross negligence or malfeasance. Therefore, instead of protecting Ovitz from a wrongful termination by Disney, Ovitz was able to receive the full benefits of a non-fault termination, even if he acted negligently or was unable to perform his duties, as long as his behavior did not reach the level of gross negligence or malfeasance. Additionally, a non-compete clause was not included within the agreement should Ovitz leave Disney's employ.

The employment agreement had a term of five years. Ovitz was to receive a salary of $1 million per year, a potential bonus each year from $0 to $10 million, and a series of stock options (the "A" options) that enabled Ovitz to purchase three million shares of Disney stock at the October 16, 1995 exercise price. The options were to vest at one million per year for three years beginning September 30, 1998. At the end of the contract term, if Disney entered into a new contract with Ovitz, he was entitled to the "B" options, an additional two million shares. There was no requirement, however, that Disney enter into a new contract with Ovitz.

Should a non-fault termination occur, however, the terms of the final version of the employment agreement appeared to be even more generous. Under a non-fault termination, Ovitz was to receive his salary for the remainder of the contract, discounted at a risk-free rate keyed to Disney's borrowing costs. He was also to receive a $7.5 million bonus for each year remaining on his contract, discounted at the same risk-free rate, even though no set bonus amount was guaranteed in the contract. Additionally, all of his "A" stock options were to vest immediately, instead of waiting for the final three years of his contract for them to vest. The final benefit of the non-fault termination was a lump sum "termination payment" of $10 million. The termination payment was equal to the payment Ovitz would receive should he complete his full five-year term with Disney, but not receive an offer for a new contract. Graef Crystal opined in the January 13, 1997, edition of California Law Business that "the contract was most valuable to Ovitz the sooner he left Disney."

### D.  OVITZ'S PERFORMANCE AS DISNEY'S PRESIDENT

Ovitz began serving as president of Disney on October 1, 1995, and became a Disney director in January 1996. Ovitz's tenure as Disney's president proved unsuccessful. Ovitz was not a good second-in-command, and he and Eisner were both aware of that fact. Eisner told defendant Watson, via memorandum, that he (Eisner) "had made an error in judgment in who I brought into the company." Other company executives were reported in the December 14, 1996 edition of the *New York Times* as saying that Ovitz had an excessively lavish office, an imperious management style, and had started a feud with NBC during his tenure. Even Ovitz admitted, during a September 30, 1996 interview on "Larry King Live," that he knew "about 1% of what I need to know." Even though admitting that he did not know his job, Ovitz studiously avoided attempts to be educated. Eisner instructed Ovitz to meet weekly with Disney's chief financial officer, defendant Bollenbach. The meetings were scheduled to occur each Monday at 2 p.m., but every week Ovitz cancelled at the last minute. . . .

### E.  THE NON-FAULT TERMINATION

Ovitz wanted to leave Disney, but could only terminate his employment if one of three events occurred: (1) he was not elected or retained as president and a director of Disney; (2) he was assigned duties materially inconsistent with his role as president; or (3) Disney reduced his annual salary or failed to grant his stock options, pay him discretionary bonuses, or make any required compensation payment. None of these three events occurred. [Thus, i]f Ovitz resigned outright, he might have been liable to Disney for damages and would not have received the benefits of the non-fault termination. He also desired to protect his reputation when exiting from his position with Disney. Eisner agreed to help Ovitz depart Disney without sacrificing any of his benefits. Eisner and Ovitz worked together as close personal friends to have Ovitz receive a non-fault termination. Eisner stated in a letter to Ovitz that: "I agree with you that we must work together to assure a smooth transition and deal with the public relations brilliantly. I am committed to make this a win-win situation, to keep our friendship intact, to be positive, to say and write only glowing things.... Nobody ever needs to know anything other than positive things from either of us. This can all work out!"

Eisner, Litvack, and Ovitz met at Eisner's apartment on December 11, 1996, to finalize Ovitz's non-fault termination. The new complaint alleges that the New Board was aware that Eisner was negotiating with Ovitz the terms of his separation. Litvack sent a letter to Ovitz on December 12, 1996, stating that, by "mutual agreement," (1) Ovitz's term of employment would end on January 31, 1997; and (2) "this letter will for all purposes of the Employment Agreement be given the same effect as though there had been a 'Non-Fault Termination,' and the Company will pay you, on or before February 5, 1997, all amounts due you under the Employment Agreement, including those under Section 11(c) thereof. In addition, the stock options granted pursuant to Option A, will vest as of January 31, 1997 and will expire in accordance with their terms on September 30, 2002." On December 12, 1996, Ovitz's departure from Disney became public. Neither the New Board of Directors nor the compensation committee had been consulted or given their approval for a non-fault termination. In addition, no record exists of any action by the New Board once the non-fault termination became public on December 12, 1996.

On December 27, 1996, Litvack sent Ovitz a new letter superseding the December 12th letter. The December 27th letter stated that Ovitz's termination would "be treated as a 'Non-Fault Termination.' " This differed from the December 12th letter, which treated Ovitz's termination "as though there had been a 'Non-Fault Termination.' " It also made the termination of Ovitz's employment and his resignation as a Disney director effective as of the close of business on December 27th, instead of on January 31, 1997, as in the December 12th letter. Additionally, it listed the amount payable to Ovitz as $38,888,230.77, and stated that the "A" options to purchase three million shares of Disney [v]ested on December 27th, instead of January 31, 1997, as in the December 12th letter. Both Eisner and Litvack signed the letter. Again, however, neither the New Board nor the compensation committee reviewed or approved the December 27th letter. No record exists of any New Board action after the December 27th letter became public, nor had any board member raised any questions or concerns since the original December 12th letter became public.

According to the new complaint, Disney's bylaws required board approval for Ovitz's non-fault termination. Eisner and Litvack allegedly did not have the authority to provide for a non-fault termination without board consent. No documents or board minutes currently exist showing an affirmative decision by the

New Board or any of its committees to grant Ovitz a non-fault termination. The New Board was already aware that Eisner was granting the non-fault termination as of December 12, 1996, the day it became public. No record of any action by the New Board affirming or questioning that decision by Eisner either before or after that date has been produced. There are also no records showing that alternatives to a non-fault termination were ever evaluated by the New Board or by any of its committees. . . .

## III. ANALYSIS

The primary issue before the Court is whether plaintiffs' new complaint survives the Rule 23.1 motion to dismiss. . . . In order [to do so the court must conclude that in the circumstances there was no need for the shareholder to make demand on the board itself to bring the suit. That is] . . . plaintiff must allege particularized facts that raise doubt about whether the challenged transaction is entitled to the protection of the business judgment rule. Plaintiffs may rebut the presumption that the board's decision is entitled to deference by raising a reason to doubt whether the board's action was taken on an informed basis or whether the directors honestly and in good faith believed that the action was in the best interests of the corporation. Thus, plaintiffs must plead particularized facts sufficient to raise (1) a reason to doubt that the action was taken honestly and in good faith or (2) a reason to doubt that the board was adequately informed in making the decision.

Defendants contend that the new complaint cannot be read reasonably to allege any fiduciary duty violation other than, at most, a breach of the directors' duty of due care. They further assert that even if the complaint states a breach of the directors' duty of care, Disney's charter provision, based on 8 Del. C. §102(b)(7), would apply and the individual directors would be protected from personal damages liability for any breach of their duty of care. A §102(b)(7) provision in a corporation's charter does not "eliminate or limit the liability of a director: (i) [f]or any breach of the director's duty of loyalty to the corporation or its stockholders; (ii) for acts or omissions not in good faith or which involve intentional misconduct or a knowing violation of the law; (iii) under §174 of this title; or (iv) for any transaction from which the director derived an improper personal benefit." A fair reading of the new complaint, in my opinion, gives rise to a reason to doubt whether the board's actions were taken honestly and in good faith, as required under the second prong of *Aronson*. Since acts or omissions not undertaken honestly and in good faith, or which involve intentional misconduct, do not fall within the protective ambit of §102(b)(7), I cannot dismiss the complaint based on the exculpatory Disney charter provision [citing *Malpiede v. Townson*, 780 A.2d 1075, 1094 (Del. 2001) (holding that, as a matter of law, §102(b)(7) bars a claim only if there is an unambiguous, residual due care claim and nothing else)].

Defendants also argue that Ovitz's employment agreement was a reasonable exercise of business judgment. They argue that Ovitz's previous position as head of CAA required a large compensation package to entice him to become Disney's president. As to the non-fault termination, defendants contend that that decision was reasonable in that the board wished to avoid protracted litigation with Ovitz. The Court is appropriately hesitant to second-guess the business judgment of a disinterested and independent board of directors. As alleged in the new complaint, however, the facts belie any assertion that the New or Old Boards exercised any business judgment or made any good faith attempt to fulfill the fiduciary duties they owed to Disney and its shareholders.

## A. THE OLD AND NEW BOARDS

According to the new complaint, Eisner unilaterally made the decision to hire Ovitz, even in the face of internal documents warning of potential adverse publicity and with three members of the board of directors initially objecting to the hiring when Eisner first broached the idea in August 1995. No draft employment agreements were presented to the compensation committee or to the Disney board for review before the September 26, 1995 meetings. The compensation committee met for less than an hour on September 26, 1995, and spent most of its time on two other topics, including the compensation of director Russell for helping secure Ovitz's employment. With respect to the employment agreement itself, the committee received only a summary of its terms and conditions. No questions were asked about the employment agreement. No time was taken to review the documents for approval. Instead, the committee approved the hiring of Ovitz and directed Eisner, Ovitz's close friend, to carry out the negotiations with regard to certain still unresolved and significant details. The allegation that Eisner and Ovitz had been close friends for over twenty-five years is not mentioned to show self-interest or domination. Instead, the allegation is mentioned because it casts doubt on the good faith and judgment behind the Old and New Boards' decisions to allow two close personal friends to control the payment of shareholders' money to Ovitz.

The Old Board met immediately after the committee did. Less than one and one-half pages of the fifteen pages of Old Board minutes were devoted to discussions of Ovitz's hiring as Disney's new president.... No presentations were made to the Old Board regarding the terms of the draft agreement. No questions were raised, at least so far as the minutes reflect. At the end of the meeting, the Old Board authorized Ovitz's hiring as Disney's president. No further review or approval of the employment agreement occurred. Throughout both meetings, no expert consultant was present to advise the compensation committee or the Old Board. Notably, the Old Board approved Ovitz's hiring even though the employment agreement was still a "work in progress." The Old Board simply passed off the details to Ovitz and his good friend, Eisner.

Negotiation over the remaining terms took place solely between Eisner, Ovitz, and attorneys representing Disney and Ovitz. The compensation committee met briefly in October to review the negotiations, but failed again to actually consider a draft of the agreement or to establish any guidelines to be used in the negotiations. The committee was apparently not otherwise involved in the negotiations....

Eisner and Ovitz reached a final agreement on December 12, 1995. They agreed to backdate the agreement, however, to October 1, 1995 [when Ovitz had actually commenced his services as President]. The final employment agreement also differed substantially from the original draft, but evidently no further committee or board review of it ever occurred. The final version of Ovitz's employment agreement was signed (according to the new complaint) without any board input beyond the limited discussion on September 26, 1995.

From the outset, Ovitz performed poorly as Disney's president. In short order, Ovitz wanted out, and, once again, his good friend Eisner came to the rescue, agreeing to Ovitz's request for a non-fault termination. Disney's board, however, was allegedly never consulted in this process. No board committee was ever consulted, nor were any experts consulted. Eisner and Litvack alone granted Ovitz's non-fault termination, which became public on December 12, 1996. Again, Disney's board did not appear to question this action, although affirmative board action seemed to be required. On December 27, 1996, Eisner and Litvack, without explanation, accelerated the effective date of the non-fault termination, from January 31, 1997, to December 27, 1996. Again, the board apparently took no action; no questions were asked as to why this was done.

Disney had lost several key executives in the months before Ovitz was hired. Moreover, the position of president is obviously important in a publicly owned corporation. But the Old Board and the compensation committee (it is alleged) each spent less than an hour reviewing Ovitz's possible hiring. According to the new complaint, neither the Old Board nor the compensation committee reviewed the actual draft employment agreement. Nor did they evaluate the details of Ovitz's salary or his severance provisions. No expert presented the board with details of the agreement, outlined the pros and cons of either the salary or non-fault termination provisions, or analyzed comparable industry standards for such agreements. Notwithstanding this alleged information vacuum, the Old Board and the compensation committee approved Ovitz's hiring, appointed Eisner to negotiate with Ovitz directly in drafting the unresolved terms of his employment, never asked to review the final terms, and were never voluntarily provided those terms.

During the negotiation over the unresolved terms, the compensation committee was involved only once, at the very early stages in October 1995. The final agreement varied significantly from the draft agreement in the areas of both stock options and the terms of the non-fault termination. Neither the compensation committee nor the Old Board sought to review, nor did they review, the final agreement. In addition, both the Old Board and the committee failed to meet in order to evaluate the final agreement before it became binding on Disney....

The new complaint, fairly read, also charges the New Board with a similar ostrich-like approach regarding Ovitz's non-fault termination. Eisner and Litvack granted Ovitz a non-fault termination on December 12, 1996, and the news became public that day. Although formal board approval appeared necessary for a non-fault termination, the new complaint alleges that no New Board member even asked for a meeting to discuss Eisner's and Litvack's decision. On December 27, 1996, when Eisner and Litvack accelerated Ovitz's non-fault termination by over a month, with a payout of more than $38 million in cash, together with the three million "A" stock options, the board again failed to do anything. Instead, it appears from the new complaint that the New Board played no role in Eisner's agreement to award Ovitz more than $38 million in cash and the three million "A" stock options, all for leaving a job that Ovitz had allegedly proven incapable of performing.

The New Board apparently never sought to negotiate with Ovitz regarding his departure. Nor, apparently, did it consider whether to seek a termination based on fault. During the fifteen-day period between announcement of Ovitz's termination and its effective date, the New Board allegedly chose to remain invisible in the process. The new complaint alleges that the New Board: (1) failed to ask why it had not been informed; (2) failed to inquire about the conditions and terms of the agreement; and (3) failed even to attempt to stop or delay the termination until more information could be collected. If the board had taken the time or effort to review these or other options, perhaps with the assistance of expert legal advisors, the business judgment rule might well protect its decision. In this case, however, the new complaint asserts that the New Board directors refused to explore any alternatives, and refused to even attempt to evaluate the implications of the non-fault termination — blindly allowing Eisner to hand over to his personal friend, Ovitz, more than $38 million in cash and the three million "A" stock options [allegedly worth over $140 million].

These facts, if true, do more than portray directors who, in a negligent or grossly negligent manner, merely failed to inform themselves or to deliberate adequately about an issue of material importance to their corporation. Instead, the facts alleged in the new complaint suggest that the defendant directors consciously and intentionally disregarded their responsibilities, adopting a "we don't care about the risks" attitude concerning a material corporate decision. Knowing or deliberate indifference by a director to his or her duty to act faithfully and with appropriate care is conduct, in my opinion, that may not have been taken honestly and in good faith to advance the best interests of the company. Put differently, all of the alleged facts, if true, imply that the defendant directors knew that they were making material decisions without adequate information and without adequate deliberation, and that they simply did not care if the decisions caused the corporation and its stockholders to suffer injury or loss. Viewed in this light, plaintiffs' new complaint sufficiently alleges a breach of the directors' obligation to act honestly and in good faith in the corporation's best interests for a Court to conclude, if the facts are true, that the defendant directors' conduct fell outside the protection of the business judgment rule.

Where a director consciously ignores his or her duties to the corporation, thereby causing economic injury to its stockholders, the director's actions are either "not in good faith" or "involve intentional misconduct" [citing Section 102(b)(7)(ii)]. Thus, plaintiffs' allegations support claims that fall outside the liability waiver provided under Disney's certificate of incorporation.

## IV.   CONCLUSION

It is of course true that after-the-fact litigation is a most imperfect device to evaluate corporate business decisions, as the limits of human competence necessarily impede judicial review. But our corporation law's theoretical justification for disregarding honest errors simply does not apply to intentional misconduct or to egregious process failures that implicate the foundational directoral obligation to act honestly and in good faith to advance corporate interests. Because the facts alleged here, if true, portray directors consciously indifferent to a material issue facing the corporation, the law must be strong enough to intervene against abuse of trust. Accordingly, all three of plaintiffs' claims for relief concerning fiduciary duty breaches and waste survive defendants' motions to dismiss.

## QUESTIONS ON *DISNEY*

1. What is the analytical significance of the alleged fact that there were material changes made to the Ovitz employment contract by management after the Board meeting of October 16? While these changes were material to the contract, would you regard them as material to Disney's business?

2. Relatedly, would you say it is poor corporate governance practice, when dealing with a senior executive contract of this sort, for the board to grant to the CEO "the authority to approve final terms and conditions as long as they are within the framework of the draft agreement that the board had approved"? According to the opinion, what factors, if any, make this an atypical situation for the board?

3. The court seems impressed that Michael Eisner agreed "to help Ovitz depart Disney without sacrificing any of his benefits." Beyond this pledge, what additional facts would you want to know to pass a judgment on whether Eisner was violating his duty in so acting?

4. What outcome might you expect as this case proceeds to trial? Why?

## NOTE ON THE FORMAL STRUCTURE OF DIRECTOR LIABILITY FOR INATTENTION

Post-*Disney*, the following formal structure of director liability for inattention apparently exists under Delaware law. First, mere director negligence — lacking that degree of attention that a reasonable person in the same or similar situation would be expected to pay to a decision — will not give rise to liability. In this circumstance, the business judgment rule will operate to foreclose liability (and generally permit dismissal at the motion to dismiss phase of the litigation). See *Gagliardi* and *American Express*, supra. Second, facts that establish gross negligence, however, may (as in *Smith v. Van Gorkom*) be the basis for a breach of duty finding and result in liability for any losses that result. However, under Section 102(b)(7), such liability for gross negligence alone can be waived (and in most public companies has been waived) through a shareholder-approved amendment to the corporate charter. Third, such waivers however *may not* waive liability that rests in part upon breach of the duty of loyalty and, under the statutory language, that inability to waive damages is extended to acts (or omissions) not done in "good faith." Therefore, there is conceptually a third level of inattention — we could call abandonment of office as some old cases did — in which a director's inattention is so profound that the court concluded that the directors lacked "good faith." In this event — this extreme level of inattention neither the business judgment rule nor the waiver authorized by §102(b)(7) will protect the defendant from liability.

This structure may be criticized as being overly developed and perhaps incoherent. What is the line between gross negligence, liability for which the legislature permits shareholder waiver and inattention so profound as to constitute lack of good faith that may not be waived? More importantly, what is the social advantage in attempting to draw such a line?

## NOTE: A DUTY OF GOOD FAITH AND SECTION 102(B)(7)

The Court of Chancery's doctrinal reliance on an alleged violation of a directorial duty of good faith in *Disney* caused some understandable, but perhaps exaggerated, commotion among corporate lawyers and corporate directors. What *is* this duty they want to know? Where does it come from? And more important, how can directors be sure they are doing whatever it is that it requires, so that they may feel secure in their hard-earned property?

For about twenty years there has been talk in Delaware Supreme Court cases about a "triad" of directorial duties: care, loyalty, and good faith. Once this "triad" formulation crept into the jurisprudence it was repeated without real explication. Interestingly, the Chancery judges in their explanations for the grounds of their decisions tended to speak about duties of loyalty and care, not a triad of duties. Yet many Chancery opinions referred to the directors' duty to act in good faith. Indeed it was two Chancery cases — *Caremark* and *Gagliardi* — that were cited by Chancellor Chandler in *Disney* as support for the existence of a duty of good faith. But generally the Chancery cases did not create a conceptual structure in which a duty of good faith existed independently of care and loyalty. The Supreme Court of Delaware, however, has referred to good faith as if it were an independent duty.

How are we to understand the conceptual structure of directors' duties? That is how do these three terms — care, loyalty, and good faith — relate to each other, and, operationally, what, if anything, does recognition of the obligation of good faith add to the conventional conception of appropriate director conduct.

In some ways, the most basic duty of every fiduciary may be said to be the duty to exercise good faith in an effort to understand and to satisfy the obligations of the office. The obligations of the office will vary depending on the purposes for which the institution was created. A trustee of an express trust may have a high responsibility to attempt to preserve capital, for example, while a director of a business corporation must exercise due care both to preserve assets and monitor the acceptance of risk in the informed hope of capital appreciation. But while the specifics required of the fiduciary may vary, depending on the institution and the circumstances, the generalities of the duties can be stated. All fiduciary offices will require the fiduciary to avoid unfair self-dealing and to exercise power for the purpose of the institution and not for the fiduciary's personal benefit. And all will require reasonable attention to the role. Thus, the predicate duty of good faith may be seen as simply a higher level of abstraction of the fiduciary obligations of care and loyalty. So for example, the director Mrs. Pritchard may be said to have violated her duty of care and attention by not attending meetings of the corporation's board and by not otherwise taking any steps to monitor her sons' fraudulent activities. But she could just as easily have been said to violate her duty of good faith, since she did not even try to do her job. Indeed, although the Disney directors were not as out of it as Mrs. Pritchard seems to have been, of the cases often read in introductory law school courses on director liabilities, her case may be closest to theirs. But if Mrs Pritchard violated her duty of care, we do not need to recur to any obligation of good faith to impress liability upon her. Why do we need this concept for the Disney directors?

The answer comes from some unfortunately broad statutory drafting in §102(b)(7) of the Delaware statute, which is quoted by the court in *Disney*. So here we see the problem: §102(b)(7) was enacted in 1985 following the surprising result in *Smith v. VanGorkom*. It provides that a corporate charter may waive director liability to the corporation for damages except for, among other things, damages in connection with a breach of loyalty (here the lawyers drafting this statute were apparently thinking of loyalty in a narrow financial conflict sense) and for acts or omissions "not in good faith." Under most conceptions of loyalty, acts not in good faith would constitute a breach of loyalty, so at best this exception seems to create a redundancy. But as *Disney* shows it does more than that.

After the *Disney* case (and before it for thoughtful corporate lawyers), one cannot offer to directors the broad assurance that §102(b)(7) presumably intended. *Disney* establishes that there can be a level of director neglect or inattention that might lead a court to find that the directors were not seriously trying to meet their duty, in which event the protection of the charter amendment authorized by §102(b)(7) may not offer protection. One cannot say very much at present concerning what constitutes that level of inattention. Certainly, as a general matter, allowing the CEO to negotiate the terms of the employment (and termination) of his second-in-command subject to rather general board oversight and review does not itself, or in general, seem like an abandonment of board responsibilities. The spectacular amounts involved in the Ovitz matter of course provide strong coloration in that instance.

But the more basic question of policy is what is the sensible justification for permitting shareholders to waive in the charter damages for director "gross negligence," but not permit waiver of even grosser negligence (by which we mean conduct such as in Disney where a court is willing to say that the Board was not sufficiently trying at all)?

In fact, one might take the view that what should be excepted from the waiver authorized by §102(b)(7) are only (i) breaches of loyalty, including any act authorized for an inappropriate purpose or for which a director received an improper personal benefit, (ii) knowingly illegal acts, or (iii) for distributions that violate §174. In other words §102(b)(7) should be amended to give it the effect that it was thought to have created. Liability for bad judgments where no financial conflict is involved or for losses caused by a failure to prevent conduct that causes a loss — should be waivable ex ante by the shareholders.

What arguments can you imagine in support of and in opposition to such a proposed amendment to §102(b)(7)?

## PREFATORY NOTE ON DISNEY POST-TRIAL OPINION

The shareholders' suit against the Walt Disney Company board of directors arising out of the decision to hire and then, barely more than a year later, to fire Michael Ovitz as Disney's number two executive came to trial in 2004. Recall that the complaint had alleged that the Disney board had been grossly inattentive with respect to both the hiring of Mr. Ovitz (i.e. the terms of the contract of employment) and his firing (i.e. the board did not know or care that the company had grounds to fire Ovitz for cause and thus avoid the almost 140 million dollar termination payment that the contract contemplated). The Disney corporate charter contains a provision of the type authorized by Section 102(b)(7) of the Delaware corporate code. Thus, the corporation had waived the right to collect damages from directors that might proximately arise from director inattention not accompanied by self-dealing or other acts not in good faith. Doctrinally, what was interesting in the case was the assertion that the extent of the board's inattention in this instance was such that it could not be said that the board had exercised "good faith" in either of the two actions challenged.

In its earlier opinion on the matter the Court had held — as a matter of pleading alone — that something more than mere negligence had been alleged; it held that, if the facts alleged were true they would constitute "deliberate disregard of the interests of the corporation." This, it was said, would not be merely negligence or violation of duty of care, but a breach of the duty to exercise good faith — not covered by 102(b)(7) or the business judgment rule.

The trial consumed 37 days of testimony. On August 9, 2005, Chancellor William Chandler issued a 174-page decision exhaustively reviewing the testimony and concluding that the plaintiffs bore the burden of proof on their claims against all defendants, including Mr. Ovitz, and that they had failed to carry that burden.

In addition to addressing the evidence in the case, the opinion offers some pertinent thoughts concerning corporate governance standards in our evolving world. The effect of the opinion will be to quiet to some extent the uncertainty concerning potential director liability created by what may be seen as the "good faith" brohaha. There has been something of a small industry in academic circles attempting to create from the earlier Disney opinions a significant new basis for director liability, or attempting, on the other hand, to interpret the attention paid to the use of the good faith term in the earlier opinions as not reflecting any movement away from the traditional solicitous attitude of the Delaware courts towards directors who are not financially interested or in cahoots with some one who is.

The opinion itself is extremely lengthy and the recitations to evidence in the case extensive. The opinion extract below eliminates from the text most footnotes in which the citation to the record evidence were placed largely by the Court. The factual findings of the opinion provide a fascinating look into the operations of a major American corporation. Also of interest in the opinion is the importance that the Court puts upon a distinction between compliance with fiduciary obligations and compliance with emerging "best practices of corporate governance." Finally, the Court contributes a useful and cogent discussion of the place of "good faith" in the panoply of fiduciary obligations.

## BACKGROUND NOTE

The Court begins the telling of the tale with the accidental death of Frank Wells in 1994. Wells had been the number two to Disney's CEO Michael Eisner for ten years and together the management team had been highly successful. There were no acceptable inside candidates for Wells' job and for a time Eisner assumed these duties. About a year later, Eisner had a health scare and the Board increased its concern that succession planning be addressed. Eisner and Ovitz, as two important and successful men in the Hollywood film and entertainment community, had known each other and been social friends for 25 years. Eisner had previously made overtures to Ovitz to join Disney's management team, without success. Ovitz had started a talent agency in 1974 with Ron Meyer and others called Creative Artists Agency (CAA). He represented many of the biggest stars in the business and was an effective negotiator. By the time he started negotiating a possible Disney position his annual income from CCA was $20 million.

MCA, another Hollywood firm that had started as a talent agency, had been acquired by Sony earlier and, in 1995, CAA was retained to advise Seagram, Inc. in connection with its proposed acquisition of 80 percent of MCA stock from

Sony. Edgar Brofman, Jr., the representative of Seagram's controlling share-holders, approached Ovitz during this period about leaving CAA and joining MCA as CEO, once Seagram acquired control. These negotiations ultimately foundered. Ovitz turned his attention back to CAA. Eisner had observed all of this from a distance and decided this was the time to approach Ovitz again. He was supported in this decision by Roy Disney and Sid Bass, two of Disney's largest individual shareholders. He asked Irwin Russell, a director, chair of the board's compensation committee, and a lawyer who had represented Eisner personally in the past, to lead the negotiations for Disney. Ovitz had his lawyer, Bob Goldman, negotiate for him.

## IN RE THE WALT DISNEY COMPANY DERIVATIVE LITIGATION
### Court of Chancery of the State of Delaware (2005)

\*　　　　\*　　　　\*　　　　\*

## I. Facts

### A. MICHAEL OVITZ JOINS THE WALT DISNEY COMPANY

\*　　　　\*　　　　\*　　　　\*

While Russell and Goldman were in the preliminary stages of negotiating the financial terms of Ovitz's contract, Eisner and Ovitz continued their talks as well. From these talks, Ovitz gathered that it was his skills and experience that would be brought to bear on Disney's current weaknesses, which he identified as poor talent relationships and stagnant foreign growth.... Ovitz wanted assurances from Eisner that Ovitz's vision was shared....Eisner was able to assuage Ovitz's concerns, because at some point during these negotiations, Ovitz came to the understanding that he and Eisner would run Disney as partners. Ovitz did recognize that Eisner was Chairman and would be his superior, but he believed that the two would work in unison in a relationship akin to the one that exists between senior and junior partners. As it would turn out, Ovitz was mistaken, for Eisner had a radically different perception of their respective roles at Disney.

### 4. Ovitz's Contract With Disney Begins to Take Form

By the beginning of August 1995, the non-contentious terms of Ovitz's employment agreement (the "OEA") were $1 million in annual salary and a performance-based, discretionary bonus. The remaining terms were not as easily agreed to and related primarily to stock options and Ovitz's insistence for down-side protection. Ovitz, using Eisner's contract as a yardstick, was asking for options on eight million shares of Disney's stock. Both Russell and Eisner, however, refused to offer eight million options and believed that no options should be offered within the first five years of Ovitz's contract.... Using both Eisner's and Wells' original employment contracts as a template, the parties reached a compromise.... Ovitz would receive a five-year contract with two tranches of options. The first tranche consisted of three million options vesting in equal parts in the third, fourth and fifth years, and if the value of those options at the end of the five years had not appreciated to $50 million, Disney would make up the difference. The second tranche consisted of two million options that would vest immediately [that is in 5 years] if Disney and Ovitz opted to renew the contract.

The proposed OEA [Original Employment Agreement] sought to protect both parties in the event that Ovitz's employment ended prematurely and provided that absent defined causes, neither party could terminate the agreement without penalty. If Ovitz, for example, walked away, for any reason other than those permitted under the OEA, he would forfeit any benefits remaining under the OEA and could be enjoined from working for a competitor. Likewise, if Disney fired Ovitz for any reason other than gross negligence or malfeasance, Ovitz would be entitled to a non-fault payment (Non-Fault Termination or "NFT"), which consisted of his remaining salary, $7.5 million a year for [term of the contract plus] any unaccrued bonuses, the immediate vesting of his first tranche of options and a $10 million cash out payment for the second tranche of options.

### 5. Crystal is Retained to Assist Russell and Watson in Evaluating the OEA

As the basic terms of the OEA were coming together, Russell authored and provided Eisner and Ovitz with a "Case Study" outlining the OEA parameters and Russell's commentary on what he believed was an extraordinary level of executive compensation. Specifically, Russell noted that it was appropriate to provide Ovitz with "downside protection and upside opportunity" and to assist Ovitz with "the adjustment in life style resulting from the lower level of cash compensation from a public company in contrast to the availability of cash distributions and perquisites from a privately held enterprise." According to Russell, Ovitz was an "exceptional corporate executive" who was a "highly successful and unique entrepreneur." Nevertheless, Russell cautioned that Ovitz's salary under the OEA was at the top level for any corporate officer and significantly above that of the CEO and that the number of stock options granted under the OEA was far beyond the standards applied within Disney and corporate America "and will raise very strong criticism." Russell rounded out his analysis by recommending an additional study so that he and Eisner could answer questions should they arise. Russell did not provide this Case Study to any other member of Disney's board of directors.

With the various financial terms of the OEA sufficiently concrete, Russell enlisted the aid of two people who could help with the final financial analysis: Raymond Watson, a current member of Disney's compensation committee and the past chairman of Disney's board of directors (and one of the men who designed the original pay structure behind Wells' and Eisner's compensation packages);[1] and Graef Crystal, an executive compensation consultant.... The three [met] on August 10.... Crystal prepared.... a comprehensive executive compensation database that would accept various inputs and run BlackScholes analyses to output a range of values for the options. At the meeting, the three men worked with various assumptions and manipulated inputs in order to generate a series of values that could be attributed to the OEA. In addition to Crystal's work, Watson had prepared several spreadsheets presenting similar assessments, but these spreadsheets did not use the Black-Scholes valuation method. At the end of the day, the men made their conclusions, discussed them, and agreed that Crystal would memorialize his findings and fax the report to Russell.

Two days later, Crystal faxed his memorandum to Russell. In the memo, Crystal concluded that the OEA would provide Ovitz with approximately $23.6 million per year for the first five years of the deal. Crystal estimated that the contract was worth $23.9 million a year, over a seven-year period, if Disney and Ovitz exercised the two-year renewal option. Crystal opined that those figures would approximate Ovitz's present compensation with CAA.... [In a slightly revised Aug. 12 memo] Crystal opined that the OEA, during the first five years, was, as he originally estimated, worth $23.6 million, but as to the value of the OEA's renewal option, Crystal revised his estimation and believed that the two additional years would increase the value of the entire OEA to $24.1 million per year. Up until this point, only three members of Disney's board of directors were in the know concerning the status of the negotiations with Ovitz or the particulars of the OEA — Eisner, Russell and Watson.

### 6. Ovitz Accepts Eisner's Offer

While Russell, Watson and Crystal were finalizing their analysis of the OEA, Eisner and Ovitz were coming to terms of their own. Eisner, having recently conferred with Russell concerning his ongoing research, gave Ovitz a take-it-or-leave-it offer: If Ovitz joined Disney as its new President, he would not assume the duties or title of COO.[2] After short deliberation, Ovitz accepted Eisner's terms, and that evening he, Eisner and Sid Bass (and their families) celebrated Ovitz's decision.

---

1. This was the first instance where a board member other than Russell or Eisner was brought into the Ovitz negotiation process.....

2. While vacationing together, Eisner told Ovitz that Sid Bass was flying into Aspen for dinner and that "either we're going to have a deal by the time he lands ... or we're not, ... [and] the deal will be gone." Ovitz was then given until 6:00 p.m. that night to concede on a number of issues; the two largest concessions were: 1) the reduction in the number of options from a single grant of five million to two separate grants, — the first grant being three million options for the first five years, and the second grant consisting of an additional two million options if the contract was renewed; and 2) Ovitz abandoning the idea of joining the Company as a Co-CEO. See Tr. 4196:10-4198:3.

As it would turn out, the celebratory mood was short lived. The next day, August 13, Eisner called a meeting at his home in Los Angeles to discuss his decision and, in addition to Ovitz and Russell, Sanford Litvack (Disney's General Counsel)[3] and Stephen Bollenbach (Disney's Chief Financial Officer) were invited to attend. At the meeting, Litvack and Bollenbach, who had just found out the day before that Eisner was negotiating with Ovitz, were not happy with the decision. Their discontent "officially" stemmed from the perception that Ovitz would disrupt the cohesion that existed between Eisner, Litvack and Bollenbach, and both Litvack and Bollenbach made it clear that they would not agree to report to Ovitz but would continue to report to Eisner. At trial, the Court was left with the perception that Litvack harbored resentment that he was not selected to be Disney's President and that this fueled, to some extent, Litvack's resistance to Ovitz assuming the post he coveted. Bollenbach's resistance was more curious. Indeed, Bollenbach had been hired before Ovitz and, at the time, his expectation was that he would report only to Eisner. Still, his testimony seemed disingenuous to the Court when he pinned his resistance on the fact that he had been part of a cohesive trio (*i.e.*, Bollenbach, Litvack, and Eisner). After all, Bollenbach had been with the Company for a total of three months before he was informed of the negotiations with Ovitz. Despite this mutiny, Eisner was able to assuage Ovitz's concern about his shrinking authority in the Company, and Ovitz, with his back against the wall, acceded to Litvack and Bollenbach's terms.

The next day, August 14, Ovitz and Eisner signed the letter agreement ("OLA").... The OLA ... was subject to approval of Disney's compensation committee[4] and board of directors. That same day, Russell contacted Sidney Poitier (for a second time) to inform him that Eisner and Ovitz reached an agreement.... Watson also contacted Ignacio "Nacho" Lozano by phone.... Lozano testified that he felt comfortable with Ovitz's ability to make the transition from a private company culture to that of a public company.... Eisner contacted each of [the other board members] by phone to inform them of the impending deal. During these calls, Eisner described his friendship with Ovitz, and Ovitz's background and qualifications.

On the same day that Eisner and Ovitz signed the OLA, the news of Ovitz's hiring was made public via a press release. Public reaction was extremely positive. Disney was applauded for the decision, and Disney's stock price increased 4.4 percent in a single day — increasing Disney's market capitalization by more than $1 billion.

---

3. Litvack was also Disney's Chief of Corporate Operations and Executive Vice President for Law and Human Resources.

4. The compensation committee was comprised of Russell, Watson, Ignacio Lozano and Sidney Poitier.

## 7.   Disney's Board of Directors Hires Michael Ovitz

Once the OLA was signed, [Disney in-house lawyer] Joseph Santaniello . . .
took charge of embodying the terms Russell and Goldman had agreed upon . . . .
Santaniello concluded that the $50 million guarantee presented negative tax
implications for the Company, as it might not have been deductible. Concluding
that the provision must be eliminated, Russell initiated discussions on how to
compensate Ovitz for this change — from this, an amalgamation of amendments
to certain terms of the OEA arose in order to replace the back-end guarantee.[5]
Russell again worked with Watson and Crystal to consider [this] . . . .[They]
applied the Black-Scholes methodology to assess the value of the extended exercisability features of the options and Watson generated his own analysis to the
same end.

On September 26, 1995, the compensation committee met *for one hour* to
consider (1) the proposed terms of the OEA, (2) the compensation packages
for various Disney employees, (3) 121 stock option grants, (4) Iger's CapCi-
ties/ABC employment agreement and (5) Russell's compensation for negotiating
the Ovitz deal. The discussion concerning the OEA focused on a term sheet (the
actual draft of the OEA was not distributed), from which Russell and Watson
outlined the process they had followed back in August and described Crystal's
analysis. Russell testified that the topics discussed were historical comparables
such as Eisner's and Wells' option grants, and the factors that he, Watson and
Crystal had considered in setting the size of the option grants and the termination
provisions of the contract. Watson testified that he provided the committee with
the spreadsheet analysis he had performed back in August and discussed his
findings. Crystal, however, did not attend the meeting and his work product
was not distributed to the Committee. At trial, Crystal testified that he was available via telephone to respond to questions if needed, but no one from the committee in fact called. After Russell's and Watson's presentations, Litvack
responded to various questions but the substance of those questions was not
recounted in any detail at trial.[6] Poitier and Lozano testified that they believed

---

5. *See id.* at 50:7-19; *see also* PTE 348 (Russell's letter to Eisner suggesting the elimination of the
$50 million guarantee and replacing it with: (1) the reduction in the option strike price from 115% to
100% of the Company's stock price on the day of the grant for the two million options that would
become exercisable in the sixth and seventh year after commencement of employment; (2) Payment of
$10 million in severance if the Company chose not to renew Ovitz's contract; and (3) alteration of the
renewal option to provide for a five year extension, $1.25 million per year in salary, the same bonus
structure as the first five years of the contract, and the grant of three million additional options).

6. Plaintiffs contend that since Litvack had no responsibility in the actual negotiations of the Ovitz
contract, the question session, which followed Russell's and Watson's presentations, and was memorialized in the committee minutes, could not have been of any substance. *See* Pls.' Post Trial Opening
Br. at 21. The Court does not agree with this contention. Litvack testified that he knew what the deal
was. *See* Litvack 384:18-385:4. He could therefore speak intelligently to questions from the committee. Whatever personal animosity Litvack harbored for Ovitz, not actually negotiating the deal did not
prevent him from answering the committee's questions with "substance."

they had received sufficient information from Russell's and Watson's presentations[7] to enable them to exercise their judgment in the best interest of the Company. When the discussions concluded, the Committee unanimously voted to approve the terms of the OEA subject to "reasonable further negotiations within the framework of the terms and conditions" described in the OEA.[8]

An executive meeting of Disney's board immediately followed ... [There the board was informed] of the reporting structure that Eisner and Ovitz agreed to, but no discussion of the discontent Litvack or Bollenbach expressed .... was recounted. Eisner led the discussion regarding Ovitz, and Watson then explained his analysis and both he and Russell responded to questions by the board. Upon resuming the regular session, the board deliberated further, then voted unanimously to elect Ovitz as President.

### 8. The October 16, 1995 Compensation Committee Meeting

In accordance with the compensation committee's resolution roughly three weeks before,[9] the compensation committee convened again on October 16, 1995, in a special meeting to discuss several issues relating to stock options. After a presentation by Litvack ... the compensation committee unanimously approved amendments to The Walt Disney Company 1990 Stock Incentive Plan ... .and also approved a new plan, known as The Walt Disney Company 1995 Stock Incentive Plan (the "1995 Plan"). Both plans were subject to further approval by the full board of directors and by shareholders.

Following approval of these plans, Litvack reviewed the terms of the proposed OEA with the compensation committee, after which the committee unanimously approved ... the award of Ovitz's options pursuant to the 1990 Plan. Ovitz's options were priced at market as of the date of the meeting. .....

---

7. Plaintiffs have demonstrated that at no point were the following matters discussed in the committee meeting: (1) the purchase of Ovitz's private jet for $187,000 over the appraised value; (2) the purchase of Ovitz's BMW at acquisition cost and not the depreciated market value; (3) the purchase of Ovitz's computers at replacement value instead of their lower book value; (4) any specific list of perquisites, despite Eisner already agreeing to provide Ovitz with numerous such benefits; and (5) that despite Ovitz's bonus being payable completely on a discretionary basis, Russell's memorandum to Ovitz indicating that the bonus would likely approximate $7.5 million annually. Although I have concluded that plaintiffs have established these facts, they are ultimately immaterial to my decision.

8. At the behest of Watson, the committee discussed the time and energy Russell had placed into the negotiations and suggested that the committee recommend to the full board that Russell be compensated $250,000. The compensation committee voted to recommend this fee and the full board, while in executive session, approved it. See PTE 39 at WD01171; PTE 29 at WD01195-96. Russell abstained from voting on the issue.

9. PTE 39 at WD01170 (mentioning that Ovitz's stock option grant would be delayed until further details were worked out between Ovitz and the Company), WD01186-88 (term sheet outlining vesting schedule, other special terms of Ovitz's options, and that Ovitz's options would be formally granted at a later date).

The amendment to the 1990 Plan (consistent with the provisions of the new 1995 Plan), together with the terms of the Stock Option Agreement, provided that, in the event of an NFT, Ovitz's options would be exercisable until the later of September 30, 2002, or twenty-four months after termination, but in no event later than October 16, 2005 (ten years from the date of grant).

### B. OVITZ'S PERFORMANCE AS PRESIDENT OF THE WALT DISNEY COMPANY

#### 1. Ovitz's Early Performance

Ovitz's tenure as President of The Walt Disney Company officially began on October 1, 1995. Eisner authored three documents shortly after Ovitz began work that shed light on his early performance on the job. The first is a letter written to Ovitz dated October 10, 1995. Eisner lauded Ovitz's initial performance, and also provided Ovitz with some written guidance with respect to Eisner's management philosophies....

The second document is a letter Eisner wrote to the board of directors, the Bass family, and his wife on October 20, 1995. In it, Eisner called Ovitz's hiring "a great coup for us and a saving grace for me ... Everybody is excited being with him, doing business with him.... He has already run a private company, and being a quick study, has quickly adapted to the public institution." ....

The third document is dated November 10, 1995, and is a memo addressed to Tony Schwartz, Eisner's biographer. In it, Eisner says that Ovitz has had a difficult time accepting Bollenbach and Litvack as his equals, but that Ovitz was adjusting, realizing that he need not "prove to himself, to the group, to the world, that he is in charge." Eisner also reaffirmed that "Michael Ovitz is the right choice. He will, in short order, be up to speed in the areas we have discussed endlessly — brand management, corporate direction, moral compass and all those difficult areas, especially for Disney, to define." ....

As late as the end of 1995, Eisner's attitude with respect to Ovitz was positive. Eisner wrote, "1996 is going to be a great year — We are going to be a great team — We every day are working better together — Time will be on our side — We will be strong, smart, and unstoppable!!!" Eisner opined that Ovitz performed well during 1995, notwithstanding the difficulties Ovitz was experiencing assimilating to Disney's culture.

#### 2. A Mismatch of Cultures and Styles

In 1996, however, the tenor of the comments surrounding Ovitz's performance and his transition to The Walt Disney Company changed. In January 1996, a corporate retreat was held at Walt Disney World in Orlando, Florida. At that retreat, Ovitz failed to integrate himself in the group of executives by declining to participate in group activities, insisting on a limousine when the other executives, including Eisner, were taking a bus, and making inappropriate demands of the park employees. In short, Ovitz "was a little elitist for the egalitarian Walt

Disney World cast members [employees]," and a poor fit with his fellow executives.

As 1996 wore on, it became apparent that the difficulties Ovitz was having at the Company were less and less likely to be resolved. By the summer of 1996, Eisner had spoken with several directors about Ovitz's failure to adapt to the Company's culture. In June 1996, Eisner, Ovitz, and Wilson were in France for a cycling trip during which "it became clear [to Wilson] that what [he] had been hearing was not just idle gossip," but that "there was a problem of Mr. Ovitz being accepted into the organization."

### 3. Approaching the Endgame

By the fall of 1996, directors began discussing that the disconnect between Ovitz and the Company was likely irreparable, and that Ovitz would have to be terminated. Additionally, the industry and popular press were beginning to publish an increasing number of articles describing dissension within The Walt Disney Company's executive suite. One of the more prominent of these articles was an article published in Vanity Fair based on an interview given by Bollenbach, which many of the directors discussed while present for the November 25, 1996 board meeting.

### 4. Specific Examples of Ovitz's Performance as President of The Walt Disney Company

Throughout this litigation, plaintiffs have argued that Ovitz acted improperly while in office. The specific examples discussed below demonstrate that the record created at trial does not support those allegations.

Plaintiffs have alleged that even before Ovitz was formally elected as President and employed by Disney, that he exercised Presidential authority in connection with the construction or renovation of his office. The record does provide support for the benign assertion that Ovitz performed some work for the Company before his hiring was official. In addition to the fact that the documents plaintiffs rely on evidence no effort by Ovitz to direct the office work or authorize expenditures for it, the testimony of both Ovitz and Eisner was that Ovitz's involvement in the project was limited. Furthermore, Ovitz's authority over the project both before and after October 1, 1995, was minimal at best, yet at the same time consistent with the input that would be expected from an executive when a new office is built for him or her.

In addition to allegations that Ovitz overstepped his authority with respect to his office, plaintiffs contend that Ovitz acted improperly in connection with discussions he had, either personally, or on behalf of the Company, with representatives from the National Football League ("NFL") with respect to bringing a team to the Los Angeles area. First and foremost, contemporary documents indicate that Disney, under Eisner's direction, was considering bringing an NFL franchise to Los Angeles before Ovitz's hiring was ... announced. Second, any work Ovitz may have done on behalf of the Company in regards to the NFL before his employment formally began is, in my mind, evidence of Ovitz's good faith efforts to benefit the Company and bring himself up to speed — not evidence of malfeasance or other ulterior motives. Third, it is clear from the record that, as soon as Eisner instructed Ovitz to cease discussions with the NFL, Ovitz complied with Eisner's directive. Again, the record fails to support allegations of misconduct by Ovitz in this regard either before or after October 1, 1995.

Plaintiffs argue that Ovitz is responsible, at least in part, for Bollenbach's decision to leave the Company, and the controversy surrounding the hiring of Jamie Tarses to ABC [by then a Disney subsidiary]. Bollenbach . . . contradicts the assertion that he left because of Ovitz. Instead, he left the Company to pursue a better opportunity with Hilton Hotels.

In mid-1996, ABC hired Jamie Tarses. It was reported in the press that Ovitz "orchestrated" Tarses' hiring even though she was under contract at NBC for roughly fifteen more months. Eisner testified that Ovitz was not at fault for the perceived negative repercussions of Tarses' hiring, saying that he "was convinced that [Ovitz] was brought into something he did not instigate." In fact, Tarses' hiring was championed by Iger and approved by Litvack.

Another "failure" plaintiffs have attempted to pin on Ovitz, but which is in reality more attributable to Iger, revolves around the film Kundun, directed by Martin Scorsese. The film was not well received by the Chinese government and, at least initially, may have caused the Company some setbacks in that rapidly expanding market. Once again, however, the testimony was clear that Ovitz did not have authority to approve the movie; instead, that authority (and the concomitant responsibility) rested wholly with Roth and Eisner. . . .

\*      \*      \*      \*

[Court goes on to review Ovitz's performance] Ovitz was assigned to oversee Disney Interactive, which created interactive video games. Eisner testified that Disney Interactive was "doing very badly, actually," but he hoped that Ovitz might be able to turn it around. Ovitz was unable to do so. In the face of Eisner's critical view of Ovitz's performance with respect to Disney Interactive, Ovitz testified that he had several ideas for Disney Interactive which could have potentially helped Disney Interactive, including a joint venture with Sony, and a purchase of part of Yahoo!®, all of which Eisner rejected. Ovitz also pursued, together with Roth, a deal intended to benefit Disney's motion picture studio with Beacon Communications, a company run by Armyan Bernstein, a writer and director. Again Eisner instructed Ovitz not to close the deal.

Ovitz wanted the Company to purchase Putnam Publishing in order to acquire the rights to author Tom Clancy. He also wanted to place other prominent authors (and former clients) such as Michael Crichton and Stephen King under contract with Disney's publishing division. Eisner rejected these efforts as ill conceived.

A similar story emerges of Ovitz's leadership over Hollywood Records. Ovitz wanted to place Janet Jackson under contract with Hollywood Records, acquire EMI (a Hollywood Records competitor) or enter into a joint venture with Sony. Once again, however, Eisner rejected all of these suggestions. Eisner and others were also critical of what they perceived to be a lack of attention paid by Ovitz to Hollywood Records, though Ovitz's files belie the assertion that Ovitz ignored his oversight of Hollywood Records.[10]

There are three competing theories as to why Ovitz was not successful. First, plaintiffs argue that Ovitz failed to follow Eisner's directives, especially in regard to acquisitions, and that generally, Ovitz did very little. Second, Ovitz contends that Eisner's micromanaging prevented Ovitz from having the authority necessary to make the changes that Ovitz thought were appropriate. In addition, Ovitz believes he was not given enough time for his efforts to bear fruit. Third, the remaining defendants simply posit that Ovitz failed to transition from a private to public company, from the "sell side to the buy side," and otherwise did not adapt to the Company culture or fit in with other executives. In the end, however, it makes no difference why Ovitz was not as successful as his reputation would have led many to expect, so long as he was not grossly negligent or malfeasant.

Many of Ovitz's efforts failed to produce results, often because his efforts reflected an opposite philosophy than that held by Eisner, Iger, and Roth. This does not mean that Ovitz intentionally failed to follow Eisner's directives or that he was insubordinate. To the contrary, it demonstrates that Ovitz was attempting to use his knowledge and experience, which (by virtue of his experience on the "sell side" as opposed to the "buy side" of the entertainment industry) was fundamentally different from Eisner's, Iger's, and Roth's, to benefit the Company. But different does not mean wrong. Total agreement within an organization is often a far greater threat than diversity of opinion. Unfortunately, the philosophical divide between Eisner and Ovitz was greater than both believed, and as two proud and stubborn individuals, neither of them was willing to consider the possibility that their point of view might be incorrect, leading to their inevitable falling out.

### 5.  Veracity and "Agenting"

At trial, plaintiffs, together with their expert on these issues, Donohue, spent a great deal of effort attempting to persuade the Court that Ovitz was a habitual liar,

---

10. See PTE 606; PTE 622; PTE 629; PTE 768; DTE 190. [Expert witness Professor] Donohue's predictable opinion that "Ovitz could have been in a coma and still collecting these empty documents" is of no benefit to the Court and, indeed, documents such as PTE 606 and PTE 622 contain marginalia with Ovitz's handwriting, which would refute Donohue's opinion that there is no indication that the files were ever read by Ovitz. See Tr. 9282:15-9284:16. Furthermore, plaintiffs' attempt to use Ovitz's statement on the Larry King Live show — that after a year on the job he knew "about one percent of what I need to know" — to demonstrate that Ovitz failed to apply himself on the job, is specious and wholly unpersuasive. PTE 323 at 7.

and that his lack of veracity would constitute good cause to terminate him without paying the NFT. Defendants respond that the purported veracity problems attributable to Ovitz do not involve material falsehoods, but instead were caused by Ovitz's tendency to "handle" or "agent" others. Eisner testified that, with respect to Iger's statement that Iger did not trust Ovitz, the lack of trust was related to Ovitz's failure to communicate with Iger, and that Ovitz "wasn't doing anything wrong."[11] Eisner also expressed that he personally did not trust Ovitz.[12] From both the tenor of the document (written shortly after the stress of his mother's death) and from Eisner's more emotionally detached trial testimony, however, it is clear that Eisner was not referring to any material falsehoods, but instead to Ovitz's salesmanship or, in other words, his "agenting."

Litvack felt the same way, saying that he did not trust Ovitz's judgment and that he did not trust Ovitz generally because Ovitz would "handle" Litvack and "put his spin on things." Litvack also said that the "worst that I could remember in terms of lies was — and I use the word 'lies' — was 'I was on the phone with someone important and couldn't be on time for the meeting.'" Other executives and directors made similar comments that they could recall no material falsehoods told to them by Ovitz.

In the absence of any concrete evidence that Ovitz told a material falsehood during his tenure at Disney, plaintiffs fall back on alleging that Ovitz's disclosures regarding his earn-out with, and past income from, CAA, were false or materially misleading. As a neutral fact-finder, I find that the evidence simply does not support either of those assertions. . . . .

### 6.  Gifts and Expenses

In moving from the talent agency he founded to a public company, Ovitz was faced with an array of new policies and rules relating to gifts and expenses. Eisner had asked Russell to speak to Ovitz about his expenses, and on January 17, 1996, Russell and Ovitz met for breakfast to discuss the topic. To follow up on their meeting, Ovitz sent a memo to Russell in January 1996 asking for help in handling

---

11. Tr. 4300:7-4301:22. This testimony demonstrates that there could be any number of reasons for which Iger would no longer trust Ovitz. Lack of veracity is but one.

12. Eisner wrote:

Michael [Ovitz] does not have the trust of anybody. I do not trust him. None of the people he works with feels comfortable with his directness and honesty. Like an athlete who has lost his way, Michael is pressing, is confused, and [is] ineffective. His heart may be in the right place, but his ego never allows it to pump. His creative instincts may be in the right place, but his insecurity and existential drive never allows a real functioning process. . . . He would be a great salesman, but his corporate disingenuous nature undermines him. And his lack of interests in longterm outcomes affects his judgment on short-term deals. The biggest problem is that nobody trusts him, for he cannot tell the truth. He says whatever comes to mind, no matter what the reality. Because of all the above his executives, outside business associates, and the Press have turned against him.

PTE 79 at DD002624.

his expenses. According to Ovitz, Russell was "fantastic" in helping Ovitz's assistant meet and confer with a knowledgeable Disney employee so that Ovitz's expenses could be properly handled.

The only evidence in the record that is admissible to prove that Ovitz did not comply with Disney's policies regarding expenses is (1) the statements by Eisner that Ovitz may not have been in compliance with those policies, and (2) the undisputed fact that Disney withheld $1 million from the cash payment of Ovitz's NFT, but ultimately returned all but roughly $140,000 of that amount.

The record contains several examples of statements by Eisner where he believed that Ovitz's compliance with Company expense policies was questionable. The trial testimony of Eisner, Russell, and especially Litvack (whom Eisner had assigned to oversee Ovitz's expenses), however, was credible and coherent in stating that Ovitz was in compliance with the Company's expense policies.

*        *        *        *

Plaintiffs have repeatedly criticized Ovitz's gift giving as self-serving and not in accordance with Company policies. Furthermore, they argue that he failed to properly report gifts that he received while serving as President of Disney. Once more, the record fails to support these assertions. As with Ovitz's expenses, Eisner asked Russell to assist Ovitz in complying with Disney's policies with respect to gifts. Litvack was also told of Eisner's concerns, and following an investigation, he found that Ovitz was in compliance with Disney's gift policies. At trial, plaintiffs' counsel asked Litvack whether he was aware of several questionable gifts, but Litvack unambiguously testified that either he had approved those gifts, or that, had he been asked, he would have approved those gifts because they related to the business of the Company. In sum, finding Litvack's and Eisner's trial testimony credible as cited above, I find that Ovitz was not in violation of The Walt Disney Company's policies relating to expenses or giving and receiving gifts.

C.  OVITZ'S TERMINATION

1.  *The Beginning of the End*

Ovitz's relationship with Eisner, and with other Disney executives and directors, continued to deteriorate through September 1996. In mid-September, Litvack, with Eisner's approval, spoke with, or more accurately cornered Ovitz. Litvack told Ovitz that he thought it was clear that Ovitz was not working out at Disney and that he should start looking for both a graceful way out of Disney and a new job. [On a second occasion Litvak communicated Eisner's idea that Ovitz should look for another opportunity to which, according to the court, Ovitz replied that Eisner] was "going to have to pull me out of here ... I'm not leaving," and that if Eisner wanted him to leave Disney, Eisner could tell him so to his face. At trial, Ovitz testified that he felt that "as far as [he] was concerned, [he] was chained to that desk and that company. [That he] wasn't going to leave there a loser," that the guy that hired him or the full board would have to fire him, and that he hoped he could still make it work and make all these problems just disappear.

Following up on the discussions between Litvack and Ovitz, Eisner and Ovitz had several meetings on or around September 21, 1996, during which they discussed Ovitz's future (or lack thereof) at Disney, and the possibility that Ovitz would seek employment at Sony [which has been floated to O. months earlier]. Eisner believed that Sony would be both willing and excited to take Ovitz in "trade" from Disney because Ovitz had a very positive longstanding relationship with many of Sony's top executives. Eisner favored the Sony "trade" because, not only would it remove Ovitz and his personality from the halls of Disney, but it would also relieve Disney of having to pay Ovitz under the OEA. . . .

The Sony discussions continued on October 8 when Ovitz wrote Eisner a note asking for formal permission to begin negotiations with Sony. After stating that he was still shocked that Eisner wanted him out, Ovitz wrote that he had resolved to look at other employment possibilities, and he wanted to make sure that he did not leave himself or Sony open to a lawsuit because his departure from Disney would leave Ovitz in breach of the OEA. On October 9 Eisner responded by letter, telling Ovitz that neither he nor anyone else at Disney had any objections to Ovitz working out a deal and eventually going to work for Sony. In fact, Eisner thought it was best that Ovitz and Disney work together to ensure a smooth departure. Additionally, Eisner wrote a letter to Mr. Idei, Sony's Chairman, trumpeting Ovitz and notifying Mr. Idei that Disney had given permission for Ovitz to enter into negotiations for a possible move to Sony. Apparently, however, only a limited number of directors knew that Ovitz was given permission to negotiate with Sony, including Litvack, Watson, Russell, Gold, and Roy Disney, and that the board as a whole was never approached about the possible Sony "trade." Of these directors, only Litvack and Russell were ever asked for their opinions on the matter. [*Ed. query*: Is this a weakness? Is such a matter one in which law or good business practice suggests board involvement?]

On November 1, Ovitz wrote a letter to Eisner notifying Eisner that things had failed to work out with Sony and that Ovitz had instead decided to recommit himself to Disney with "an even greater commitment of [his] own energies" than he had before and an "increased appreciation" of the Disney organization. There are varying accounts of why Ovitz did not end up employed at Sony, but the important fact is that Ovitz remained at Disney.

## 2. The September 30, 1996 Board Meeting

During the course of the Sony discussions the Disney board convened a meeting on September 30, 1996, while attending a Disney anniversary at the Walt Disney World Resort in Orlando, Florida. Ovitz was in attendance at the board meeting, and it is undisputed that neither Ovitz's future with Disney nor his conversations to date with Eisner and Litvack were discussed at the general board meeting. Eisner, however, testified that he spoke with various directors either during an executive session held that same day at which Ovitz was not present, or in small groups during the weekend, to notify them that there were continuing problems with Ovitz's performance. Additionally, other directors testified that Eisner apprised them of the developing situation with Ovitz either during or prior to September 1996. Although Eisner never sat down at a full board meeting to discuss the persistent and growing Ovitz problem, it is clear that he made an effort to notify and talk with a large majority, if not all of the directors.

On the night of September 30, Eisner and Ovitz made their now famous appearance on *The Larry King Live Show* in which Eisner refuted the then current Hollywood gossip that there was a growing rift between himself and Ovitz and emphatically stated that if given the chance, he would hire Ovitz again. It is clear now that this entire interview was a shameless public relations move during which both Eisner and Ovitz did not candidly answer Larry King's questions with the goal of deflating the negative rumors surrounding their failed partnership.

On October 1, the day after the Larry King interview, Eisner sent a letter that he had been working on since the summer, to Russell and Watson detailing Eisner's mounting difficulties with Ovitz, including Ovitz's failure to adapt to Disney's corporate culture in even the slightest fashion, Eisner's lack of trust for Ovitz, and Ovitz's complete failure to alleviate Eisner's workload.[13] Apparently, an incident at Eisner's mother's funeral, which involved Ovitz getting into an argument on a New York City street over a parking space, spurred Eisner to finally send this letter. The letter stated that:

> If I should be hit by a truck, the company simply cannot make [Ovitz] CEO or leave him as president with a figurehead CEO. It would be catastrophic. I hate saying it, but his strength of personality together with his erratic behavior and pathological problems, and I hate saying that, is a mixture leading to disaster for this company.

Eisner stated that his goal in writing the letter was to keep Ovitz from succeeding him at Disney should the opportunity arise. Because of that purpose, the letter contained a good deal of hyperbole to help Eisner better "unsell" Ovitz as his successor. Neither Russell nor Watson divulged at any time the contents of the letter with other members of the board.

Eisner was informed on November 1 that Ovitz's negotiations with Sony had failed to result in Ovitz leaving Disney. Once Eisner discovered that the Sony

---

13. PTE 79; *see also supra* text "Veracity and 'Agenting'" at 49. Although I have found that Ovitz was not a liar, Eisner's persistently-vocalized reservations about Ovitz's veracity are not inconsistent with that finding. I conclude that while Ovitz gave this Court no reason to believe that he lied, that it is entirely possible that his actions while at Disney and his general character led Eisner to believe that Ovitz was not completely honest. Eisner, however, was unable to point to specific instances where Ovitz was untruthful.

negotiations had failed... [he]decided that Ovitz must be gone by the end of the year.

*      *      *      *

Instead of sending this letter to Ovitz, Eisner met with Ovitz personally on November 13 and they discussed much of what was contained in the letter, especially Ovitz's alleged management and ethics problems. Notes taken by Eisner following this meeting stated that the meeting was "2 hours and 15 minutes of [Eisner] telling [Ovitz] that it was not going to work." Eisner believed that Ovitz just would not listen to what he was trying to tell him and instead, Ovitz insisted that he would stay at Disney, going so far as to state that he would chain himself to his desk.

### 3. Options for Ovitz's Termination

.... Eisner and Litvack had ... been discussing whether Ovitz could be terminated, and more importantly, whether he could be terminated for cause. Eisner hoped to obtain a termination for cause because he believed that although Ovitz "had not done the job that would warrant [the NFT] payment" Disney was obliged to honor the OEA. Honoring the OEA meant that if Ovitz was terminated without cause, he would receive the NFT payment that the OEA called for, which consisted of the balance of Ovitz's salary, an imputed amount of bonuses, a $10 million termination fee and the immediate vesting of his three million stock options at the time. Litvack advised Eisner from the very beginning that he did not believe that there was cause to terminate Ovitz under the OEA.

As the end of November approached, Eisner again asked Litvack if Disney had cause to fire Ovitz and avoid the costly NFT payment. Litvack proceeded to examine more carefully the issue of whether cause existed under the OEA. Litvack reviewed the OEA, refreshed himself on the meaning of gross negligence and malfeasance and reviewed all of the facts concerning Ovitz's performance of which he was aware. Litvack freely admits that he did not do any legal research in answering the cause question; nor did he order an outside investigation to be undertaken or an outside opinion to be authored.... Litvack, for the second time, concluded that there was no cause to terminate Ovitz. In fact, despite Ovitz's poor performance and concerns about his honesty, Litvack believed that the question of whether Ovitz could be terminated for cause was not a close question and, in fact, Litvack described it as "a no-brainer." Litvack, however, produced no written work product or notes to show to the board that would explain or defend his conclusion, and because he did not ask for an outside opinion to be authored, there was no written work product at all. When Litvack notified Eisner that he did not believe cause existed, Eisner testified that he "checked with almost anybody that [he] could find that had a legal degree, and there was just no light in that possibility. It was a total dead end from day one."

In a perfect, more responsible world, both Litvack and Eisner would have had sufficient documentation not only to back up their conclusion that Ovitz could not be terminated for cause, but they would have also had sufficient evidence of the research and legwork they did to arrive at that conclusion. Despite the paucity of evidence, it is clear to the Court that both Eisner and Litvack wanted to fire Ovitz for cause to avoid the costly NFT payment, and perhaps out of personal motivations. The Court is convinced, based upon these two factors, that Eisner and Litvack did in fact make a concerted effort to determine if Ovitz could be terminated for cause, and that despite these efforts, they were unable to manufacture the desired result.

In addition to determining that there was no cause to fire Ovitz as defined in the OEA, Litvack also testified that it would be inappropriate and unethical for Disney to try to bluff Ovitz into accepting an amount less than agreed to in the OEA in case of an NFT. Litvack believed that it would be a bad idea to attempt to coerce Ovitz (by threatening a for-cause termination) into negotiating for a smaller NFT package than was provided for in the OEA because Disney, when pressed by Ovitz's attorneys, would have to admit that there in fact was no cause and possibly subject Disney to a wrongful termination suit. Litvack also believed that a failed attempt to bluff Ovitz out of the NFT could be quite harmful to Disney's reputation because it would appear as if Disney was trying to get out of contractual obligations (which it would have been), and that would make it difficult for Disney to do business and be viewed as an honest business partner.

### 4.  The November 25, 1996 Board Meeting

The Disney board held its next meeting on November 25, and Ovitz was present. . . . . The only action recorded in the minutes concerning Ovitz is his unanimous renomination to a new three-year term to the board. Gold testified, however, that by this time the board knew that Ovitz would be fired, but because Ovitz was present at the meeting it would have been akin to a "public hanging" to fail to re-nominate him.

. . . directly following the board meeting there was some discussion concerning Ovitz at the executive session . . . . There are no minutes to show who attended the executive session, but I am reasonably certain that at least Eisner, Gold, Bowers, Watson and Stern were in attendance. In the absence of further evidence, I must conclude that no other directors attended this session. . . . . Eisner notified the directors in attendance . . . . that it was his intention to fire Ovitz by year's end. . . . .

. . . . there is some controversy as to whether any details of the NFT and the cause question were discussed at this meeting. Eisner testified that, in addition to the other items, he informed those in attendance of what the NFT would cost Disney. Gold tells a somewhat more elaborate (and certainly more selfserving) version of the meeting in which Gold asks Eisner whether Ovitz's termination would be for cause, and Eisner assures Gold, in the presence of the other directors, that Litvack had advised Eisner that there were no grounds for a "for cause" termination. . . .

Outside of Gold and Stern, nobody else present at the executive session recalled Gold raising the issue of fault with Eisner or having witnessed Gold speak with Litvack.

*                 *                 *                 *

[Court reports that Director Wilson, who was a personal friend of Ovitz, went on holiday cruise with Ovitz family, during which, under directions from Eisner, he brought up with Ovitz the necessity for him to leave by the end of the year. In a contemporaneous report of these conversations with Eisner . . . ] Wilson recalled describing Ovitz as a "wounded animal . . . in a corner," and stated that by this he meant that Ovitz could become dangerous to the organization if the relationship with Disney continued. Wilson also recalled stating that Ovitz was a "loyal friend and devastating enemy," and advising that Eisner should be reasonable and magnanimous, both financially and publicly, so Ovitz could save face.

On December 3, having returned from his Thanksgiving trip, Ovitz, armed with his newfound understanding that his time at Disney was rapidly coming to an end, met with Eisner to discuss the terms of his departure. Eisner memorialized this meeting in a note to Russell which read "I met with Michael Ovitz today who wants to bring our discussions to a conclusion this week, wants you and Bob Goldman to settle out his contract immediately and sign it by weeks end." Essentially, this note asked Russell to take charge of managing the Ovitz departure. Ovitz asked that he not have to deal personally with Litvack during the termination process, although he had no qualms about Litvack being involved. Ovitz also asked for several concessions from Disney, including keeping his seat on the board, obtaining a consulting/advising arrangement with Disney, the continued use of an office and staff (but not on the Disney lot), continued health insurance and home security, continued use of the company car and the repurchase of his plane.

Although Eisner and Ovitz did not see eye to eye on Ovitz's requests, Eisner initially objected only to Ovitz's continued use of the company car, telling Russell, "I don't want to nit pick here, but we are paying him a fortune." The memo to Russell does not reflect Eisner's objections to Ovitz's other requests. Eisner, however, testified that "by the time I got from number one to number five [of listing Ovitz's requests] I had already realized it was a bad idea, and the next day I called him and told him that . . . it would be impossible." Eisner also told Russell that:

> Any deal we make that is one cent more than the contract should include a non raid clause with teeth, a non compete in areas he advises us in, and a non disclose or bad mouth me or the company for five years at least. It would be great if you paid some of his money out over time which he would lose if he broke that deal.

Shortly after this meeting, Ovitz spoke with Russell on the phone, and Russell described the conversation as "a very, very troubling and unusual conversation."

Russell stated that during their conversation, Ovitz made clear that he understood that the door to Disney was closed, but he was still "pleading his heart out . . . [with] tears in his voice." Over the next week, Disney, and more accurately, Eisner, rejected every request that Ovitz had made, informing him that all he would receive is what he had contracted for in the OEA and nothing more. Other than the extra benefits which Ovitz requested and Disney summarily denied, there seems to have been no negotiation between anyone in Ovitz's camp and anyone at Disney concerning whether there would be a for cause termination or an NFT, and nobody seems to have even mentioned to Ovitz or his representatives the possibility of a for cause termination.

### 5.   Ovitz's Bonus and His Termination

On December 10, the Executive Performance Plan Committee ("EPPC") met to consider annual bonuses for Disney's most highly compensated executive officers. The EPPC was chaired by Gold, its other members Lozano, Poitier and Russell, attended, although Poitier and Lozano attended by phone. Also in attendance were Eisner, Watson, Litvack, Santaniello, and Marsha Reed. Russell informed all those in attendance of his conversations with Ovitz's representatives and that Ovitz was going to be terminated, but that he was not going to be terminated for cause. At this meeting, Russell recommended that Ovitz, despite his poor performance and imminent termination, should receive a $7.5 million bonus for his services during the 1996 fiscal year because Disney had done so well during the fiscal year and because Disney had a large bonus pool. The EPPC approved this recommendation and it appears that Russell may have even advised the EPPC (despite the *clear* language in the OEA stating that the *bonus was discretionary*) that Disney was contractually obligated to pay Ovitz his bonus. Despite the fact that all of those in attendance should have known better, nobody spoke up to correct the mistaken perception that Ovitz had to receive a bonus, let alone a $7.5 million bonus.

The following evening, Eisner met with Ovitz at Eisner's mother's apartment in New York City. By the time this meeting occurred, it had already been decided that Ovitz was being terminated, without cause, and would be receiving his contractual NFT payment, and that he would not be receiving any of the additional items that he asked for. The purpose of this meeting was to agree to a press release to announce the termination, let Ovitz know that he would not receive any additional items, and as Eisner described it, it served as "the final parting." Eisner and Ovitz apparently came to some understanding that neither Ovitz nor Disney was to defame each other in the press, and that the separation was to be undertaken with dignity and respect for both sides. Ovitz's termination was memorialized the following day in a letter signed by Litvack and dated December 12. Litvack testified that Russell negotiated the terms in the letter, but Litvack signed this document on Eisner's instructions.

The board was not shown the December 12 letter, nor did it meet to approve its terms.

*          *          *          *

During the week that Ovitz was terminated (December 11-16), articles began appearing in the press with quotes from Ovitz or his representatives describing why Ovitz left Disney and detailing to some extent the size of his severance package. For example, a December 14 article in the Baltimore Sun reported that "Resigning Disney President Michael Ovitz said yesterday through a representative that Disney is giving him a $90 million severance package." Other articles describing Ovitz's frustrations at Disney stated that Ovitz "wasn't game to struggle against a bad situation," and that "Ovitz was frustrated by his poorly defined role, Eisner's reluctance to share power and repeated clashes with other senior Disney executives ... notably [Litvack] and [Bollenbach]," and that "the reality was that Eisner did not let go ... [and that] Eisner thwarted [Ovitz] by not giving him detailed responsibilities or the power to manage the various Disney divisions." The articles also stated that Ovitz's departure was mutual, and some went so far as to state that Ovitz's departure was his own idea. Additionally, it was reported that Ovitz had hired a public relations consultant named Steven Rivers to put a positive spin on the termination for Ovitz. Ovitz, however, testified that he did not employ Rivers or any other PR firm at this time. Eisner believed that he had been generous in his treatment of Ovitz, as well as his agreement to make the termination seem mutual, and felt that these articles were:

> an incredible betrayal not of a contract, not of any kind of written agreement, but that I had bent over backwards, and not because he was my friend. I would do it with anybody that was leaving under these circumstances, and he just, you know, threw it right in the company's face. And I was reading every single day about what idiots we were, the Disney Company, and how he had done this enormous feat.

On December 16, Eisner reacted to these stories by sending an e-mail to John Dreyer, Disney's communications chief, which among other things stated that Ovitz was a "psychopath" and "totally incompetent." Eisner described the letter as his effort at "venting" and that "although [he] didn't know what the words meant, [he] was just so angry."

Following the official termination, the EPPC met on December 20 with the sole purpose of rescinding Ovitz's $7.5 million bonus. Litvack stated that after the December 10 EPPC meeting, he had questioned Russell as to whether the bonus was mandatory, and that Russell had sent Litvack a memo (which had been drafted almost a year earlier as an introduction to the OEA) on December 18, and in that document it became apparent that the bonus was not in fact mandatory. Russell also had a discussion with Gold on December 18 during which he told

Gold that his recommendation that Ovitz be paid a bonus was stupid and that he was worried that members of the EPPC were under the mistaken belief that the bonus was contractual. Gold testified that within a week of the December 10 meeting, Litvack and Russell came to him "sheepishly, and said 'we've made a mistake.'" On December 20 a special telephonic meeting of the EPPC was convened with the purpose of rescinding Ovitz's $7.5 million bonus, which the EPPC had voted in favor of just ten days earlier. Gold, Lozano, Russell, Watson, Eisner and Litvack attended the meeting.

..... The EPPC then revoked Ovitz's bonus. After the revocation, Gold questioned Litvack if he had not also made a mistake as to whether Ovitz could be terminated for cause and Litvack told Gold that he was sure that he had not. Gold also contends that Litvack said his view was supported by outside counsel. Litvack denies ever having made this representation.

After Ovitz's bonus was rescinded, Eisner, in a December 27 letter, accelerated Ovitz's departure date from January 31, 1997, to December 27, 1996, and Ovitz's tenure as both an executive and director of Disney ended on that date.

*          *          *          *

*          *          *          *

D.  EXPERT WITNESSES

[The Court finds the testimony of various experts offered at trial as unhelpful. In large part these were academic experts seen as offering opinions on the law as applied to the facts of the case (as the experts understood them to be). The Court concluded that it was not appropriate for the court to rely upon such testimony.]

II.  LEGAL STANDARDS

The outcome of this case is determined by whether the defendants complied with their fiduciary duties in connection with the hiring and termination of Michael Ovitz. At the outset, the Court emphasizes that the best practices of corporate governance include compliance with fiduciary duties. Compliance with fiduciary duties, however, is not always enough to meet or to satisfy what is expected by the best practices of corporate governance.

The fiduciary duties owed by directors of a Delaware corporation are the duties of due care and loyalty. Of late, much discussion among the bench, bar, and academics alike, has surrounded a so-called third fiduciary duty, that of good faith. Of primary importance in this case are the fiduciary duty of due care and the duty of a director to act in good faith. Other than to the extent that the duty of loyalty is implicated by a lack of good faith, the only remaining issues to be decided herein with respect to the duty of loyalty are those relating to Ovitz's actions in connection with his own termination. These considerations will be addressed *seriatim*, although issues of good faith are (to a certain degree) inseparably and necessarily intertwined with the duties of care and loyalty, as well as a principal reason the distinctness of these duties make a difference — namely § 102(b)(7) of the Delaware General Corporation Law.[14]

## A. THE BUSINESS JUDGMENT RULE

A comprehensive review of the history of the business judgment rule is not necessary here, but a brief discussion of its boundaries and proper use is appropriate. Delaware law is clear that the business and affairs of a corporation are managed by or under the direction of its board of directors. The business judgment rule serves to protect and promote the role of the board as the ultimate manager of the corporation. Because courts are ill equipped to engage in post hoc substantive

---

14. Perhaps these categories of care and loyalty, so rigidly defined and categorized in Delaware for many years, are really just different ways of analyzing the same issue. Professor Sean Griffith said it best when he recently wrote:

> At first glance, the duties of care and loyalty appear quite distinctive. . . .
> A bit of digging beneath these surface differences, however, reveals the richly interconnected roots of the two doctrinal paradigms. Start with the duty of care: directors must conduct themselves as ordinarily prudent persons managing their own affairs. So far so good, but a moment's reflection reveals that an ordinarily prudent person becomes an ordinarily prudent director only once we assume an element of loyalty. How do ordinarily prudent directors conduct their affairs? A decision is taken with due care, when from an array of alternatives, the directors employ a procedure to pick the one that best advances *the interests of the corporation.* Now pause for a moment to consider what a funny way this is of conceiving what an ordinarily prudent person would do *in the conduct of her own affairs.* We might typically assume that an ordinarily prudent person, in evaluating a set of alternatives, picks the one that provides the most benefit and least cost to *herself.* A director's decisionmaking process, however, can be evaluated only by changing the referent from herself to the corporation. The question of prudence, in other words, is framed with a tacit element of loyalty.
> . . . .
> . . . [Shareholders and courts] are worried about the directors' loyalty because we are concerned that their disloyalty will result in a poor bargain for the corporation. We are concerned, in other words, that conflicted directors will strike bargains for the corporation that an ordinarily prudent person would not strike for herself. This can be seen most clearly if the non-arms-length transactions that raise duty of loyalty concerns are imagined as arms-length transactions with third parties. Would an ordinarily prudent person lease a corporate asset to a third party on exceedingly generous terms? Would an ordinarily prudent person lavish compensation on a third party and permit the third party to divert investment opportunities that would otherwise come her way? These are duty of loyalty concerns framed as duty of care questions. The phrasing is natural because, at its core, the duty of loyalty is just a bet that some situations are likely to lead to careless or imprudent transactions for the corporation, which is to say that the duty of care is a motivating concern for the duty of loyalty. Here again the duties overlap.

Sean J. Griffith, *Good Faith Business Judgment: A Theory of Rhetoric in Corporate Law Jurisprudence,* 55 DUKE L. J. (forthcoming 2005) (manuscript of May 25, 2005 at 39-42 available at *http://papers.ssrn.com/sol3/papers.cfm?abstract_id=728431*) (emphasis in original, citations omitted).

review of business decisions, the business judgment rule "operates to preclude a court from imposing itself unreasonably on the business and affairs of a corporation."

## B.  WASTE

Corporate waste is very rarely found in Delaware courts because the applicable test imposes such an onerous burden upon a plaintiff — proving "an exchange that is so one sided that no business person of ordinary, sound judgment could conclude that the corporation has received adequate consideration."[15] In other words, waste is a rare, "unconscionable case[] where directors irrationally squander or give away corporate assets."[16]

## C.  THE FIDUCIARY DUTY OF DUE CARE

The fiduciary duty of due care requires that directors of a Delaware corporation "use that amount of care which ordinarily careful and prudent men would use in similar circumstances,"[17] and "consider all material information reasonably available" in making business decisions, and that deficiencies in the directors' process are actionable only if the directors' actions are grossly negligent.[18] Chancellor Allen described the two contexts in which liability for a breach of the duty of care can arise:

> First, such liability may be said to follow *from a board decision* that results in a loss because that decision was ill advised or "negligent". Second, liability to the corporation for a loss may be said to arise from an *unconsidered failure of the board to act* in circumstances in which due attention would, arguably, have prevented the loss.[19]

---

15. *Brehm*, 746 A.2d at 263; *In re The Walt Disney Co. Derivative Litig. ("Disney I")*, 731 A.2d 342, 362 (Del. Ch. 1998) (quoting *Glazer v. Zapata Corp.*, 658 A.2d 176, 183 (Del. Ch. 1993)).

16. *Brehm*, 76 A.2d at 263.

17. *Graham*, 188 A.2d at 130.

18. *Brehm*, 746 A.2d at 259; *Official Comm. Of Unsecured Creditors of Integrated Health Services, Inc. v. Elkins, et al. ("IHS")*, 2004 WL 1949290, at *9 n.37 (Del. Ch. Aug. 24, 2004); *In re Nat'l Auto Credit, Inc. S'holders Litig.*, 2003 WL 139768, at *12 (Del. Ch. Jan. 10, 2003). In *Cede III*, the Supreme Court affirmed and adopted Chancellor Allen's "presumed findings" that the directors of Technicolor "were grossly negligent in failing to reach an informed decision when they approved the agreement of merger, and . . . thereby breached their duty of care." 634 A.2d at 366. By way of example, a board of directors need not read "*in haec verba* every contract or legal document that it approves, but if it is to successfully absolve itself from charges of [violations of the duty of care], there must be some credible evidence that the directors knew what they were doing, and ensured that their purported action was given effect." *Van Gorkom*, 488 A.2d 858, 883 n.25 (Del. 1985).

19. *Caremark*, 698 A.2d at 967 (emphasis in original).

Chancellor Allen then explained with respect to board decisions:

> ... [These] cases will typically be subject to review under the director-protective business judgment rule, assuming the decision made was the product of a *process* that was *either* deliberately considered in good faith or was otherwise rational. What should be understood, but may not widely be understood by courts or commentators who are not often required to face such questions, is that compliance with a director's duty of care can never appropriately be judicially determined by reference to *the content of the board decision* that leads to a corporate loss, apart from consideration of the good faith or rationality of the process employed. That is, whether a judge or jury considering the matter after the fact, believes a decision substantively wrong, or degrees of wrong extending through "stupid" to "egregious" or "irrational", provides no ground for director liability, so long as the court determines that the process employed was either rational or employed in a *good faith* effort to advance corporate interests. To employ a different rule — one that permitted an "objective" evaluation of the decision — would expose directors to substantive second guessing by ill-equipped judges or juries, which would, in the long-run, be injurious to investor interests. Thus, the business judgment rule is process oriented and informed by a deep respect for all *good faith* board decisions.
>
> Indeed, one wonders on what moral basis might shareholders attack a *good faith* business decision of a director as "unreasonable" or "irrational". Where a director *in fact exercises a good faith effort to be informed and to exercise appropriate judgment*, he or she should be deemed to satisfy fully the duty of attention.[20]

With respect to liability for director inaction, Chancellor Allen wrote that in order for the inaction to be so great as to constitute a breach of the director's duty of care, a plaintiff must show a "lack of good faith as evidenced by sustained or systematic failure of a director to exercise reasonable oversight." The Chancellor rationalized this extremely high standard of liability for violations of the duty of care through inaction by concluding that:

> [A] demanding test of liability in the oversight context is probably beneficial to corporate shareholders as a class, as it is in the board decision context, since it makes board service by qualified persons more likely, while continuing to act as a stimulus to *good faith performance of duty* by such directors.[21]

In the duty of care context with respect to corporate fiduciaries, gross negligence has been defined as a "'reckless indifference to or a deliberate disregard of the whole body of stockholders' or actions which are 'without the bounds of reason.'" Because duty of care violations are actionable only if the directors acted with gross negligence, and because in most instances money damages are unavailable to a plaintiff who could theoretically prove a duty of care violation, duty of care violations are rarely found.

20. *Id.* at 967-68 (internal citations and footnotes omitted, emphasis in original).
21. *Id.* (emphasis in original).

D.   THE FIDUCIARY DUTY OF LOYALTY

The fiduciary duty of loyalty was described in the seminal case of *Guth v. Loft, Inc.*, in these strict and unyielding terms . . .

More recently, the Delaware Supreme Court stated that there is no safe-harbor for divided loyalties in Delaware, and that the duty of loyalty, in essence, "mandates that the best interest of the corporation and its shareholders take[] precedence over any interest possessed by a director, officer or controlling shareholder and not shared by the stockholders generally."[22] The classic example that implicates the duty of loyalty is when a fiduciary either appears on both sides of a transaction or receives a personal benefit not shared by all shareholders.

In the specific context at issue here with respect to a classic duty of loyalty claim, Ovitz, as a fiduciary of Disney, was required to act in an "adversarial and arms-length manner" when negotiating his termination and not abuse or manipulate the corporate process by which that termination was granted. He was obligated to act in good faith and "not advantage himself at the expense of the Disney shareholders."

E.   SECTION 102(B)(7)

Following the Delaware Supreme Court's landmark decision in *Van Gorkom*, the Delaware General Assembly acted swiftly to enact 8 *Del. C.* § 102(b)(7). Section 102(b)(7) states that a corporation may include in its certificate of incorporation:

(7) A provision eliminating or limiting the personal liability of a director to the corporation or its stockholders for monetary damages for breach of fiduciary duty as a director, provided that such provision shall not eliminate or limit the liability of a director: (i) For any breach of the director's duty of loyalty to the corporation or its stockholders; (ii) for acts or omissions not in good faith or which involve intentional misconduct or a knowing violation of law; (iii) under § 174 of this title; or (iv) for any transaction from which the director derived an improper personal benefit. No such provision shall eliminate or limit the liability of a director for any act or omission occurring prior to the date when such provision becomes effective. All references in this paragraph to a director shall also be deemed to refer (x) to a member of the governing body of a corporation which is not authorized to issue capital stock, and (y) to such other person or persons, if any, who, pursuant to a provision of the certificate of incorporation in accordance with § 141(a) of this title, exercise or perform any of the powers or duties otherwise conferred or imposed upon the board of directors by this title.

22. *Cede III*, 634 A.2d at 361 (citing *Pogostin v. Rice*, 480 A.2d 619, 624 (Del. 1984)).

The purpose of Section 102(b)(7) was explained by the Delaware Supreme Court in this manner:

> The purpose of Section 102(b)(7) was to *permit shareholders* — who are entitled to rely upon directors to discharge their fiduciary duties at all times — to adopt a provision in the certificate of incorporation to exculpate directors from any personal liability for the payment of monetary damages for breaches of their duty of care, but not for duty of loyalty violations, good faith violations and certain other conduct.[23]

Recently, Vice Chancellor Strine wrote that, "[o]ne of the primary purposes of §102(b)(7) is to encourage directors to undertake risky, but potentially value-maximizing, business strategies, so long as they do so in good faith."[24] Or in other words, §102(b)(7) is most useful "when, despite the directors' good intentions, [the challenged transaction] did not generate financial success and ... the possibility of hindsight bias about the directors' prior ability to foresee that their business plans would not pan out" could improperly influence a *post hoc* judicial evaluation of the directors' actions.[25]

The vast majority of Delaware corporations have a provision in their certificate of incorporation that permits exculpation to the extent provided for by §102(b)(7). This provision prohibits recovery of monetary damages from directors for a successful shareholder claim, either direct or derivative, that is exclusively based upon establishing a violation of the duty of due care.[26] The existence of an exculpation provision authorized by §102(b)(7) does not, however, eliminate a director's fiduciary duty of care, because a court may still grant injunctive relief for violations of that duty.[27]

An exculpation provision such as that authorized by §102(b)(7) is in the nature of an affirmative defense.[28] As a result, it is the burden of the director defendants to demonstrate that they are entitled to the protections of the relevant charter provision.[29]

---

23. *Emerald Partners*, 787 A.2d at 90 (emphasis in original); *see Malpiede*, 780 A.2d at 1095.

24. *Prod. Res. Group, L.L.C. v. NCT Group, Inc.*, 863 A.2d 772, 777 (Del. Ch. 2004).

25. *Id.*

26. *Emerald Partners*, 787 A.2d at 91.

27. *Malpiede*, 780 A.2d at 1095; E. Norman Veasey, et al., *Delaware Supports Directors With a Three-Legged Stool of Limited Liability, Indemnification, and Insurance*, 42 BUS. LAW. 399, 403 (1987) ("[S]ection 102(b)(7) does not eliminate the duty of care that is properly imposed upon directors. Directors continue to be charged under Delaware law with a duty of care in the decision-making process and in their oversight responsibilities. The duty of care continues to have vitality in remedial contexts as opposed to actions for personal monetary damages against directors as individuals."). *Cf. Strassburger v. Earley*, 752 A.2d 557, 581 (Del. Ch. 2000) (holding that rescissory damages, although an equitable remedy, is not appropriate for breaches solely of the duty of care).

28. *Emerald Partners*, 787 A.2d at 91-92.

29. *See id.; Emerging Communications*, 2004 WL 1305745, at *42.

F.  ACTING IN GOOD FAITH

Decisions from the Delaware Supreme Court and the Court of Chancery are far from clear with respect to whether there is a separate fiduciary duty of good faith.[30] Good faith has been said to require an "honesty of purpose," and a genuine care for the fiduciary's constituents,[31] but, at least in the corporate fiduciary context, it is probably easier to define bad faith rather than good faith.[32] This may be so because Delaware law presumes that directors act in good faith when making business judgments.[33] Bad faith has been defined as authorizing a transaction "for some purpose *other than* a genuine attempt to advance corporate welfare or [when the transaction] is *known to constitute* a violation of applicable positive law."[34] In other words, an action taken with the intent to harm the corporation is a disloyal act in bad faith. A similar definition was used seven

---

30. It does no service to our law's clarity to continue to separate the duty of loyalty from its essence; nor does the recognition that good faith is essential to loyalty demean or subordinate that essential requirement. There might be situations when a director acts in subjective good faith and is yet not loyal (*e.g.*, if the director is interested in a transaction subject to the entire fairness standard and cannot prove financial fairness), but there is no case in which a director can act in subjective bad faith towards the corporation and act loyally.... For example, one cannot act loyally as a corporate director by causing the corporation to violate the positive laws it is obliged to obey.

*Guttman*, 823 A.2d at 506 n.34. *See In re Gaylord Container Corp. S'holders Litig.*, 753 A.2d 462, 475 n.41 (Del. Ch. 2000); *In re ML/EQ Real Estate P'ship Litig.*, 1999 WL 1271885, at *4 n.20 (Del. Ch. Dec. 21, 1999); *Barkan v. Amsted Indus. Inc.*, 567 A.2d 1279, 1286 (Del. 1989); *Blasius Indus. Inc. v. Atlas Corp.*, 564 A.2d 651, 663 (Del. 1988) (holding that because the acts taken by the directors thwarted the shareholder franchise, even if the directors acted in good faith, those actions "constituted an unintended violation of the duty of loyalty that the board owed to the shareholders."); *cf. IHS*, 2004 WL 1949290, at *9 (analyzing good faith claims under the rubrics of care and loyalty, as appropriate, instead of as a separate duty).

31. E. Norman Veasey, *Reflections on Key Issues of the Professional Responsibilities of Corporate Lawyers in the Twenty-First Century*, 12 WASH. U. J. L. & POL'Y 1, 9 (2003).

32. Despite the existence of significant jurisprudence with respect to good faith in the contractual context of the covenant of good faith and fair dealing, *see, e.g., Desert Equities, Inc. v. Morgan Stanley Leveraged Equity Fund, II, L.P.*, 624 A.2d 1199 (Del. 1993), Delaware decisions have shown a reluctance to importing these contractual standards into the corporate fiduciary realm.

33. *See Allaun*, 147 A. 257; *Van Gorkom*, 488 A.2d at 873.

34. *Gagliardi*, 683 A.2d at 1051 n.2 (citing Miller v. AT&T, 507 F.2d 759 (3d Cir. 1974), emphasis in original). Chancellor Allen then explained that "[t]here can be no personal liability of a director for losses arising from 'illegal' transactions if a director were financially disinterested, acted in good faith, and relied on advice of counsel reasonably selected in authorizing a transaction." *Id.* In *Cinerama, Inc. v. Technicolor, Inc.*, 1991 WL 111134, at *15 (Del. Ch. June 24, 1991), Chancellor Allen to a certain extent equated good faith with loyalty when he stated that there was "persuasive evidence" of bad faith on the part of one of the Technicolor directors (Sullivan) because he had met and cooperated with the acquiror before the acquiror had met with the CEO. Sullivan also received a $150,000 "finder's fee" for his assistance from the post-merger Technicolor. *Id.* at *7. This portion of the decision was not appealed because Cinerama abandoned its claims that the directors acted in bad faith. *Cede III*, 634 A.2d at 359. *See also* Veasey, *infra* n.457 at 448 (noting that intentional violations of law implicate good faith by stating that "the utter failure to follow the minimum expectations of Sarbanes-Oxley, or the NYSE or NASDAQ Rules... might ... raise a good faith issue").

years earlier, when Chancellor Allen wrote that bad faith (or lack of good faith) is when a director acts in a manner "unrelated to a pursuit of the corporation's best interests."[35] It makes no difference the reason why the director intentionally fails to pursue the best interests of the corporation.[36]

Bad faith can be the result of "any emotion [that] may cause a director to [intentionally] place his own interests, preferences or appetites before the welfare of the corporation," including greed, "hatred, lust, envy, revenge, . . . shame or pride."[37] Sloth could certainly be an appropriate addition to that incomplete list if it constitutes a systematic or sustained shirking of duty.[38] Ignorance, in and of itself, probably does not belong on the list, but ignorance attributable to any of the moral failings previously listed could constitute bad faith. It is unclear, based upon existing jurisprudence, whether motive is a necessary element for a successful claim that a director has acted in bad faith, and, if so, whether that motive must be shown explicitly or whether it can be inferred from the directors' conduct.

Shrouded in the fog of this hazy jurisprudence, the defendants' motion to dismiss this action was denied because I concluded that the complaint, together with all reasonable inferences drawn from the well-plead allegations contained therein, could be held to state a non-exculpated breach of fiduciary duty claim, insofar as it alleged that Disney's directors *"consciously and intentionally disregarded their responsibilities*, adopting a 'we don't care about the risks' attitude concerning a material corporate decision."

---

35. *In re RJR Nabisco, Inc. S'holder Litig.*, 1989 WL 7036, at *15 (Del. Ch. Jan. 31, 1989); *cf. Strassburger*, 752 A.2d at 581 (holding that certain directors breached their duty of loyalty by "indifference to their duty to protect the interests of the corporation and its minority shareholders," because their primary loyalty was instead given to the interests of their employer).

36. *See Guttman* 823 A.2d at 506 n.34 ("The reason for the disloyalty (the faithlessness) is irrelevant, the underlying motive (be it venal, familial, collegial, or nihilistic) for conscious actions not in the corporation's best interest does not make it faithful, as opposed to faithless."); *Nagy v. Bistricer*, 770 A.2d 43, 48 n.2 (Del. Ch. 2000) (The duty of good faith, "[i]f it is useful at all as an independent concept, [good faith's] utility may rest in its constant reminder . . . that, regardless of his motive, a director who consciously disregards his duties to the corporation and its stockholders may suffer a personal judgment for monetary damages for any harm he causes," even if for a reason "other than personal pecuniary interest.") *Emerging Communications*, 2004 WL 1305745, at *38 (holding that certain defendants violated their duty of "loyalty and/or good faith" because of the uncertainty in defining those terms).

37. *Guttman*, 823 A.2d at 506 n.34; *cf. Malpiede*, 780 A.2d at 1085 n.29 (holding that plaintiffs did not adequately allege a breach of the "duty of loyalty and good faith" merely by pleading conclusory statements that the target's board rejected an offer based upon "(1) the interested director's desire to consummate [the deal proposed by the other bidder], (2) a desire to benefit [the majority shareholders] with a quick deal, (3) 'dislike' of [the spurned bidder], or (4) a personal desire to complete the sale process.").

38. *See* Hillary A. Sale, *Delaware's Good Faith*, 89 CORNELL L. REV. 456, 488-91 (2004) (advocating application of federal scienter standards from the Rule 10b-5 context to an analysis of whether directors have satisfied their duty of acting in good faith when the allegations stem from directors' deliberate indifference).

Upon long and careful consideration, I am of the opinion that the concept of *intentional dereliction of duty*, a *conscious disregard for one's responsibilities*, is an appropriate (although not the only) standard for determining whether fiduciaries have acted in good faith. Deliberate indifference and inaction *in the face of a duty to act* is, in my mind, conduct that is clearly disloyal to the corporation. It is the epitome of faithless conduct.

To act in good faith, a director must act at all times with an honesty of purpose and in the best interests and welfare of the corporation. The presumption of the business judgment rule creates a presumption that a director acted in good faith. In order to overcome that presumption, a plaintiff must prove an act of bad faith by a preponderance of the evidence. To create a definitive and categorical definition of the universe of acts that would constitute bad faith would be difficult, if not impossible. And it would misconceive how, in my judgment, the concept of good faith operates in our common law of corporations. Fundamentally, the duties traditionally analyzed as belonging to corporate fiduciaries, loyalty and care, are but constituent elements of the overarching concepts of allegiance, devotion and faithfulness that must guide the conduct of every fiduciary. The good faith required of a corporate fiduciary includes not simply the duties of care and loyalty, in the narrow sense that I have discussed them above, but all actions required by a true faithfulness and devotion to the interests of the corporation and its shareholders. A failure to act in good faith may be shown, for instance, where the fiduciary intentionally acts with a purpose other than that of advancing the best interests of the corporation, where the fiduciary acts with the intent to violate applicable positive law, or where the fiduciary intentionally fails to act in the face of a known duty to act, demonstrating a conscious disregard for his duties. There may be other examples of bad faith yet to be proven or alleged, but these three are the most salient. As evidenced by previous rulings in this case both from this Court and the Delaware Supreme Court, issues of the Disney directors' good faith (or lack thereof) are central to the outcome of this action. With this background, I now turn to applying the appropriate standards to defendants' conduct.

## III. ANALYSIS

Stripped of the presumptions in their favor that have carried them to trial, plaintiffs must now rely on the evidence presented at trial to demonstrate by a preponderance of the evidence that the defendants violated their fiduciary duties and/or committed waste. More specifically, in the area of director action, plaintiffs must prove by a preponderance of the evidence that the presumption of the business judgment rule does not apply either because the directors breached their fiduciary duties, acted in bad faith or that the directors made an "unintelligent or unadvised judgment,"[39] by failing to inform themselves of all

---

39. *Mitchell*, 167 A. at 833; *Van Gorkom*, 488 A.2d at 872.

material information reasonably available to them before making a business decision.[40]

If plaintiffs cannot rebut the presumption of the business judgment rule, the defendants will prevail. If plaintiffs succeed in rebutting the presumption of the business judgment rule, the burden then shifts to the defendants to prove by a preponderance of the evidence that the challenged transactions were entirely fair to the corporation.[41]

As it relates to director inaction, plaintiffs will prevail upon proving by a preponderance of the evidence that the defendants breached their fiduciary duties by not acting. In order to invoke the protections of the provision in the Company's certificate of incorporation authorized by 8 Del. C. §102(b)(7), the defendants must prove by a preponderance of the evidence that they are entitled to the protections of that provision.

## A. OVITZ DID NOT BREACH HIS DUTY OF LOYALTY

As previously mentioned, the only issue remaining in this case with respect to the traditional duty of loyalty (aside from whether there is an overlap between loyalty and good faith) is whether Ovitz breached his fiduciary duty of loyalty in the course of his termination. Before trial, Ovitz moved for summary judgment on this claim, a motion I denied on the ground that genuine issues of material fact existed which prevented entry of summary judgment in favor of Ovitz at that time. More specifically, I recognized:

> ... *if* Ovitz received a[n] NFT, [then] he had a contractual right to receive the payout he did receive. But Ovitz did not have a contractual right to receive a[n] NFT.... Instead, Ovitz's receipt of a[n] NFT was conditioned upon a one-time determination (to be made by [the Company]) that was not guaranteed by his contract, and Ovitz appears to have actively engaged in negotiations and decisionmaking that affected [the Company]'s determination to grant the NFT.
>
> Ovitz negotiated his exit from [the Company] with Eisner, Russell, and others. He made a conscious decision not to resign and to seek the benefits that his contract made available to him only under certain prescribed circumstances. Ovitz allegedly colluded with those on the other side of the bargaining table ... in bringing about the circumstances that would entitle him to his NFT benefits. In so doing, he allegedly manipulated corporate processes and thereby violated his fiduciary duties to [the Company].[42]

Now, upon consideration of the evidence presented at trial, and based upon the findings of fact made above, it is clear that plaintiffs have failed to demonstrate by a preponderance of the evidence that Ovitz breached his duty of loyalty.

---

40. *Brehm*, 746 A.2d at 259; *Van Gorkom*, 488 A.2d at 872; *Kaplan v. Centex Corp.*, 284 A.2d 119, 124 (Del. 1971).

41. *Cede III*, 663 A.2d at 1162; *Emerald Partners*, 787 A.2d at 91.

42. *Id.* at *7.

Ovitz did not breach his fiduciary duty of loyalty by receiving the NFT payment because he played no part in the decisions: (1) to be terminated and (2) that the termination would not be for cause under the OEA.[43] Ovitz did possess fiduciary duties as a director and officer while these decisions were made, but by not improperly interjecting himself into the corporation's decisionmaking process nor manipulating that process, he did not breach the fiduciary duties he possessed in that unique circumstance. Furthermore, Ovitz did not "engage" in a transaction with the corporation — rather, the corporation imposed an unwanted transaction upon him.

\*                    \*                    \*                    \*

### B.   DEFENDANTS DID NOT COMMIT WASTE

Plaintiffs pursued a claim for waste at trial . . . . the standard for waste is a very high one that is difficult to meet. Plaintiffs refer to Professor Murphy's opinion that the OEA improperly incentivized Ovitz to leave the Company and receive an NFT, rather than complete the term of the OEA, to support their argument for waste. Of course, Professor Murphy's opinion relies on the assumptions that either Ovitz would be able to procure for himself an NFT, or that Eisner had agreed to terminate him even before Ovitz was hired.

The record does not support these assertions in any conceivable way. Apart from his job performance, Ovitz was never in a position to determine if he would be terminated, and if so, whether it would be with or without cause. As it relates to job performance, I find it patently unreasonable to assume that Ovitz intended to perform just poorly enough to be fired quickly, but not so poorly that he could be terminated for cause.

\*                    \*                    \*                    \*

More importantly, however, I conclude that given his performance, Ovitz could not have been fired for cause under the OEA. Any early termination of his employment, therefore, had to be in the form of an NFT. In reaching this conclusion, I rely on the expert reports of both Feldman and Fox, whose factual assumptions are generally consonant with my factual findings above. Nevertheless, by applying the myriad of definitions for gross negligence and malfeasance discussed by Donohue, Feldman and Fox, I also independently conclude, based upon the facts as I have found them, that Ovitz did not commit gross negligence or malfeasance while serving as the Company's President.

\*                    \*                    \*                    \*

As a result, terminating Ovitz and paying the NFT did not constitute waste because he could not be terminated for cause and because many of the defendants gave credible testimony that the Company would be better off without Ovitz, . . . . In other words, defendants did not commit waste.

43. *See supra* text "Ovitz's Bonus and His Termination" at 80.

C. THE OLD BOARD'S DECISION TO HIRE OVITZ AND THE COMPENSATION
COMMITTEE'S APPROVAL OF THE OEA WAS NOT GROSSLY NEGLIGENT
AND NOT IN BAD FAITH

The members of the "Old Board" (Eisner, Bollenbach, Litvack, Russell, Roy
Disney, Gold, Nunis, Poitier, Stern, Walker, Watson, Wilson, Bowers, Lozano
and Mitchell) were required to comply with their fiduciary duties on behalf of the
Company's shareholders while taking the actions that brought Ovitz to the Company. For the future, many lessons of what not to do can be learned from defendants' conduct here. Nevertheless, I conclude that the only reasonable application
of the law to the facts as I have found them, is that the defendants did not act in bad
faith, and were at most ordinarily negligent, in connection with the hiring of Ovitz
and the approval of the OEA. In accordance with the business judgment rule
(because, as it turns out, business judgment was exercised), ordinary negligence
is insufficient to constitute a violation of the fiduciary duty of care. I shall elaborate upon this conclusion as to each defendant.

*1. Eisner*

Eisner was clearly the person most heavily involved in bringing Ovitz to the
Company and negotiating the OEA. He was a long-time friend of Ovitz and the
instigator and mastermind behind the machinations that resulted in Ovitz's hiring
and the concomitant approval of the OEA. In that aspect, Eisner is the most
culpable of the defendants. He was pulling the strings; he knew what was
going on. On the other hand, at least as the duty of care is typically defined in
the context of a business judgment (such as a decision to select and hire a corporate president), of all the defendants, he was certainly the most informed of all
reasonably available material information, making him the least culpable in that
regard.

\*          \*          \*          \*

As a general rule, a CEO has no obligation to continuously inform the board
of his actions as CEO, or to receive prior authorization for those actions.[44]
Nevertheless, a reasonably prudent CEO (that is to say, a reasonably prudent

---

44. In a corporation of the Company's size and scope, the only logical way for the corporation to
operate is that the everyday governance should be "under the direction" of the board of directors rather
than "by" the board. More than twenty years ago, this Court wrote (and it is even more true today):

A fundamental precept of Delaware corporation law is that it is the board of directors,
and neither shareholders nor managers, that has ultimate responsibility for the management of the enterprise. Of course, given the large, complex organizations though which
modern multifunction business corporations often operate, the law recognizes that corporate boards, comprised as they traditionally have been of persons dedicating less than
all of their attention to that role, cannot themselves manage the operations of the firm, but
may satisfy their obligations by thoughtfully appointing officers, establishing or approving goals and plans and monitoring performance. Thus Section 141(a) of DGCL
expressly permits a board of directors to delegate managerial duties to officers of the

CEO with a board willing to think for itself and assert itself against the CEO when necessary) would not have acted in as unilateral a manner as did Eisner when essentially committing the corporation to hire a second-in-command, appoint that person to the board, and provide him with one of the largest and richest employment contracts ever enjoyed by a non-CEO. I write, "essentially committing," because although I conclude that legally, Ovitz's hiring was not a "done deal" as of the August 14 OLA,[45] it was clear to Eisner, Ovitz, and the directors who were informed, that as a practical matter, it certainly was a "done deal."[46]

*      *      *      *

Notwithstanding the foregoing, Eisner's actions in connection with Ovitz's hiring should not serve as a model for fellow executives and fiduciaries to follow. His lapses were many. He failed to keep the board as informed as he should have. He stretched the outer boundaries of his authority as CEO by acting without specific board direction or involvement. He prematurely issued a press release that placed significant pressure on the board to accept Ovitz and approve his compensation package in accordance with the press release. To my mind, these actions fall far short of what shareholders expect and demand from those entrusted with a fiduciary position. Eisner's failure to better involve the board in the process of Ovitz's hiring, usurping that role for himself, although not in violation of law,[47] does not comport with how fiduciaries of Delaware corporations are expected to act.

Despite all of the legitimate criticisms that may be leveled at Eisner, especially at having enthroned himself as the omnipotent and infallible monarch of his personal Magic Kingdom, I nonetheless conclude, after carefully considering and weighing all the evidence, that Eisner's actions were taken in good faith. That is, Eisner's actions were taken with the subjective belief that those actions were in the best interests of the Company — he believed that his taking charge and acting swiftly and decisively to hire Ovitz would serve the best interests of the Company notwithstanding the high cost of Ovitz's hiring and notwithstanding

---

corporation, except to the extent that the corporation's certificate of incorporation or bylaws may limit or prohibit such a delegation.

*Grimes v. Donald*, 402 A.2d 1205, 1211 (Del. Ch. 1979) (quoting *Abercrombie v. Davies*, 123 A.2d 893, 899 (Del. Ch. 1956)), *aff'd sub nom. Harrison v. Chapin*, 415 A.2d 1068 (Del. 1980).

45. The OLA's opening paragraph stated, "This will confirm our arrangement under which you will become employed by [the Company]. *Subject to the formal approval of the Company's Board of Directors and its Compensation Committee*, we have agreed that . . . ." PTE 60 at DD002932 (emphasis added). The footnote in the summary judgment opinion in this case, *Disney III*, 2004 WL 2050138, at *6 n.54, that Ovitz was likely legally bound by the OLA as of October 1, 1995, is not contradicted by my conclusion here that the Company was not legally bound until at least September 26, 1995.

46. Tr. 2807:13-23; 3572:3-23; 3708:7-17; 6827:8-19; 7693:24-7694:6; 8198:5-21.

47. Eisner's authority to take these actions was not restricted in any way by statute, the Company's certificate of incorporation, bylaws, or a board resolution.

that two experienced executives who had arguably been passed over for the position (Litvack and Bollenbach) were not completely supportive.[48] . . . .

## 2. Russell

Apart from Eisner, Russell, who was familiar with the Company's compensation policies and practices from his service as chairman of the Company's compensation committee, was the next most heavily involved director in hiring Ovitz, as he was the main negotiator on behalf of the Company. Russell was also closely involved with Watson and Crystal in shaping and extensively analyzing Ovitz's proposed compensation. Russell spoke to Poitier on two occasions in mid-August 1995 to discuss the terms of Ovitz's compensation, and he knew that Watson would speak with Lozano. Additionally, on September 26, 1995, Russell led the discussion at the compensation committee meeting regarding the proposed terms for the OEA, and then reported on that meeting during the full board meeting shortly thereafter.

The compensation committee's charter indicates that the committee has the power to "establish the salaries" of the Company's CEO and COO/President, together with benefits and incentive compensation, including stock options, for those same individuals. In addition to this power, the committee's charter charges it with the duty to "approve employment contracts, or contracts at will," for "all corporate officers who are members of the Board of Directors regardless of salary."

Plaintiffs have argued that Russell exceeded the scope of his authority as chairman of the compensation committee by negotiating with Ovitz on behalf of the Company.[49] Although it is true that nothing in the compensation committee's charter specifically grants authority to the committee to negotiate (as opposed to simply approve) employment contracts, there is no language in the charter that would indicate that the committee does not have this power. Indeed, the contrary appears to be the case. The charter distinguishes between "establish[ing]" salaries for the CEO and COO/President and "approv[ing]" salaries for those individuals, together with many others.

In negotiating with Ovitz, Russell became privy to a great deal of information with respect to Ovitz. Ovitz's representatives relayed some of that information to Russell. General information about Ovitz also was common knowledge to those in the entertainment industry. Russell did not independently and objectively verify

48. Eisner's stellar track record as the Company's Chairman and CEO over the preceding eleven years (from 1984 to 1995) bolsters his belief that his decisions generally benefit the Company and its shareholders.

49. *See* Tr. 2676:11-2678:19. Although it would have been ideal if the other members of the compensation committee were more substantively involved in those negotiations, it would certainly be unwieldy as a practical matter to require the entire committee, together and as a whole, to negotiate on the Company's behalf.

the representations made by Ovitz's negotiators that his income from CAA was $20 to $25 million annually because Russell, based upon his pre-existing knowledge, believed that representation to be accurate.[50] Nonetheless, I conclude that Russell negotiated with Ovitz at arms' length.

*        *        *        *

### 3. Watson

Watson's main role in Ovitz's hiring and his election as President of the Company was helping Russell evaluate the financial ramifications of the OEA. Watson is a past Chairman of the Company's board, and served in that position when Eisner and Wells were hired in 1984. Watson was familiar with Crystal, having worked with him on Eisner's and Wells' contracts in 1984 and again in 1989.

Watson conducted extensive analyses of Ovitz's proposed compensation package, sharing those analyses with Crystal and Russell at their meeting on August 10, and in their later discussions stemming from that meeting. He was also involved in determining how to replace the proposed option guarantee with the extended exercisability of Ovitz's options (together with other features). He also spoke with Lozano (although the date is unclear) sometime before the September 26, 1995 compensation committee meeting in order to inform him somewhat of his and Russell's analyses and discussions. Watson attended the September 26, 1995 compensation committee meeting and voted in favor of the resolution approving the terms of the OEA.

Watson was familiar with making executive compensation decisions at the Company. Nothing in his conduct leads me to believe that he took an "ostrich-like" approach to considering and approving the OEA. Nothing in his conduct leads me to believe that Watson consciously and intentionally disregarded his duties to the Company. Nothing in his conduct leads me to believe that Watson had anything in mind other than the best interests of the Company when evaluating and consenting to Ovitz's compensation package. Finally, nothing in his conduct leads me to believe that Watson failed to inform himself of all material information reasonably available before making these decisions. In short, I conclude that plaintiffs have not demonstrated by a preponderance of the evidence that Watson either breached his fiduciary duty of care or acted in anything other than good faith in connection with the hiring of Ovitz and the approval of the economic terms of the OEA.

### 4. Poitier and Lozano

Poitier and Lozano were the remaining members of the compensation committee that considered the economic terms of the OEA. It is not disputed that they were far less involved in the genesis of the OEA than were Russell, and to a lesser

---

50. Tr. 2352:3-2363:13; 2402:6-21; 2755:2-2757:10.

extent, Watson. The question in dispute is whether their level of involvement in the OEA was so low as to constitute gross negligence and, therefore, a breach of their fiduciary duty of care, or whether their actions evidence a lack of good faith. As will be shown, I conclude that neither of these men acted in a grossly negligent manner or in bad faith.

*          *          *          *

There is no question that Poitier and Lozano's involvement in the process of Ovitz's hiring came very late in the game. As found above, Poitier received a call from Russell on August 13 (and another the next day), during which they discussed the terms of the proposed OLA. Lozano spoke with Watson regarding this same subject. It appears that neither Poitier nor Lozano had any further involvement with the hiring process, apart from these phone calls, until the September 26, 1995 compensation committee meeting.

At that meeting, both Poitier and Lozano received the term sheet that explained the key terms of Ovitz's contract, and they were present for and participated in the discussion that occurred. Both then voted to approve the terms of the OEA, and both credibly testified that they believed they possessed sufficient information at that time to make an informed decision. Plaintiffs largely point to two perceived inadequacies in this meeting (and in Poitier and Lozano's business judgment) — first, that insufficient time was spent reviewing the terms of Ovitz's contract and, second, that Poitier and Lozano were not provided with sufficient documentation, including Crystal's correspondence, Watson's calculations, and a draft of the OEA. These arguments understandably hearken back to *Van Gorkom*, where the Supreme Court condemned the Trans Union board for agreeing to a material transaction after a board meeting of about two hours and without so much as a term sheet of the transaction as contemplated. Although the parallels between *Van Gorkom* and this case at first appear striking, a more careful consideration will reveal several important distinctions between the two.

First and foremost, the nature of the transaction in *Van Gorkom* is fundamentally different, and orders of magnitude more important, than the transaction at issue here. In *Van Gorkom*, the Trans Union board was called into a special meeting on less than a day's notice, without notice of the reason for the meeting, to consider a merger agreement that would result in the sale of the entire company. As footnoted above, Delaware law, *as a matter of statute*, requires directors to take certain actions in connection with a merger of the corporation, as was being contemplated by Trans Union. No statute required the Company's board to take action in connection with Ovitz's hiring. The Company's governing documents provide that the officers of the corporation will be selected by the board of directors, . . . . the charter of the compensation committee states that the committee is responsible for establishing and approving the salary of the Company's President. That is exactly what happened. The board meeting was not called on short notice, and the directors were well aware that Ovitz's hiring would be discussed at the meeting as a result of the August 14 press release more than a month before. Furthermore, analyzing the transactions in terms of monetary value, and even accepting plaintiffs' experts' bloated valuations for comparison purposes, it is beyond question that the $734 million sale of Trans Union was material and significantly larger than the financial ramifications to the Company of Ovitz's hiring.

Second, the Trans Union board met for about two hours to discuss and deliberate on this monumental transaction in the life of Trans Union. A precise amount of time for the length of the compensation committee meeting, and more specifically, the length of the discussion regarding the OEA, is difficult to establish. The minutes of the compensation committee's meeting and the full board's meeting indicate that the compensation committee meeting convened at 9:00 a.m., and that the full board's meeting convened at 10:00 a.m., leaving no more than an hour for the compensation committee to meet. Lozano, although he had little recollection of the meeting, believed that the compensation committee meeting ran long — until 10:30 a.m. As I found above, the meeting lasted about an hour. Russell testified that the discussion of the OEA took about 25-30 minutes, significantly more time than the brief discussion reflected in the minutes would seem to indicate. Lozano believed that the committee spent "perhaps four times as much time on Mr. Ovitz's contract than we did on Mr. Russell's compensation."

I am persuaded by Russell and Lozano's recollection that the OEA was discussed for a not insignificant length of time. Is that length of time markedly less than the attention given by the Trans Union board to the merger agreement they were statutorily charged with approving or rejecting? Yes. Is that difference probative on the issue of whether the compensation committee adequately discussed the OEA? Not in the least. When the Trans Union board met for those two hours, it was the very first time any of those directors had discussed a sale of the company. Here, all the members of the committee were aware in advance that Ovitz's hiring would be discussed, and the members of the committee had also previously had more than minimal informal discussions amongst themselves as to the *bona fides* of the OEA before the meeting ever occurred. Furthermore, as mentioned above, the nature and scope of the transactions are fundamentally different.

Third, the Trans Union board had absolutely no documentation before it when it considered the merger agreement. The board was completely reliant on the misleading and uninformed presentations given by Trans Union's officers (Van Gorkom and Romans). In contrast, the compensation committee was provided with a term sheet of the key terms of the OEA and a presentation was made by Russell (assisted by Watson), who had personal knowledge of the relevant information by virtue of his negotiations with Ovitz and discussions with Crystal. Additionally, the testimony and documentary evidence support this conclusion. It is true that the compensation committee did not review and discuss the then existing draft of the full text of the OEA. This, however, is not required. Nor is it necessary for an expert to make a formal presentation at the committee meeting in order for the board to rely on that expert's analysis, although that certainly would have been the better course of action.

Furthermore, the Company's compensation committee reasonably and wisely left the task of negotiating and drafting the actual text of the OEA in the hands of the Company's counsel.

Fourth, Trans Union's senior management completely opposed the merger; In contrast, the Company's senior management generally saw Ovitz's hiring as a boon for the Company, notwithstanding Litvack and Bollenbach's initial personal feelings. In sum, although Poitier and Lozano did very little in connection with Ovitz's hiring and the compensation committee's approval of the OEA, they did not breach their fiduciary duties. I conclude that they were informed by Russell and Watson of all *material* information reasonably available, even though they were not privy to every conversation or document exchanged amongst Russell, Watson, Crystal and Ovitz's representatives.

Much has been made throughout the various procedural iterations of this case about Crystal's involvement (or lack thereof) in the compensation committee's deliberations and decisionmaking. Although there are many criticisms that could and have been made (including by Crystal himself) regarding Crystal's failure to calculate *ex ante* the cost of a potential NFT, nothing in the record leads me to conclude that any member of the compensation committee had actual knowledge that would lead them to believe (as to Poitier and Lozano, their understanding of Crystal's advice was based on information relayed by Russell and Watson) that Crystal's analysis was inaccurate or incomplete. Without that knowledge, I conclude that the compensation committee acted in good faith and relied on Crystal in good faith, and that the fault for errors or omissions in Crystal's analysis must be laid at his feet, and not upon the compensation committee.

The compensation committee reasonably believed that the analysis of the terms of the OEA was within Crystal's professional or expert competence, and together with Russell and Watson's professional competence in those same areas, the committee relied on the information, opinions, reports and statements made by Crystal, even if Crystal did not relay the information, opinions, reports and statements in person to the committee as a whole. Crystal's analysis was not so deficient that the compensation committee would have reason to question it. Furthermore, Crystal appears to have been selected with reasonable care, especially in light of his previous engagements with the Company in connection with past executive compensation contracts that were structurally, at least, similar to the OEA. For all these reasons, the compensation committee also is entitled to the protections of 8 *Del. C.* §141(e) in relying upon Crystal.

Viewed objectively, the compensation committee was asked to make a decision knowing that: 1) Ovitz was a third party with whom Russell negotiated at arms' length; 2) regardless of whether Ovitz truly was "the most powerful man in Hollywood," he was a highly-regarded industry figure; 3) Ovitz was widely believed to possess skills and experience that would be very valuable to the Company, especially in light of the CapCities/ABC acquisition, Wells' death, and Eisner's medical problems; 4) in order to accept the Company's presidency,

Ovitz was leaving and giving up his very successful business, which would lead a reasonable person to believe that he would likely be highly successful in similar pursuits elsewhere in the industry; 5) the CEO and others in senior management were supporting the hiring; and 6) the potential compensation was not economically material to the Company.

Poitier and Lozano did not intentionally disregard a duty to act, nor did they bury their heads in the sand knowing a decision had to be made. They acted in a manner that they believed was in the best interests of the corporation. Delaware law does not require (nor does it prohibit) directors to take as active a role as Russell and Watson took in connection with Ovitz's hiring. There is no question that in comparison to those two, the actions of Poitier and Lozano may appear casual or uninformed, but I conclude that they did not breach their fiduciary duties and that they acted in good faith in connection with Ovitz's hiring.

### 5.  The Remaining Members of the Old Board

[The Court concludes that the remaining members of the board cannot, based on the evidence, be found to have acted in bad faith.]

### D.  EISNER AND LITVACK DID NOT ACT IN BAD FAITH IN CONNECTION WITH OVITZ'S TERMINATION, AND THE REMAINDER OF THE NEW BOARD HAD NO DUTIES IN CONNECTION THEREWITH

The New Board[51] was likewise charged with complying with their fiduciary duties in connection with any actions taken, or required to be taken, in connection with Ovitz's termination. The key question here becomes whether the board was under a duty to act in connection with Ovitz's termination, because if the directors were under no duty to act, then they could not have acted in bad faith by not acting, nor would they have failed to inform themselves of all material information reasonably available before making a decision, because no decision was required to be made. Furthermore, the actions taken by the Company's officers (namely Eisner and Litvack) in connection with Ovitz's termination must be viewed through the lens of whether the board was under a duty to act. If the board was under no such duty, then the officers are justified in acting alone. If the board was under a duty to act and the officers improperly usurped that authority, the analysis would obviously be different.

### 1.  The New Board Was Not Under a Duty to Act

Determining whether the New Board was required to discuss and approve Ovitz's termination requires careful consideration of the Company's governing

---

51. The New Board consisted of Eisner, Ovitz, Roy Disney, Gold, Litvack, Nunis, Poitier, Russell, Stern, Walker, Watson, Wilson, Bowers, Lozano, Mitchell, O'Donovan and Murphy.

instruments..... Article Tenth of the Company's certificate of incorporation states:

> The officers of the Corporation shall be chosen in such a manner, shall hold their offices for such terms and shall carry out such duties as are determined solely by the Board of Directors, subject to the right of the Board of Directors to remove any officer or officers at any time with or without cause.

The Company's bylaws state at Article IV:

> Section 1. General. The officers of the Corporation shall be chosen by the Board of Directors and shall be a Chairman of the Board of Directors (who must be a director), a President, a Secretary and a Treasurer.
>     ....
> Section 2. Election. The Board of Directors at its first meeting held after each Annual Meeting of stockholders shall elect the officers of the Corporation who shall hold their offices for such terms and shall exercise such powers and perform such duties as shall be determined from time to time solely by the Board of Directors, which determination may be by resolution of the Board of Directors or in any bylaw provision duly adopted or approved by the Board of Directors; and all officers of the Corporation shall hold office until their successors are chosen and qualified, or until their earlier resignation or removal. Any officer elected by the Board of Directors may be removed at any time by the Board of Directors with or without cause. Any vacancy occurring in any office of the Corporation may be filled only by the Board of Directors.
> Section 3. Chairman of the Board of Directors. The Chairman of the Board of Directors shall be the Chief Executive Officer of the Corporation, shall preside at all meetings of the Board of Directors and of stockholders and shall, subject to the provisions of the Bylaws and the control of the Board of Directors, have general and active management, direction, and supervision over the business of the Corporation and over its officers. ... He shall perform all duties incident to the office of chief executive and such other duties as from time to time may be assigned to him by the Board of Directors. He shall have the right to delegate any of his powers to any other officer or employee.
> Section 4. President. The President shall report and be responsible to the Chairman of the Board. The President shall have such powers and perform such duties as from time to time may be assigned or delegated to him by the Board of Directors or are incident to the office [of] President.

Other relevant language comes from the board resolution that elected Ovitz as President, which states: "RESOLVED, that Michael S. Ovitz be, and hereby is, elected President of the Corporation, effective October 1, 1995, to serve in such capacity at the pleasure of this Board of Directors."

Having considered these documents, I come to the following conclusions: 1) the board of directors has the sole power to elect the officers of the Company; 2) the board of directors has the sole power to determine the "duties" of the officers of the Company (either through board resolutions or bylaws); 3) the Chairman/ CEO has "general and active management, direction, and supervision over the business of the Corporation and over its officers," and that such management, direction and supervision is subject to the control of the board of directors; 4) the Chairman/CEO has the power to manage, direct and supervise the lesser officers and employees of the Company; 5) the board has the *right*, but not the *duty* to remove the officers of the Company with or without cause, and that right is non-exclusive; and 6) because that right is non-exclusive, and because the Chairman/ CEO is affirmatively charged with the management, direction and supervision of the officers of the Company, together with the powers and duties incident to the office of chief executive, the Chairman/CEO, subject to the control of the board of directors,[52] also possesses the *right* to remove the inferior officers and employees of the corporation.

The New Board unanimously believed that Eisner, as Chairman and CEO, possessed the power to terminate Ovitz without board approval or intervention. Nonetheless, the board was informed of and supported Eisner's decision. The board's simultaneous power to terminate Ovitz, reserved to the board by the certificate of incorporation, did not divest Eisner of the authority to do so, or vice-versa. Eisner used that authority, and terminated Ovitz — a decision, coupled with the decision to honor the OEA, that resulted in the Company's obligation to pay the NFT. Because Eisner unilaterally terminated Ovitz, as was his right, the New Board was not required to act in connection with Ovitz's termination.

Therefore, the fact that no formal board action was taken with respect to Ovitz's termination is of no import. . . . . For these reasons, the members of the New Board

---

52. Care should be taken to not read too much into the phrase, "subject to the control of the board of directors," as this "restriction" is simply a reflection of basic agency principles, and not a limitation on the powers and authority that would otherwise be incident to the office of chief executive. A chief executive officer has authority to govern the corporation subject to the control of the board of directors — that is, the chief executive officer may act as a general agent for the benefit of the corporation and in the manner in which the chief executive officer believes the board of directors desires him to act, but may not act in a manner contrary to the express desires of the board of directors. See RESTATEMENT (SECOND) OF AGENCY §§ 33, 39, 73 (1958). More generally, the rule has been stated thusly:

> Implied authority (including 'incidental' and 'inferred' authority) of the agent to act is a natural consequence of the express authority granted. It is implied from what is actually manifested to the agent by the principal. It is obvious that implied authority cannot, by its very nature, be inconsistent with express authority because any expression of actual authority must control.

WILLIAM A. GREGORY, THE LAW OF AGENCY AND PARTNERSHIP § 15 (3d ed. 2001).

For example, as it would apply to this case, the chief executive officer possesses the authority to remove inferior employees (including officers) so long as the board of directors does not expressly limit or negate the chief executive officer's implied or inherent authority to do so. No member of the New Board expressed, either contemporaneously or at trial, any objection to Ovitz's termination. . . . .

(other than Eisner and Litvack, who will be discussed individually below) did not breach their fiduciary duties and did not act in bad faith in connection with Ovitz's termination and his receipt of the NFT benefits included in the OEA.

### 2. Litvack

Litvack, as an officer of the corporation and as its general counsel, consulted with, and gave advice to, Eisner, on two questions relevant to Ovitz's termination. They are, first, whether Ovitz could or should have been terminated for cause and, second, whether a board meeting was required to ratify or effectuate Ovitz's termination or the payment of his NFT benefits. For the reasons I have already stated, Litvack properly concluded that the Company did not have good cause under the OEA to terminate Ovitz. He also properly concluded that no board action was necessary in connection with the termination.

\*          \*          \*          \*

In conclusion, Litvack gave the proper advice and came to the proper conclusions when it was necessary. He was adequately informed in his decisions, and he acted in good faith for what he believed were the best interests of the Company.

### 3. Eisner

Having concluded that Eisner alone possessed the authority to terminate Ovitz and grant him the NFT, I turn to whether Eisner acted in accordance with his fiduciary duties and in good faith when he terminated Ovitz. As will be shown hereafter, I conclude that Eisner did not breach his fiduciary duties and did act in good faith in connection with Ovitz's termination and concomitant receipt of the NFT.

When Eisner hired Ovitz in 1995, he did so with an eye to preparing the Company for the challenges that lay ahead, especially in light of the CapCities/ABC acquisition and the need for a legitimate potential successor to Eisner. To everyone's regret, including Ovitz, things did not work out as blissfully as anticipated. Eisner was unable to work well with Ovitz, and Eisner refused to let Ovitz work without close and constant supervision. Faced with that situation, Eisner essentially had three options: 1) keep Ovitz as President and continue trying to make things work; 2) keep Ovitz at Disney, but in a role other than President; or 3) terminate Ovitz.

In deciding which route to take, Eisner, consistent with his discretion as CEO, considered keeping Ovitz as the Company's President an unacceptable solution. Shunting Ovitz to a different role within the Company would have almost certainly entitled Ovitz to the NFT, or at the very least, a costly lawsuit to determine whether Ovitz was so entitled. Eisner would have also rightly questioned whether there was another position within the Company where Ovitz could be of use. Eisner was then left with the only alternative he considered feasible — termination.

Faced with the knowledge that termination was the best alternative and knowing that Ovitz had not performed to the high expectations placed upon him when he was hired, Eisner inquired of Litvack on several occasions as to whether a for-cause termination was possible such that the NFT payment could be avoided, and then relied in good faith on the opinion of the Company's general counsel.... In the end, however, he bit the bullet and decided that the best decision would be to terminate Ovitz and pay the NFT.

After reflection on the more than ample record in this case, I conclude that Eisner's actions in connection with the termination are, for the most part, consistent with what is expected of a faithful fiduciary....

## CONCLUSION

For the reasons set forth in the Court's Opinion of this date, judgment is hereby entered in the above captioned action against plaintiffs and in favor of defendants on all counts. The parties shall bear their own costs.

IT IS SO ORDERED.

## 9.5    Corporate Opportunity Doctrine

## 9.5.1    Determining Which Opportunities "Belong" to the Corporation

*§9.5.1, page 330: Add the following material at the end of the section:*

### IN RE EBAY, INC. SHAREHOLDERS LITIGATION
2004 Del. Ch. LEXIS 4 (2004)

CHANDLER, Chancellor

Shareholders of eBay, Inc. filed these consolidated derivative actions against certain eBay directors and officers for usurping corporate opportunities. Plaintiffs allege that eBay's investment banking advisor, Goldman Sachs Group, engaged in "spinning," a practice that involves allocating shares of lucrative initial public offerings of stock to favored clients. In effect, the plaintiff shareholders allege that Goldman Sachs bribed certain eBay insiders, using the currency of highly profit-able investment opportunities — opportunities that should have been offered to, or provided for the benefit of, eBay rather than the favored insiders. Plaintiffs accuse Goldman Sachs of aiding and abetting the corporate insiders breach of their fiduciary duty of loyalty to eBay.

The individual eBay defendants, as well as Goldman Sachs, have moved to dismiss these consolidated actions....

## I. BACKGROUND FACTS

The facts, as alleged in the complaint, are straightforward. In 1995, defendants Pierre M. Omidyar and Jeffrey Skoll founded nominal defendant eBay as Delaware corporation, as a sole proprietorship. eBay is a pioneer in online trading platforms, providing a virtual auction community for buyers and sellers to list items for sale and to bid on items of interest. In 1998, eBay retained Goldman Sachs and other investment banks to underwrite an initial public offering of common stock. Goldman Sachs was the lead underwriter. The stock was priced at $18 per share. Goldman Sachs purchased about 1.2 million shares. Shares of eBay stock became immensely valuable during 1998 and 1999, rising to $175 per share in early April 1999. Around that time, eBay made a secondary offering, issuing 6.5 million shares of common stock at $170 per share for a total of $1.1 billion. Goldman Sachs again served as lead underwriter. Goldman Sachs was asked in 2001 to serve as eBay's financial advisor in connection with an acquisition by eBay of PayPal, Inc. For these services, eBay has paid Goldman Sachs over $8 million.

During this same time period, Goldman Sachs "rewarded" the individual defendants by allocating to them thousands of IPO shares, managed by Goldman Sachs, at the initial offering price. Because the IPO market during this particular period of time was extremely active, prices of initial stock offerings often doubled or tripled in a single day. Investors who were well-connected, either to Goldman Sachs or to similarly situated investment banks serving as IPO underwriters, were able to flip these investments into instant profit by selling the equities in a few days or even in a few hours after they were initially purchased.

The essential allegation of the complaint is that Goldman Sachs provided these IPO share allocations to the individual defendants to show appreciation for eBay's business and to enhance Goldman Sachs' chances of obtaining future eBay business. In addition to co-founding eBay, defendant Omidyar has been eBay's CEO, CFO and President. He is eBay's largest stockholder, owning more than 23% of the company's equity. Goldman Sachs allocated Omidyar shares in at least forty IPOs at the initial offering price. Omidyar resold these securities in the public market for millions of dollars in profit. Defendant Whitman owns 3.3% of eBay stock and has been President, CEO and a director since early 1998. Whitman also has been a director of Goldman Sachs since 2001. Goldman Sachs allocated Whitman shares in over a 100 IPOs at the initial offering price. Whitman sold these equities in the open market and reaped millions of dollars in profit. Defendant Skoll, in addition to co-founding eBay, has served in various positions at the company, including Vice-President of Strategic Planning and Analysis and President. He served as an eBay director from December 1996 to March 1998. Skoll is eBay's second largest stockholder, owning about 13% of the company. Goldman Sachs has allocated Skoll shares in at least 75 IPOs at the initial offering price, which Skoll promptly resold on the open market, allowing him to realize millions of dollars in profit. Finally, defendant Robert C. Kagle has served as an eBay director since June 1997. Goldman Sachs allocated Kagle shares in at least 25 IPOs at the initial offering price. Kagle promptly resold these equities, and recorded millions of dollars in profit.

## II.  ANALYSIS

### A.  DEMAND FUTILITY

[The court concluded that four arguably independent directors had received rich options for their service and that the defendants, holding together about 40 percent of eBay stock, were sufficiently in control that for pleading purposes the four nondefendant directors would not be considered independent for demand futility purposes.]

### B.  CORPORATE OPPORTUNITY

Plaintiffs have stated a claim that defendants usurped a corporate opportunity of eBay. Defendants insist that Goldman Sachs' IPO allocations to eBay's insider directors were "collateral investments opportunities" that arose by virtue of the inside directors status as wealthy individuals. They argue that this is not a corporate opportunity within the corporation's line of business or an opportunity in which the corporation had an interest or expectancy. These arguments are unavailing.

First, no one disputes that eBay financially was able to exploit the opportunities in question. Second, eBay was in the business of investing in securities. The complaint alleges that eBay "consistently invested a portion of its cash on hand in marketable securities." According to eBay's 1999 10-K, for example, eBay had more than $550 million invested in equity and debt securities. eBay invested more than $181 million in "short-term investments" and $373 million in "long-term investments." Thus, investing was "a line of business" of eBay. Third, the facts alleged in the complaint suggest that investing was integral to eBay's cash management strategies and a significant part of its business. Finally, it is no answer to say, as do defendants, that IPOs are risky investments. It is undisputed that eBay was never given an opportunity to turn down the IPO allocations as too risky.

Defendants also argue that to view the IPO allocations in question as corporate opportunities will mean that every advantageous investment opportunity that comes to an officer or director will be considered a corporate opportunity. On the contrary, the allegations in the complaint in this case indicate that unique, below-market price investment opportunities were offered by Goldman Sachs to the insider defendants as financial inducements to maintain and secure corporate business. This was not an instance where a broker offered advice to a director about an investment in a marketable security. The conduct challenged here involved a large investment bank that regularly did business with a company steering highly lucrative IPO allocations to select insider directors and officers at that company, allegedly both to reward them for past business and to induce them to direct future business to that investment bank. This is a far cry from the defendants' characterization of the conduct in question as merely "a broker's investment recommendations" to a wealthy client.

Nor can one seriously argue that this conduct did not place the insider defendants in a position of conflict with their duties to the corporation. One can realistically characterize these IPO allocations as a form of commercial discount or rebate for past or future investment banking services. Viewed pragmatically, it is easy to understand how steering such commercial rebates to certain insider directors places those directors in an obvious conflict between their self-interest and the corporation's interest. It is noteworthy, too, that the Securities and Exchange Commission has taken the position that "spinning" practices violate the obligations of broker-dealers under the "Free-riding and Withholding Interpretation" rules. As the SEC has explained, "the purpose of the interpretation is to protect the integrity of the public offering system by ensuring that members make a bona fide public distribution of 'hot issue' securities and do not withhold such securities for their own benefit or use the securities to reward other persons who are in a position to direct future business to the member."

Finally, even if one assumes that IPO allocations like those in question here do not constitute a corporate opportunity, a cognizable claim is nevertheless stated on the common law ground that an agent is under a duty to account for profits obtained personally in connection with transactions related to his or her company. The complaint gives rise to a reasonable inference that the insider directors accepted a commission or gratuity that rightfully belonged to eBay but that was improperly diverted to them. Even if this conduct does not run afoul of the corporate opportunity doctrine, it may still constitute a breach of the fiduciary duty of loyalty. Thus, even if one does not consider Goldman Sachs' IPO allocations to these corporate insiders — allocations that generated millions of dollars in profit — to be a corporate opportunity, the defendant directors were nevertheless not free to accept this consideration from a company, Goldman Sachs, that was doing significant business with eBay and that arguably intended the consideration as an inducement to maintaining the business relationship in the future. [Citing *Restatement (Second) of Agency* §388 (1957).]

### C.   AIDING AND ABETTING CLAIM

Plaintiffs' complaint adequately alleges the existence of a fiduciary relationship, that the individual defendants breached their fiduciary duty and that plaintiffs have been damaged because of the concerted actions of the individual defendants and Goldman Sachs. Goldman Sachs, however, disputes whether it "knowingly participated" in the eBay insiders' alleged breach of fiduciary duty. The allegation, however, is that Goldman Sachs had provided underwriting and investment advisory services to eBay for years and that it knew that each of the individual defendants owed a fiduciary duty to eBay not to profit personally at eBay's expense and to devote their undivided loyalty to the interests of eBay.

Goldman Sachs also knew or had reason to know of eBay's investment of excess cash in marketable securities and debt. Goldman Sachs was aware (or charged with a duty to know) of earlier SEC interpretations that prohibited steering "hot issue" securities to persons in a position to direct future business to the broker-dealer. Taken together, these allegations allege a claim for aiding and abetting sufficient to withstand a motion to dismiss.

III.  CONCLUSION

For all of the above reasons, I deny the defendants' motions to dismiss the complaint in this consolidated action.

IT IS SO ORDERED.

## BEAM v. MARTHA STEWART
### 833 A.2d 961 (Del. Ch. 2003)

CHANDLER, Chancellor

Monica A. Beam, a shareholder of Martha Stewart Living Omnimedia, Inc. ("MSO"), brings this derivative action against the defendants, all current directors and a former director of MSO, and against MSO as a nominal defendant. The defendants have filed three separate motions seeking (1) to dismiss Counts II, III, and IV under Court of Chancery Rule 12(b)(6) for failure to state claims upon which relief may be granted; (2) to dismiss the amended complaint under Court of Chancery Rule 23.1 for failure to comply with the demand requirement and for failure adequately to plead demand excusal; or alternatively (3) to stay this action in favor of litigation currently pending in the U.S. District Court for the Southern District of New York. n1 This is the Court's ruling on these motions. . . .

Plaintiff Monica A. Beam is a shareholder of MSO and has been since August 2001. . . .

Defendant Martha Stewart ("Stewart") is a director of the company and its founder, chairman, chief executive officer, and by far its majority shareholder. MSO's common stock is comprised of Class A and Class B shares. Class A shares are traded on the New York Stock Exchange and are entitled to cast one vote per share on matters voted upon by common stockholders. Class B shares are not publicly traded and are entitled to cast ten votes per share on all matters voted upon by common stockholders. Stewart owns or beneficially holds 100% of the B shares in conjunction with a sufficient number of A shares that she controls roughly 94.4% of the shareholder vote. Stewart, a former stockbroker, has in the past twenty years become a household icon, known for her advice and expertise on virtually all aspects of cooking, decorating, entertaining, and household affairs generally. . . .

Defendant L. John Doerr ("Doerr"), is a former director of MSO. His tenure as a director ended in March 2002. Doerr is the general partner of a venture capital firm, Kleiner, Perkins, Caufield & Byers ("Kleiner, Perkins").

The plaintiff seeks relief in relation to three distinct types of activities. The first involves the well-publicized matters surrounding Stewart's alleged improper trading of shares of ImClone Systems, Inc. ("ImClone") and her public statements in the wake of those allegations. The second relates to the private sale of sizeable blocks of MSO stock by both Stewart and Doerr in early 2002. The third challenges the board's decisions with regard to the provision of "split-dollar" insurance for Stewart. . . .

### B.  PRIVATE SALES OF MSO STOCK

In January 2002, Stewart and the Martha Stewart Family Partnership sold 3,000,000 shares of Class A stock to entities designated in the amended complaint as "ValueAct." In March 2002, Kleiner, Perkins, acting through its general partner, Doerr, sold 1,999,403 shares of MSO to ValueAct. . . .

### A.  MOTIONS TO DISMISS COUNTS II, III, AND IV — COURT
###      OF CHANCERY RULE 12(B)(6)

In ruling on a motion to dismiss under Rule 12(b)(6), the Court considers only the allegations in the amended complaint, and any documents incorporated by reference therein. . . .

### 2.  *Count III — Stock Sales by Stewart and Doerr*

Count III of the amended complaint alleges that Stewart and Doerr breached their fiduciary duty of loyalty, usurping a corporate opportunity by selling large blocks of MSO stock to ValueAct. Defendants Stewart and Doerr are essentially in the same position with respect to Count III. The basic requirements for establishing usurpation of a corporate opportunity were articulated by the Delaware Supreme Court in *Broz v. Cellular Information Systems, Inc.*:

> [A] corporate officer or director may not take a business opportunity for his own if: (1) the corporation is financially able to exploit the opportunity; (2) the opportunity is within the corporation's line of business; (3) the corporation has an interest or expectancy in the opportunity; [**23] and (4) by taking the opportunity for his own, the corporate fiduciary will thereby be placed in a position [inimical] to his duties to the corporation.

In this analysis, no single factor is dispositive. Instead the Court must balance all factors as they apply to a particular case. For purposes of the present motion, I assume that the sales of stock to ValueAct could be considered to be a "business opportunity." I now address each of the four factors articulated in *Broz*.

### a.   Financial Ability of MSO to Exploit the Opportunity

The amended complaint asserts that MSO was able to exploit this opportunity because the Company's certificate of incorporation had sufficient authorized, yet unissued, shares of Class A common stock to cover the sale to ValueAct. Defendants do not deny that the Company could have sold previously unissued shares to ValueAct. I therefore conclude that the first factor has been met.

### b.   Within MSO's Line of Business

An opportunity is within a corporation's line of business if it is "an activity as to which [the corporation] has fundamental knowledge, practical experience and ability to pursue." Because I have already determined that MSO had sufficient authorized but unissued shares available and because no special expertise is required to issue stock, I find that the "ability to pursue" prong is met. The question then becomes whether selling its own stock is an activity as to which the Company has fundamental knowledge and practical experience.

Plaintiff states that the Company's line of business is "creating 'how-to' content and domestic merchandise for homemakers and other consumers." Nevertheless, the Court recognizes that raising capital is a fundamental activity in which businesses are often engaged. MSO made its initial public offering in October 1999. Therefore, in a strictly literal sense, the Company, like any stock corporation, "has fundamental knowledge and practical experience" in the activity of selling its stock in exchange for capital contributions. This conclusion, however, does not help plaintiff in this instance. MSO is a consumer products company, not an investment company. Simply stated, selling stock is not the same line of business as selling advice to homemakers. Further, I would presume that a company's "line of business" is one that is intended to be profitable. By definition, a company's issuance of its stock does not generate income. For the foregoing reasons, I therefore conclude that the sale of stock by Stewart and Doerr was not within MSO's line of business.

### c.   MSO's Interest or Expectancy in the Stock Sales

A corporation has an interest or expectancy in an opportunity if there is "some tie between that property and the nature of the corporate business." Requiring a tie to the "nature of the corporate business" implicates many of the issues discussed above regarding MSO's line of business. The *Broz* Court found that the company in that case, CIS (a company in the business of providing cellular phone service to the Midwest), had no interest or expectancy in the Michigan-2 license in question because CIS was divesting its cellular license holdings and its business plan did not contemplate any new acquisitions. Here, plaintiff does not allege any facts that would imply that MSO was in need of additional capital, seeking additional capital, or even remotely interested in finding new investors. Had MSO wished to do so, it had a readily available, liquid market in which to accomplish that aim, as MSO's Class A stock is traded on the New York Stock Exchange.

I fail to see any connection between the potential sale of stock to ValueAct and the nature of MSO's business. Further, issuance of new shares without a need or desire for new capital is perceived to have negative effects on preexisting shareholders, as the new capital may not be effectively used to increase earnings at the same time that the preexisting shareholders' proportionate interests in the corporation have decreased. Plaintiff presents no indication that MSO had any expectation, interest, or necessity to raise capital through new issuances of stock, nor can I reasonably infer such from the amended complaint. In the absence of specific allegations indicative of corporate interest or expectancy, I must conclude that this factor of the *Broz* test has not been met.

### d. Whether the Stock Sales Placed Stewart and Doerr in a Position Inimical to Their Duties to MSO

"The corporate opportunity doctrine is implicated only in cases where the fiduciary's seizure of an opportunity results in a conflict between the fiduciary's duties to the corporation and the self-interest of the director as actualized by the exploitation of the opportunity. Given that I have concluded that MSO had no interest or expectancy in the issuance of new stock to ValueAct, I fail to see, based on the allegations before me, how Stewart and Doerr's sales placed them in a position inimical to their duties to the Company. Were I to decide otherwise, directors of every Delaware corporation would be faced with the ever-present specter of suit for breach of their duty of loyalty if they sold stock in the company on whose Board they sit.

Additionally, Delaware courts have recognized a policy that allows officers and directors of corporations to buy and sell shares of that corporation at will so long as they act in good faith. A corporation generally "has no interest in its outstanding stock or in dealing in its shares among its stockholders." Plaintiff cites only one case purported to be to the contrary — *Thorpe v. CERBCO, Inc.* *Thorpe* involved a bidder who approached the management of Insituform East, Inc. desirous to purchase the company. In bad faith, management withheld this information from the outside directors, lied by saying that the bidder had not expressed interest in purchasing the company, threatened to block any sale of the entire company, and simply informed the board a bidder wished to buy the inside directors' controlling interest. I would attempt to compare the well-pled facts in this case to those in *Thorpe*, but I am unable to do so because the amended complaint fails to provide *any* factual detail about the circumstances surrounding the stock sales, alleging only that the transactions occurred.

Delaware jurisprudence favors certainty and predictability. Directors must "make decisions based on the situation as it exists at the time a given opportunity is presented." In the absence of allegations based on well-pled facts that call into question the propriety of Stewart and Doerr's sales at the time they made them, it is impossible to infer that they acted in bad faith in selling their shares or placed themselves in a position inimical to their duties to MSO. Given the allegations before me, the fourth factor of the *Broz* test is not met.

On balancing the four factors, I conclude that plaintiff has failed to plead facts sufficient to state a claim that Stewart and Doerr usurped a corporate opportunity for themselves in violation of their fiduciary duty of loyalty to MSO. Count III is dismissed in its entirety under Rule 12(b)(6) for failure to state a claim upon which relief can be granted.

## NOTE ON PRESENTING POSSIBLE CORPORATE OPPORTUNITIES TO THE BOARD OF DIRECTORS

When an officer or director is presented with a business opportunity that may be a corporate opportunity, one way to proceed is to present the opportunity to the board of directors for its judgment. This is especially prudent if the director or officer wished to argue that the corporation was itself not able or not interested in taking advantage of this opportunity. Financial inability is an especially weak reed for a fiduciary to rely upon when outside financing may be available to the firm to take advantage of a profitable opportunity. While presenting the opportunity to the board seems clearly the safer practice for the fiduciary and the better corporate governance practice, it is not required under Delaware law. In *Beam v. Martha Stewart OmniMedia*, Chancellor Chandler noted the following:

> There is some controversy in the parties' briefs as to whether the opportunity for the ValueAct sales was presented to the board by Stewart or Doerr. In *Broz*, the Supreme Court clearly stated, "It is not the law of Delaware that presentation to the board is a necessary prerequisite to a finding that a corporate opportunity has not been usurped." *Id.* at 157. Presenting an opportunity to the board simply provides, "a kind of 'safe harbor' for the director, which removes the specter of a *post hoc* judicial determination that the director or officer has improperly usurped a corporate opportunity." *Id.* I have concluded that the amended complaint fails to plead properly that Stewart and Doerr usurped a corporate opportunity, regardless of whether it was ever presented to the board. Since they were under no separate obligation to present it, the count cannot be sustained whether a presentation was made or not.

In *Beam*, the purported opportunity was said to be the chance to sell corporate stock. This is an odd corporate opportunity claim and not one in which the Board — which ordinarily will always have the power to issue new shares itself — will have an interest in. An opportunity to buy corporate stock of the issuer, which may in some circumstances affect corporate control, might be very different.

# Chapter 10
# Shareholder Lawsuits

## 10.1 Distinguishing Between Direct and Derivative Claims

*§10.1, page 351: Add the following material at the end of the section:*

### NOTE ON *TOOLEY v. DONALDSON, LUFKIN & JENRETTE, INC.*

In *Tooley v. Donaldson, Lufkin & Jenrette, Inc.,* 845 A.2d 1031 (Del. 2004), the Delaware Supreme Court attempted to clarify the distinction between direct (class) suits by shareholders and derivative suits brought by shareholders in the name of the corporation.

The suit was brought by minority shareholders as a direct (class) action alleging that the board had breached a fiduciary duty to them by agreeing to a twenty-two-day delay in closing a proposed merger. In the merger, the shareholders were to get cash, and the claim was that the extension of time to close deprived them of the time value of the merger proceeds for the period of the delay.

The Court of Chancery dismissed, stating that if any claim was stated it was a claim belonging to the corporation since it was a claim held equally by all shareholders. The court focused on language in earlier cases that emphasized that a shareholder had to suffer some special injury in order to state a direct claim. The Supreme Court affirmed the dismissal but in doing so restated the test for determining whether a suit is to be treated as derivative or direct: "We set forth in this Opinion the law to be applied henceforth in determining whether a stockholder's claim is derivative or direct. The issue must turn *solely* on the following questions: (1) who suffered the alleged harm (the corporation or the suing shareholders); and who would receive the benefit of any recovery or other remedy (the corporation or the stockholders individually)?" Thus the Supreme Court removed from the analysis the question of special injury as being the mark of a direct claim.

In the event the Supreme Court held that no claim of any sort was stated by the complaint, since the shareholders had no individual right to have the merger occur at all. From the corporation's point of view as well there simply was no wrong alleged. Nevertheless, if there had been a claim stated, it would have been a direct (not withstanding no special injury to the representative plaintiff). This case shows the limited utility of the special injury concept (which will work well enough in some situations to identify an individual or direct claim). Here, while the claim was shared by all shareholders and thus was not "special," it was nevertheless individual (if a legal right had been asserted at all).

The restatement in *Tooley* is clarifying, but does not constitute a change in the law from that set forth in the Note in this section.


## 10.4   Balancing the Rights of Boards to Manage the Corporation and Shareholders' Rights to Obtain Judicial Review


## 10.4.2   Special Litigation Committees

*§10.4.2, page 380: Insert the following material before* How Does the Court Exercise Business Judgment?:

*In re Oracle Corp. Derivative Litigation* demonstrates the highly individualized inquiry that the Chancery Court may pursue in probing the independence of a Special Litigation (SLC)Committee that requests the dismissal of a shareholder derivative action. The opinion is well-written and entertaining. The questions it raises are whether the defendants could reasonably have anticipated that a Delaware judge would find the independence of academic directors compromised by multiple overlapping "old school ties," financial and otherwise, and what a defending board should do next time to ensure that it appoints an independent SLC that can pass the independence test. Note, too, that *In re Oracle* should be read in conjunction with *Emerging Communications*, in which the Chancery Court conducts a similarly tough-minded investigation into the independence of a special board committee appointed to negotiate on behalf of public shareholders in a freezeout transaction.

### IN RE ORACLE CORP. DERIVATIVE LITIGATION
824 A.2d 917 (Del. Ch. 2003)

STRINE, Vice Chancellor

In this opinion, I address the motion of the special litigation committee ("SLC") of Oracle Corporation to terminate this action, "the Delaware Derivative Action," and other such actions pending in the name of Oracle against certain Oracle directors and officers. These actions allege that these Oracle directors engaged in insider trading while in possession of material, non-public information showing that Oracle would not meet the earnings guidance it gave to the market for the third quarter of Oracle's fiscal year 2001. The SLC bears the burden of persuasion on this motion and must convince me that there is no material issue of fact calling into doubt its independence. This requirement is set forth in *Zapata Corp. v. Maldonado*[1] and its progeny....

The question of independence "turns on whether a director is, *for any substantial reason,* incapable of making a decision with only the best interests of the corporation in mind." ... That is, the independence test ultimately "focus[es] on impartiality and objectivity." ... In this case, the SLC has failed to demonstrate that no material factual question exists regarding its independence.

During discovery, it emerged that the two SLC members — both of whom are professors at Stanford University — are being asked to investigate fellow Oracle directors who have important ties to Stanford, too. Among the directors who are accused by the derivative plaintiffs of insider trading are: (1) another Stanford professor, who taught one of the SLC members when the SLC member was a Ph.D. candidate and who serves as a senior fellow and a steering committee member alongside that SLC member at the Stanford Institute for Economic Policy Research or "SIEPR"; (2) a Stanford alumnus who has directed millions of dollars of contributions to Stanford during recent years, serves as Chair of SIEPR's Advisory Board and has a conference center named for him at SIEPR's facility, and has contributed nearly $600,000 to SIEPR and the Stanford Law School, both parts of Stanford with which one of the SLC members is closely affiliated; and (3) Oracle's CEO, who has made millions of dollars in donations to Stanford through a personal foundation and large donations indirectly through Oracle, and who was considering making donations of his $100 million house and $170 million for a scholarship program as late as August 2001, at around the same time period the SLC members were added to the Oracle board. Taken together, these and other facts cause me to harbor a reasonable doubt about the impartiality of the SLC.

It is no easy task to decide whether to accuse a fellow director of insider trading. For Oracle to compound that difficulty by requiring SLC members to consider accusing a fellow professor and two large benefactors of their university of conduct that is rightly considered a violation of criminal law was unnecessary and inconsistent with the concept of independence recognized by our law. The possibility that these extraneous considerations biased the inquiry of the SLC is too substantial for this court to ignore. I therefore deny the SLC's motion to terminate....

The Delaware Derivative Complaint centers on alleged insider trading by four members of Oracle's board of directors — Lawrence Ellison, Jeffrey Henley, Donald Lucas, and Michael Boskin (collectively, the "Trading Defendants"). Each of the Trading Defendants had a very different role at Oracle.

Ellison is Oracle's Chairman, Chief Executive Officer, and its largest stockholder, owning nearly twenty-five percent of Oracle's voting shares. By virtue of his ownership position, Ellison is one of the wealthiest men in America. By virtue

---

1. *430 A.2d 779 (Del. 1981).*

of his managerial position, Ellison has regular access to a great deal of information about how Oracle is performing on a week-to-week basis.

Henley is Oracle's Chief Financial Officer, Executive Vice President, and a director of the corporation. Like Ellison, Henley has his finger on the pulse of Oracle's performance constantly.

Lucas is a director who chairs Oracle's Executive Committee and its Finance and Audit Committee. . . .

Boskin is a director, Chairman of the Compensation Committee, and a member of the Finance and Audit Committee. As with Lucas, Boskin's access to information was limited mostly to historical financials and did not include the week-to-week internal projections and revenue results that Ellison and Henley received.

According to the plaintiffs, each of these Trading Defendants possessed material, non-public information demonstrating that Oracle would fail to meet the earnings and revenue guidance it had provided to the market in December 2000. In that guidance, Henley projected — subject to many disclaimers, including the possibility that a softening economy would hamper Oracle's ability to achieve these results — that Oracle would earn 12 cents per share and generate revenues of over $2.9 billion in the third quarter of its fiscal year 2001 ("3Q FY 2001"). Oracle's 3Q FY 2001 ran from December 1, 2000 to February 28, 2001.

The plaintiffs allege that this guidance was materially misleading and became even more so as early results for the quarter came in. . . .

In addition, the plaintiffs contend more generally that the Trading Defendants received material, non-public information that the sales growth for Oracle's other products was slowing in a significant way, which made the attainment of the earnings and revenue guidance extremely difficult. This information grew in depth as the quarter proceeded, as various sources of information that Oracle's top managers relied upon allegedly began to signal weakness in the company's revenues. These signals supposedly included a slowdown in the "pipeline" of large deals that Oracle hoped to close during the quarter and weak revenue growth in the first month of the quarter.

During the time when these disturbing signals were allegedly being sent, the Trading Defendants engaged in the following trades:

- On January 3, 2001, Lucas sold 150,000 shares of Oracle common stock at $30 per share, reaping proceeds of over $4.6 million. These sales constituted 17% of Lucas's Oracle holdings.
- On January 4, 2001, Henley sold one million shares of Oracle stock at approximately $32 per share, yielding over $32.3 million. These sales represented 7% of Henley's Oracle holdings.
- On January 17, 2001, Boskin sold 150,000 shares of Oracle stock at over $33 per share, generating in excess of $5 million. These sales were 16% of Boskin's Oracle holdings.
- From January 22 to January 31, 2001, Ellison sold over 29 million shares at prices above $30 per share, producing over $894 million. Despite the huge

proceeds generated by these sales, they constituted the sale of only 2% of Ellison's Oracle holdings.

Into early to mid-February, Oracle allegedly continued to assure the market that it would meet its December guidance. Then, on March 1, 2001, the company announced that rather than posting 12 cents per share in quarterly earnings and 25% license revenue growth as projected, the company's earnings for the quarter would be 10 cents per share and license revenue growth only 6%. The stock market reacted swiftly and negatively to this news, with Oracle's share price dropping as low as $15.75 before closing at $16.88 — a 21% decline in one day. These prices were well below the above $30 per share prices at which the Trading Defendants sold in January 2001. . . .

### B. THE PLAINTIFFS' CLAIMS IN THE DELAWARE DERIVATIVE ACTION

The plaintiffs make two central claims in their amended complaint in the Delaware Derivative Action. First, the plaintiffs allege that the Trading Defendants breached their duty of loyalty by misappropriating inside information and using it as the basis for trading decisions. This claim rests its legal basis on the venerable case of *Brophy v. Cities Service Co.*[5] Its factual foundation is that the Trading Defendants were aware (or at least possessed information that should have made them aware) that the company would miss its December guidance by a wide margin and used that information to their advantage in selling at artificially inflated prices.

Second, as to the other defendants — who are the members of the Oracle board who did not trade — the plaintiffs allege a *Caremark*[6] violation, in the sense that the board's indifference to the deviation between the company's December guidance and reality was so extreme as to constitute subjective bad faith. . . .

### D. THE FORMATION OF THE SPECIAL LITIGATION COMMITTEE

On February 1, 2002, Oracle formed the SLC in order to investigate the Delaware Derivative Action and to determine whether Oracle should press the claims raised by the plaintiffs, settle the case, or terminate it. Soon after its formation, the SLC's charge was broadened to give it the same mandate as to all the pending derivative actions, wherever they were filed.

The SLC was granted full authority to decide these matters without the need for approval by the other members of the Oracle board.

### E. THE MEMBERS OF THE SPECIAL LITIGATION COMMITTEE

Two Oracle board members were named to the SLC. Both of them joined the Oracle board on October 15, 2001, more than a half a year after Oracle's 3Q FY

5. *31 Del. Ch. 241, 70 A.2d 5 (Del. Ch. 1949).*
6. *In re Caremark Int'l Derivative Litig., 698 A.2d 959 (Del. Ch. 1996).*

2001 closed. The SLC members also share something else: both are tenured professors at Stanford University.

Professor Hector Garcia-Molina is Chairman of the Computer Science Department at Stanford and holds the Leonard Bosack and Sandra Lerner Professorship in the Computer Science and Electrical Engineering Departments at Stanford. . . .

The other SLC member, Professor Joseph Grundfest, is the W.A. Franke Professor of Law and Business at Stanford University. He directs the University's well-known Directors' College[8] and the Roberts Program in Law, Business, and Corporate Governance at the Stanford Law School. Grundfest is also the principal investigator for the Law School's Securities Litigation Clearinghouse. Immediately before coming to Stanford, Grundfest served for five years as a Commissioner of the Securities and Exchange Commission. Like Garcia-Molina, Grundfest's appointment at Stanford was a homecoming, because he obtained his law degree and performed significant post-graduate work in economics at Stanford.

As will be discussed more specifically later, Grundfest also serves as a steering committee member and a senior fellow of the Stanford Institute for Economic Policy Research, and releases working papers under the "SIEPR" banner.

For their services, the SLC members were paid $250 an hour, a rate below that which they could command for other activities, such as consulting or expert witness testimony. Nonetheless, during the course of their work, the SLC members became concerned that (arguably scandal-driven) developments in the evolving area of corporate governance as well as the decision in *Telxon v. Meyerson,* . . . might render the amount of their compensation so high as to be an argument against their independence. Therefore, Garcia-Molina and Grundfest agreed to give up any SLC-related compensation if their compensation was deemed by this court to impair their impartiality. . . .

The SLC members were recruited to the board primarily by defendant Lucas, with help from defendant Boskin. . . . The wooing of them began in the summer of 2001. Before deciding to join the Oracle board, Grundfest, in particular, did a good deal of due diligence. His review included reading publicly available information, among other things, the then-current complaint in the Federal Class Action. . . .

The SLC's investigation was, by any objective measure, extensive. The SLC reviewed an enormous amount of paper and electronic records. SLC counsel interviewed seventy witnesses, some of them twice. SLC members participated in several key interviews, including the interviews of the Trading Defendants.

Importantly, the interviewees included all the senior members of Oracle's management most involved in its projection and monitoring of the company's financial performance, including its sales and revenue growth. These interviews combined with a special focus on the documents at the company bearing on these subjects, including e-mail communications.

---

8. In the interests of full disclosure, I spoke at the Directors' College in spring 2002.

The SLC also asked the plaintiffs in the various actions to identify witnesses the Committee should interview. The Federal Class Action plaintiffs identified ten such persons and the Committee interviewed all but one, who refused to cooperate. The Delaware Derivative Action plaintiffs and the other derivative plaintiffs declined to provide the SLC with any witness list or to meet with the SLC.

During the course of the investigation, the SLC met with its counsel thirty-five times for a total of eighty hours. In addition to that, the SLC members, particularly Professor Grundfest, devoted many more hours to the investigation.

In the end, the SLC produced an extremely lengthy Report totaling 1,110 pages (excluding appendices and exhibits) that concluded that Oracle should not pursue the plaintiffs' claims against the Trading Defendants or any of the other Oracle directors serving during the 3Q FY 2001.... I endeavor a rough attempt to capture the essence of the Report in understandable terms....

... [T]he SLC concluded that even a hypothetical Oracle executive who possessed all information regarding the company's performance in December and January of 3Q FY 2001 would not have possessed material, non-public information that the company would fail to meet the earnings and revenue guidance it provided the market in December. Although there were hints of potential weakness in Oracle's revenue growth, especially starting in mid-January 2001, there was no reliable information indicating that the company would fall short of the mark, and certainly not to the extent that it eventually did....

Consistent with its Report, the SLC moved to terminate this litigation. The plaintiffs were granted discovery focusing on three primary topics: the independence of the SLC, the good faith of its investigative efforts, and the reasonableness of the bases for its conclusion that the lawsuit should be terminated. Additionally, the plaintiffs received a large volume of documents comprising the materials that the SLC relied upon in preparing its Report.

## III. THE APPLICABLE PROCEDURAL STANDARD

In order to prevail on its motion to terminate the Delaware Derivative Action, the SLC must persuade me that: (1) its members were independent; (2) that they acted in good faith; and (3) that they had reasonable bases for their recommendations.[17] If the SLC meets that burden, I am free to grant its motion or may, in my discretion, undertake my own examination of whether Oracle should terminate and permit the suit to proceed if I, in my oxymoronic judicial "business judgment," conclude that procession is in the best interests of the company.[18] This two-step analysis comes, of course, from *Zapata*....

As I understand it, this standard requires me to determine whether, on the basis of the undisputed factual record, I am convinced that the SLC was independent,

17. *Zapata v. Maldonado, 430 A.2d 779, 788-89 (Del. 1981); Katell v. Morgan Stanley Group, 1995 Del. Ch. LEXIS 76, 1995 WL 376952 at *5 (Del. Ch. June 15, 1995).*
18. *Zapata, 430 A.2d at 789.*

acted in good faith, and had a reasonable basis for its recommendation. If there is a material factual question about these issues causing doubt about any of these grounds, I read *Zapata* and its progeny as requiring a denial of the SLC's motion to terminate. . . .

In its Report, the SLC took the position that its members were independent. In support of that position, the Report noted several factors including:

- the fact that neither Grundfest nor Garcia-Molina received compensation from Oracle other than as directors;
- the fact that neither Grundfest nor Garcia-Molina were on the Oracle board at the time of the alleged wrongdoing;
- the fact that both Grundfest and Garcia-Molina were willing to return their compensation as SLC members if necessary to preserve their status as independent;
- the absence of any other material ties between Oracle, the Trading Defendants, and any of the other defendants, on the one hand, and Grundfest and Garcia-Molina, on the other; and
- the absence of any material ties between Oracle, the Trading Defendants, and any of the other defendants, on the one hand, and the SLC's advisors, on the other.

Noticeably absent from the SLC Report was any disclosure of several significant ties between Oracle or the Trading Defendants and Stanford University, the university that employs both members of the SLC. In the Report, it was only disclosed that:

- defendant Boskin was a Stanford professor;
- the SLC members were aware that Lucas had made certain donations to Stanford; and
- among the contributions was a donation of $50,000 worth of stock that Lucas donated to Stanford Law School after Grundfest delivered a speech to a venture capital fund meeting in response to Lucas's request. It happens that Lucas's son is a partner in the fund and that approximately half the donation was allocated for use by Grundfest in his personal research. . . .

In view of the modesty of these disclosed ties, it was with some shock that a series of other ties among Stanford, Oracle, and the Trading Defendants emerged during discovery. Although the plaintiffs have embellished these ties considerably beyond what is reasonable, the plain facts are a striking departure from the picture presented in the Report.

Before discussing these facts, I begin with certain features of the record — as I read it — that are favorable to the SLC. Initially, I am satisfied that neither of the SLC members is compromised by a fear that support for the procession of this suit would endanger his ability to make a nice living. Both of the SLC members are distinguished in their fields and highly respected. Both have tenure, which could not have been stripped from them for making a determination that this lawsuit should proceed.

Nor have the plaintiffs developed evidence that either Grundfest or Garcia-Molina have fundraising responsibilities at Stanford. . . .

Defendant Michael J. Boskin is the T.M. Friedman Professor of Economics at Stanford University. During the Administration of President George H.W. Bush, Boskin occupied the coveted and important position of Chairman of the President's Council of Economic Advisors. He returned to Stanford after this government service, continuing a teaching career there that had begun many years earlier.

During the 1970s, Boskin taught Grundfest when Grundfest was a Ph.D. candidate. Although Boskin was not Grundfest's advisor and although they do not socialize, the two have remained in contact over the years, speaking occasionally about matters of public policy.

Furthermore, both Boskin and Grundfest are senior fellows and steering committee members at the Stanford Institute for Economic Policy Research, which was previously defined as "SIEPR." According to the SLC, the title of senior fellow is largely an honorary one. According to SIEPR's own web site, however, "senior fellows actively participate in SIEPR research and participate in its governance." . . .

Likewise, the SLC contends that Grundfest went MIA as a steering committee member, having failed to attend a meeting since 1997. The SIEPR web site, however, identifies its steering committee as having the role of "advising the director [of SIEPR] and guiding [SIEPR] on matters pertaining to research and academics." . . . Because Grundfest allegedly did not attend to these duties, his service alongside Boskin in that capacity is, the SLC contends, not relevant to his independence.

That said, the SLC does not deny that both Boskin and Grundfest publish working papers under the SIEPR rubric and that SIEPR helps to publicize their respective works. Indeed, as I will note later in this opinion, Grundfest, in the same month the SLC was formed, addressed a meeting of some of SIEPR's largest benefactors — the so-called "SIEPR Associates." The SLC just claims that the SIEPR affiliation is one in which SIEPR basks in the glow of Boskin and Grundfest, not the other way around, and that the mutual service of the two as senior fellows and steering committee members is not a collegial tie of any significance.

With these facts in mind, I now set forth the ties that defendant Lucas has to Stanford. . . .

As noted in the SLC Report, the SLC members admitted knowing that Lucas was a contributor to Stanford. They also acknowledged that he had donated $50,000 to Stanford Law School in appreciation for Grundfest having given a speech at his request. About half of the proceeds were allocated for use by Grundfest in his research.

But Lucas's ties with Stanford are far, far richer than the SLC Report lets on. To begin, Lucas is a Stanford alumnus, having obtained both his undergraduate and graduate degrees there. By any measure, he has been a very loyal alumnus.

In showing that this is so, I start with a matter of some jousting between the SLC and the plaintiffs. Lucas's brother, Richard, died of cancer and by way of his will established a foundation. Lucas became Chairman of the Foundation and serves as a director along with his son, a couple of other family members, and some non-family members. A principal object of the Foundation's beneficence has been Stanford. The Richard M. Lucas Foundation has given $11.7 million to Stanford since its 1981 founding. Among its notable contributions, the Foundation funded the establishment of the Richard M. Lucas Center for Magnetic Resonance Spectroscopy and Imaging at Stanford's Medical School. Donald Lucas was a founding member and lead director of the Center.

The SLC Report did not mention the Richard M. Lucas Foundation or its grants to Stanford. In its briefs on this motion, the SLC has pointed out that Donald Lucas is one of nine directors at the Foundation and does not serve on its Grant Review Committee. Nonetheless, the SLC does not deny that Lucas is Chairman of the board of the Foundation and that the board approves all grants.

Lucas's connections with Stanford as a contributor go beyond the Foundation, however. From his own personal funds, Lucas has contributed $4.1 million to Stanford, a substantial percentage of which has been donated within the last half-decade. Notably, Lucas has, among other things, donated $424,000 to SIEPR and approximately $149,000 to Stanford Law School. Indeed, Lucas is not only a major contributor to SIEPR, he is the Chair of its Advisory Board. At SIEPR's facility at Stanford, the conference center is named the Donald L. Lucas Conference Center.

From these undisputed facts, it is inarguable that Lucas is a very important alumnus of Stanford and a generous contributor to not one, but two, parts of Stanford important to Grundfest: the Law School and SIEPR.

With these facts in mind, it remains to enrich the factual stew further, by considering defendant Ellison's ties to Stanford. . . .

There can be little doubt that Ellison is a major figure in the community in which Stanford is located. The so-called Silicon Valley has generated many success stories, among the greatest of which is that of Oracle and its leader, Ellison. One of the wealthiest men in America, Ellison is a major figure in the nation's increasingly important information technology industry. Given his wealth, Ellison is also in a position to make—and, in fact, he has made—major charitable contributions.

Some of the largest of these contributions have been made through the Ellison Medical Foundation, which makes grants to universities and laboratories to support biomedical research relating to aging and infectious diseases. Ellison is the sole director of the Foundation. Although he does not serve on the Foundation's Scientific Advisory Board that sifts through grant applications, he has reserved the right—as the Foundation's sole director—to veto any grants, a power he has not yet used but which he felt it important to retain. The Scientific Advisory Board is comprised of distinguished physicians and scientists from many institutions, but not including Stanford.

Although it is not represented on the Scientific Advisory Board, Stanford has nonetheless been the beneficiary of grants from the Ellison Medical Foundation — to the tune of nearly $10 million in paid or pledged funds. Although the Executive Director of the Foundation asserts by way of an affidavit that the grants are awarded to specific researchers and may be taken to another institution if the researcher leaves, . . . the grants are conveyed under contracts between the Foundation and Stanford itself and purport by their terms to give Stanford the right (subject to Foundation approval) to select a substitute principal investigator if the original one becomes unavailable. . . .

During the time Ellison has been CEO of Oracle, the company itself has also made over $300,000 in donations to Stanford. Not only that, when Oracle established a generously endowed educational foundation — the Oracle Help Us Help Foundation — to help further the deployment of educational technology in schools serving disadvantaged populations, it named Stanford as the "appointing authority," which gave Stanford the right to name four of the Foundation's seven directors. . . . Stanford's acceptance reflects the obvious synergistic benefits that might flow to, for example, its School of Education from the University's involvement in such a foundation, as well as the possibility that its help with the Foundation might redound to the University's benefit when it came time for Oracle to consider making further donations to institutions of higher learning.

Taken together, these facts suggest that Ellison (when considered as an individual and as the key executive and major stockholder of Oracle) had, at the very least, been involved in several endeavors of value to Stanford. . . .

The SLC contends that even together, these facts regarding the ties among Oracle, the Trading Defendants, Stanford, and the SLC members do not impair the SLC's independence. In so arguing, the SLC places great weight on the fact that none of the Trading Defendants have the practical ability to deprive either Grundfest or Garcia-Molina of their current positions at Stanford. Nor, given their tenure, does Stanford itself have any practical ability to punish them for taking action adverse to Boskin, Lucas, or Ellison — each of whom, as we have seen, has contributed (in one way or another) great value to Stanford as an institution. As important, neither Garcia-Molina nor Grundfest are part of the official fundraising apparatus at Stanford; thus, it is not their on-the-job duty to be solicitous of contributors, and fundraising success does not factor into their treatment as professors.

In so arguing, the SLC focuses on the language of previous opinions of this court and the Delaware Supreme Court that indicates that a director is not independent only if he is dominated and controlled by an interested party, such as a Trading Defendant. . . .

More subtly, the SLC argues that university professors simply are not inhibited types, unwilling to make tough decisions even as to fellow professors and large contributors. What is tenure about if not to provide professors with intellectual freedom, even in non-traditional roles such as special litigation committee members? No less ardently — but with no record evidence that reliably supports its ultimate point — the SLC contends that Garcia-Molina and Grundfest are extremely distinguished in their fields and were not, in fact, influenced by the facts identified heretofore. Indeed, the SLC argues, how could they have been influenced by many of these facts when they did not learn them until the post-Report discovery process? If it boils down to the simple fact that both share with Boskin the status of a Stanford professor, how material can this be when there are 1,700 others who also occupy the same position? . . .

The plaintiffs confronted these arguments with less nuance than was helpful. Rather than rest their case on the multiple facts I have described, the plaintiffs chose to emphasize barely plausible constructions of the evidence, such as that Grundfest was lying when he could not recall being asked to participate in the Ellison Scholars Program. From these more extreme arguments, however, one can distill a reasoned core that emphasizes what academics might call the "thickness" of the social and institutional connections among Oracle, the Trading Defendants, Stanford, and the SLC members. These connections, the plaintiffs argue, were very hard to miss — being obvious to anyone who entered the SIEPR facility, to anyone who read the *Wall Street Journal, Fortune,* or the *Washington Post,* and especially to Stanford faculty members interested in their own university community and with a special interest in Oracle. Taken in their totality, the plaintiffs contend, these connections simply constitute too great a bias-producing factor for the SLC to meet its burden to prove its independence. . . .

Having framed the competing views of the parties, it is now time to decide.

I begin with an important reminder: the SLC bears the burden of proving its independence. It must convince me. . . .

. . . Delaware law should not be based on a reductionist view of human nature that simplifies human motivations on the lines of the least sophisticated notions of the law and economics movement. *Homo sapiens* is not merely *homo economicus.* We may be thankful that an array of other motivations exist that influence human behavior; not all are any better than greed or avarice, think of envy, to name just one. But also think of motives like love, friendship, and collegiality, think of those among us who direct their behavior as best they can on a guiding creed or set of moral values. . . .

Nor should our law ignore the social nature of humans. To be direct, corporate directors are generally the sort of people deeply enmeshed in social institutions. Such institutions have norms, expectations that, explicitly and implicitly, influence and channel the behavior of those who participate in their operation. . . . Some things are "just not done," or only at a cost, which might not be so severe as a loss of position, but may involve a loss of standing in the institution. In being appropriately sensitive to this factor, our law also cannot assume — absent some proof of the point — that corporate directors are, as a general matter, persons of unusual social bravery, who operate heedless to the inhibitions that social norms generate for ordinary folk.

For all these reasons, this court has previously held that the Delaware Supreme Court's teachings on independence can be summarized thusly:

> At bottom, the question of independence turns on whether a director is, *for any substantial reason,* incapable of making a decision with only the best interests of the corporation in mind. That is, the Supreme Court cases ultimately focus on impartiality and objectivity.[49] . . .

In examining whether the SLC has met its burden to demonstrate that there is no material dispute of fact regarding its independence, the court must bear in mind the function of special litigation committees under our jurisprudence. . . .

Special litigation committees are permitted as a last chance for a corporation to control a derivative claim in circumstances when a majority of its directors cannot impartially consider a demand. By vesting the power of the board to determine what to do with the suit in a committee of independent directors, a corporation may retain control over whether the suit will proceed, so long as the committee meets the standard set forth in *Zapata.*

In evaluating the independence of a special litigation committee, this court must take into account the extraordinary importance and difficulty of such a committee's responsibility. It is, I daresay, easier to say no to a friend, relative, colleague, or boss who seeks assent for an act *(e.g.,* a transaction) that has not yet occurred than it would be to cause a corporation to sue that person. . . .

The difficulty of making this decision is compounded in the special litigation committee context because the weight of making the moral judgment necessarily falls on less than the full board. A small number of directors feels the moral gravity — and social pressures — of this duty alone. . . .

Thus, in assessing the independence of the Oracle SLC, I necessarily examine the question of whether the SLC can independently make the difficult decision entrusted to it: to determine whether the Trading Defendants should face suit for insider trading-based allegations of breach of fiduciary duty. An affirmative answer by the SLC to that question would have potentially huge negative consequences for the Trading Defendants, not only by exposing them to the possibility of a large damage award but also by subjecting them to great reputational harm. To have Professors Grundfest and Garcia-Molina declare that Oracle should press insider trading claims against the Trading Defendants would have been, to put it mildly, "news." Relatedly, it is reasonable to think that an SLC determination that the Trading Defendants had likely engaged in insider trading

---

49. *Parfi Holding AB v. Mirror Image Internet, Inc., 794 A.2d 1211, 1232 (Del. Ch. 2001)* (footnotes omitted) (emphasis in original), *rev'd in part on other grounds, 817 A.2d 149 (Del. 2002), cert. denied, 123 S. Ct. 2076 (2003).*

would have been accompanied by a recommendation that they step down as fiduciaries until their ultimate culpability was decided.

The importance and special sensitivity of the SLC's task is also relevant for another obvious reason: investigations do not follow a scientific process like an old-fashioned assembly line....

Therefore, I necessarily measure the SLC's independence contextually, and my ruling confronts the SLC's ability to decide impartially whether the Trading Defendants should be pursued for insider trading. This contextual approach is a strength of our law, as even the best minds have yet to devise across-the-board definitions that capture all the circumstances in which the independence of directors might reasonably be questioned. By taking into account all circumstances, the Delaware approach undoubtedly results in some level of indeterminacy, but with the compensating benefit that independence determinations are tailored to the precise situation at issue....

...I conclude that the SLC has not met its burden to show the absence of a material factual question about its independence. I find this to be the case because the ties among the SLC, the Trading Defendants, and Stanford are so substantial that they cause reasonable doubt about the SLC's ability to impartially consider whether the Trading Defendants should face suit. The concern that arises from these ties can be stated fairly simply, focusing on defendants Boskin, Lucas, and Ellison in that order, and then collectively.

As SLC members, Grundfest and Garcia-Molina were already being asked to consider whether the company should level extremely serious accusations of wrongdoing against fellow board members. As to Boskin, both SLC members faced another layer of complexity: the determination of whether to have Oracle press insider trading claims against a fellow professor at their university. Even though Boskin was in a different academic department from either SLC member, it is reasonable to assume that the fact that Boskin was also on faculty would — to persons possessing typical sensibilities and institutional loyalty — be a matter of more than trivial concern. Universities are obviously places of at-times intense debate, but they also see themselves as communities. In fact, Stanford refers to itself as a "community of scholars." ... To accuse a fellow professor — whom one might see at the faculty club or at inter-disciplinary presentations of academic papers — of insider trading cannot be a small thing — even for the most callous of academics.

As to Boskin, Grundfest faced an even more complex challenge than Garcia-Molina. Boskin was a professor who had taught him and with whom he had maintained contact over the years. Their areas of academic interest intersected, putting Grundfest in contact if not directly with Boskin, then regularly with Boskin's colleagues. Moreover, although I am told by the SLC that the title of senior fellow at SIEPR is an honorary one, the fact remains that Grundfest willingly accepted it and was one of a select number of faculty who attained that status. And, they both just happened to also be steering committee members. Having these ties, Grundfest (I infer) would have more difficulty objectively determining whether Boskin engaged in improper insider trading than would a person who was not a fellow professor, had not been a student of Boskin, had not kept in touch with Boskin over the years, and who was not a senior fellow and steering committee member at SIEPR.

In so concluding, I necessarily draw on a general sense of human nature. It may be that Grundfest is a very special person who is capable of putting these kinds of things totally aside. But the SLC has not provided evidence that that is the case. In this respect, it is critical to note that I do not infer that Grundfest would be less likely to recommend suit against Boskin than someone without these ties. Human nature being what it is, it is entirely possible that Grundfest would in fact be tougher on Boskin than he would on someone with whom he did not have such connections. The inference I draw is subtly, but importantly, different. What I infer is that a person in Grundfest's position would find it difficult to assess Boskin's conduct without pondering his own association with Boskin and their mutual affiliations. Although these connections might produce bias in either a tougher or laxer direction, the key inference is that these connections would be on the mind of a person in Grundfest's position, putting him in the position of either causing serious legal action to be brought against a person with whom he shares several connections (an awkward thing) or not doing so (and risking being seen as having engaged in favoritism toward his old professor and SIEPR colleague).

The same concerns also exist as to Lucas. For Grundfest to vote to accuse Lucas of insider trading would require him to accuse SIEPR's Advisory Board Chair and major benefactor of serious wrongdoing — of conduct that violates federal securities laws. Such action would also require Grundfest to make charges against a man who recently donated $50,000 to Stanford Law School after Grundfest made a speech at his request. . . .

And, for both Grundfest and Garcia-Molina, service on the SLC demanded that they consider whether an extremely generous and influential Stanford alumnus should be sued by Oracle for insider trading. Although they were not responsible for fundraising, as sophisticated professors they undoubtedly are aware of how important large contributors are to Stanford, and they share in the benefits that come from serving at a university with a rich endowment. A reasonable professor giving any thought to the matter would obviously consider the effect his decision might have on the University's relationship with Lucas, it being (one hopes) sensible to infer that a professor of reasonable collegiality and loyalty cares about the well-being of the institution he serves.

In so concluding, I give little weight to the SLC's argument that it was unaware of just how substantial Lucas's beneficence to Stanford has been. I do so for two key reasons. Initially, it undermines, rather than inspires, confidence that the SLC did not examine the Trading Defendants' ties to Stanford more closely in preparing its Report. The Report's failure to identify these ties is important because it is the SLC's burden to show independence. In forming the SLC, the Oracle board should have undertaken a thorough consideration of the facts bearing on the independence of the proposed SLC members from the key objects of the investigation....

In concluding that the facts regarding Lucas's relationship with Stanford are materially important, I must address a rather odd argument of the SLC's. The argument goes as follows. Stanford has an extremely large endowment. Lucas's contributions, while seemingly large, constitute a very small proportion of Stanford's endowment and annual donations. Therefore, Lucas could not be a materially important contributor to Stanford and the SLC's independence could not be compromised by that factor.

But missing from that syllogism is any acknowledgement of the role that Stanford's solicitude to benefactors like Lucas might play in the overall size of its endowment and campus facilities. Endowments and buildings grow one contribution at a time, and they do not grow by callous indifference to alumni who (personally and through family foundations) have participated in directing contributions of the size Lucas has. . . .

In view of the ties involving Boskin and Lucas alone, I would conclude that the SLC has failed to meet its burden on the independence question. The tantalizing facts about Ellison merely reinforce this conclusion. The SLC, of course, argues that Ellison is not a large benefactor of Stanford personally, that Stanford has demonstrated its independence of him by rejecting his child for admission, and that, in any event, the SLC was ignorant of any negotiations between Ellison and Stanford about a large contribution. For these reasons, the SLC says, its ability to act independently of Ellison is clear.

I find differently. The notion that anyone in Palo Alto can accuse Ellison of insider trading without harboring some fear of social awkwardness seems a stretch. That being said, I do not mean to imply that the mere fact that Ellison is worth tens of billions of dollars and is the key force behind a very important social institution in Silicon Valley disqualifies all persons who live there from being independent of him. Rather, it is merely an acknowledgement of the simple fact that accusing such a significant person in that community of such serious wrongdoing is no small thing.

Given that general context, Ellison's relationship to Stanford itself contributes to my overall doubt, when heaped on top of the ties involving Boskin and Lucas. During the period when Grundfest and Garcia-Molina were being added to the Oracle board, Ellison was publicly considering making extremely large contributions to Stanford. Although the SLC denies knowledge of these public statements, Grundfest claims to have done a fair amount of research before joining the board, giving me doubt that he was not somewhat aware of the possibility that Ellison might bestow large blessings on Stanford. This is especially so when I cannot rule out the possibility that Grundfest had been told by Lucas about, but has now honestly forgotten, the negotiations over the Ellison Scholars Program.

Furthermore, the reality is that whether or not Ellison eventually decided not to create that Program and not to bequeath his house to Stanford, Ellison remains a plausible target of Stanford for a large donation. This is especially so in view of

Oracle's creation of the Oracle Help Us Help Foundation with Stanford and Ellison's several public indications of his possible interest in giving to Stanford. And, while I do not give it great weight, the fact remains that Ellison's medical research foundation has been a source of nearly $10 million in funding to Stanford. Ten million dollars, even today, remains real money.

Of course, the SLC says these facts are meaningless because Stanford rejected Ellison's child for admission. I am not sure what to make of this fact, but it surely cannot bear the heavy weight the SLC gives it. The aftermath of denying Ellison's child admission might, after all, as likely manifest itself in a desire on the part of the Stanford community never to offend Ellison again, lest he permanently write off Stanford as a possible object of his charitable aims — as the sort of thing that acts as not one, but two strikes, leading the batter to choke up on the bat so as to be even more careful not to miss the next pitch. Suffice to say that after the rejection took place, it did not keep Ellison from making public statements in *Fortune* magazine on August 13, 2001 about his consideration of making a huge donation to Stanford, at the same time when the two SLC members were being courted to join the Oracle board.

As an alternative argument, the SLC contends that neither SLC member was aware of Ellison's relationship with Stanford until after the Report was completed. Thus, this relationship, in its various facets, could not have compromised their independence. Again, I find this argument from ignorance to be unavailing. An inquiry into Ellison's connections with Stanford should have been conducted before the SLC was finally formed and, at the very least, should have been undertaken in connection with the Report. In any event, given how public Ellison was about his possible donations it is difficult not to harbor troublesome doubt about whether the SLC members were conscious of the possibility that Ellison was pondering a large contribution to Stanford. In so concluding, I am not saying that the SLC members are being untruthful in saying that they did not know of the facts that have emerged, only that these facts were in very prominent journals at the time the SLC members were doing due diligence in aid of deciding whether to sign on as Oracle board members. The objective circumstances of Ellison's relations with Stanford therefore generate a reasonable suspicion that seasoned faculty members of some sophistication — including the two SLC members — would have viewed Ellison as an active and prized target for the University. The objective circumstances also require a finding that Ellison was already, through his personal Foundation and Oracle itself, a benefactor of Stanford. . . .

Before closing, it is necessary to address two concerns. The first is the undeniable awkwardness of opinions like this one. By finding that there exists too much doubt about the SLC's independence for the SLC to meet its *Zapata* burden, I make no finding about the subjective good faith of the SLC members, both of whom are distinguished academics at one of this nation's most prestigious institutions of higher learning. . . . Nothing in this record leads me to conclude that either of the SLC members acted out of any conscious desire to favor the Trading

Defendants or to do anything other than discharge their duties with fidelity. But that is not the purpose of the independence inquiry.

That inquiry recognizes that persons of integrity and reputation can be compromised in their ability to act without bias when they must make a decision adverse to others with whom they share material affiliations. To conclude that the Oracle SLC was not independent is not a conclusion that the two accomplished professors who comprise it are not persons of good faith and moral probity, it is solely to conclude that they were not situated to act with the required degree of impartiality. *Zapata* requires independence to ensure that stockholders do not have to rely upon special litigation committee members who must put aside personal considerations that are ordinarily influential in daily behavior in making the already difficult decision to accuse fellow directors of serious wrongdoing. . . .

The SLC's motion to terminate is DENIED. IT IS SO ORDERED.

## MORE ON INDEPENDENT DIRECTORS

### BEAM v. MARTHA STEWART
833 A.2d 961 (Del. Ch. 2003)

CHANDLER, Chancellor

Monica A. Beam, a shareholder of Martha Stewart Living Omnimedia, Inc. ("MSO"), brings this derivative action against the defendants, all current directors and a former director of MSO, and against MSO as a nominal defendant. The defendants have filed three separate motions seeking (1) to dismiss Counts II, III, and IV under Court of Chancery Rule 12(b)(6) for failure to state claims upon which relief may be granted; (2) to dismiss the amended complaint under Court of Chancery Rule 23.1 for failure to comply with the demand requirement and for failure adequately to plead demand excusal; or alternatively (3) to stay this action in favor of litigation currently pending in the U.S. District Court for the Southern District of New York. This is the Court's ruling on these motions. . . .

Plaintiff Monica A. Beam is a shareholder of MSO and has been since August 2001. . . .

Defendant Martha Stewart ("Stewart") is a director of the company and its founder, chairman, chief executive officer, and by far its majority shareholder. MSO's common stock is comprised of Class A and Class B shares. Class A shares are traded on the New York Stock Exchange and are entitled to cast one vote per share on matters voted upon by common stockholders. Class B shares are not publicly traded and are entitled to cast ten votes per share on all matters voted upon by common stockholders. Stewart owns or beneficially holds 100% of the B shares in conjunction with a sufficient number of A shares that she controls roughly 94.4% of the shareholder vote. Stewart, a former stockbroker, has in the past twenty years become a household icon, known for her advice and expertise on virtually all aspects of cooking, decorating, entertaining, and household affairs generally.

Defendant Sharon L. Patrick ("Patrick") is a director of MSO and its president and chief operating officer. The amended complaint reports that in 2001, MSO paid Patrick a salary of $700,000, a $280,000 bonus, and granted her options for 130,000 Class A shares. She also serves as the secretary of M. Stewart, Inc., which is described in the complaint as "one of Stewart's personal companies." Prior to Patrick's employment at MSO, she was a consultant to the magazine, *Martha Stewart Living*, and developed extensive experience in the media, entertainment, and consulting businesses. Patrick is also a longtime personal friend of Stewart.

Defendant Arthur C. Martinez ("Martinez") has been a director of MSO since January 2001. Martinez is the former chairman of the board of directors and chief executive officer of Sears Roebuck and Co. . . . A March 2001 article in *Directors & Boards* reported that Patrick and Stewart both consider Martinez to be "an old friend." Also, Martinez was recruited to serve on MSO's board by then-board member Charlotte Beers ("Beers"), another "longtime friend and confidante" of Stewart.

Defendant Darla D. Moore ("Moore") has been a director of MSO since September 2001, when Beers resigned and Moore replaced her. Moore's professional background includes a partnership at Rainwater, Inc., a private investment firm, a managing directorship with Chase Bank, and service as a trustee of Magellan Health Services, Inc. Moore, too, is reported to be a longtime friend of both Stewart and Beers, as evidenced by a 1996 *Fortune* magazine article highlighting the close friendship among the three women and by the amended complaint's report of Moore's attendance at a wedding reception in 1995, which was attended by both Stewart and Samuel Waksal and hosted by Stewart's lawyer, Allen Grubman.

Defendant Naomi O. Seligman ("Seligman") has been a director of MSO since 1999. She is a co-founder and senior partner of Cassius Advisors and a co-founder and former senior partner of Research Board, Inc. Seligman serves as a director of several public companies, including John Wiley & Sons ("JWS"), a publisher. The amended complaint relates a *Wall Street Journal* report that Seligman contacted the chief executive officer of JWS on behalf of Stewart to express concern over an unflattering biography of Stewart that was scheduled for publication by JWS.

Defendant Jeffery W. Ubben ("Ubben") has been a director of MSO since January 2002. He is the founder and managing partner of ValueAct Capital Partners, L.P. and a director of Insurance Auto Auctions, Inc. Ubben has formerly served as a managing partner and as a portfolio manager, working in the investment industry since at least 1987.

Defendant L. John Doerr ("Doerr"), is a former director of MSO. His tenure as a director ended in March 2002. Doerr is the general partner of a venture capital firm, Kleiner, Perkins, Caufield & Byers ("Kleiner, Perkins").

The amended complaint states that compensation paid to MSO's directors includes all of the following:

- $20,000 as an annual retainer;
- $1,000 for each meeting attended in person;
- $500 for each meeting attended telephonically; and
- $5,000 annually for serving as chairman of any committee.

Twenty-five percent of directors' fees are paid in shares of MSO's Class A common stock, with the remaining 75% payable either in Class A shares or cash at the choice of the director. In addition, MSO has a stock option plan for the directors.

The plaintiff seeks relief in relation to three distinct types of activities. The first involves the well-publicized matters surrounding Stewart's alleged improper trading of shares of ImClone Systems, Inc. ("ImClone") and her public statements in the wake of those allegations. The second relates to the private sale of sizeable blocks of MSO stock by both Stewart and Doerr in early 2002. The third challenges the board's decisions with regard to the provision of "split-dollar" insurance for Stewart. . . .

### B.  MOTIONS TO DISMISS THE AMENDED COMPLAINT — COURT OF CHANCERY RULE 23.1

Defendants have moved to dismiss the amended complaint under Court of Chancery Rule 23.1 for failure to make demand upon MSO's board of directors or adequately to plead why demand would be futile. On a motion to dismiss pursuant to Rule 23.1, the Court considers the same documents, similarly accepts well-pled allegations as true, and makes reasonable inferences in favor of the plaintiff — all as it does in considering a motion to dismiss under Rule 12(b)(6). Rule 23.1, however, confers substantive rights that result in derivative complaints being subjected to more stringent pleading requirements. The plaintiff must state with particularity the efforts made to cause the company's board of directors to take action on the matters of concern to the plaintiff — to state how demand was made. n46 If, as in this action, the plaintiff has failed to make a demand on the board, the plaintiff must state with particularity the reasons that demand should be excused.

Plaintiff concedes that demand was not made but asserts that demand would be futile because the board of directors is incapable of acting independently and disinterestedly in evaluating demand with respect to plaintiff's claims. As a practical matter, because Counts II through IV are dismissed for failure to state a claim, I need only determine whether demand would be futile with respect to Count I. Count I alleges that Stewart breached her fiduciary duties to MSO and its shareholders by selling (perhaps illegally) shares of ImClone in December of 2001 and by public statements she made regarding that sale. Because this claim does not challenge an action of the board of directors of MSO, the appropriate test for demand futility is that articulated in *Rales v. Blasband*. Particularly, the Court's task is to evaluate whether the particularized allegations "create a reasonable doubt that, as of the time the complaint [was] filed, the board of directors could have properly exercised its independent and disinterested business judgment in responding to a demand. *Rales* requires that a majority of the board be able to consider and appropriately to respond to a demand "free of personal financial interest and improper extraneous influences." Demand is excused as futile if the Court finds there is "a reasonable doubt that a majority of the Board would be disinterested or independent in making a decision on demand.The original complaint was filed on August 15, 2002. At that time the board members were defendants Stewart, Patrick, Martinez, Seligman, Moore, and Ubben. Thus, these six individuals constitute the board for purposes of evaluating demand futility. Demand is required if, in view of all the particularized allegations in the complaint and drawing all reasonable inferences in favor of the plaintiff, there is no reasonable doubt of the ability of a majority, here four of the six directors, to respond to demand appropriately.

### 1.  Inside Directors: Stewart and Patrick

Defendants do not suggest that either Stewart or Patrick should be considered disinterested, independent, and able to consider demand on Count I without interference of improper extraneous influences. Still, Rule 23.1 places the burden on the plaintiff to specify in the complaint the reasons why demand would be futile.

The amended complaint alleges that in her sales of ImClone stock and subsequent statements on the subject, Stewart not only breached her fiduciary duties to MSO and its shareholders but may have committed criminal acts. It seems that these allegations indicate a significant likelihood that Stewart may be both civilly and criminally liable with respect to these actions. This is sufficient to raise a reasonable doubt of Stewart's disinterest in the challenged acts. I find that Stewart must be considered incapable of appropriately considering demand with respect to Count I.

Patrick is the president, chief operating officer, and a director of MSO. Her 2001 compensation included $980,000 in salary and bonuses along with a grant of options to purchase 130,000 Class A shares of MSO. Based on the magnitude of compensation described flowing to Patrick from her work at MSO, I find that Patrick has a material interest in her own continued employment. Because Stewart is the company's chairman and chief executive, controls over 94% of the shareholder vote, and is the "personification of [MSO's] brands as well as [its] senior executive and primary creative force," Stewart certainly has the ability to affect Patrick's employment and compensation at MSO. As described above, Stewart is personally interested in the subject matter of Count I. This raises a reasonable doubt whether Patrick can evaluate and respond to demand on Count I without being influenced by improper consideration of the extraneous matter of how pursuit of that claim would affect Stewart's interests. . . .

## 2.  Outside Directors: Martinez, Moore, Seligman, and Ubben

Stewart has overwhelming voting control of MSO, controlling over 94% of the shareholder vote. It is reasonable to infer that she can remove or replace any or all of the directors. This ability does not by itself demonstrate that Stewart has the capacity to control the outside directors, but is not without relevance to whether there is a reasonable doubt of the outside directors' independence of Stewart. What is required in addition are allegations demonstrating that remaining on MSO's board is material to the outside directors such that they would be incapable of considering demand without this extraneous consideration having an inappropriate effect on their decisionmaking process. No such allegations are made in the amended complaint. The amended complaint does specify the various retainers, meeting fees, and other perquisites afforded the directors, but it is not obvious from the allegations that such compensation would be sufficient to entice any of the outside directors to ignore fiduciary duties to MSO and its shareholders. Nor does plaintiff suggest that the outside directors have a history of blindly following Stewart's will or even accepting her recommendations without adequate independent study and investigation.

The amended complaint also describes two of the outside directors, Martinez and Moore, as having longstanding friendships with Stewart. Notwithstanding defendants' arguments to the contrary, some professional or personal friendships, which may border on or even exceed familial loyalty and closeness, may raise a reasonable doubt whether a director can appropriately consider demand. This is particularly true when the allegations raise serious questions of either civil or criminal liability of such a close friend. Not all friendships, or even most of them, rise to this level and the Court cannot make a *reasonable* inference that a particular friendship does so without specific factual allegations to support such a conclusion.

The factual allegations regarding Stewart's friendship with Martinez are inadequate to raise a reasonable doubt of his independence. While employed by Sears, Martinez developed business ties to MSO due to Sears' marketing of a substantial quantity of MSO products. Martinez was recruited to serve on MSO's board of directors by Beers, who is described as Stewart's longtime personal friend and confidante and who was at that time an MSO director. Shortly after Martinez joined MSO's board, Patrick was quoted in a magazine article saying, "Arthur [Martinez] is an old friend to both me and Martha [Stewart]." Weighing against these factors, the amended complaint discloses that Martinez has been an executive and director for major corporations since at least 1990. At present he serves as a director for four prominent corporations, including MSO, and is the chairman of the Federal Reserve Bank of Chicago. One might say that Martinez's reputation for acting as a careful fiduciary is essential to his career — a matter in which he would surely have a material interest. Furthermore, the amended complaint does not give a single example of any action by Martinez that might be construed as evidence of even a slight inclination to disregard his duties as a fiduciary for *any* reason. In this context, I cannot reasonably infer, on the basis of several years of business interactions and a single affirmation of friendship by a third party, that the friendship between Stewart and Martinez raises a reasonable doubt of Martinez's ability to evaluate demand independently of Stewart's personal interests.

The allegations regarding the friendship between Moore and Stewart are somewhat more detailed, yet still fall short of raising a reasonable doubt about Moore's ability properly to consider demand on Count I. In 1995, Stewart's lawyer, Allen Grubman, hosted a wedding reception for his daughter. Among those in attendance at the reception were Moore, Stewart, and Waksal. In addition, *Fortune* magazine published an article in 1996 that focused on the close personal friendships among Moore, Stewart, and Beers. In September 2001, when Beers resigned from MSO's board of directors, Moore was selected to replace her. Although the amended complaint lists fewer positions of fiduciary responsibility for Moore than were listed for Martinez, it is clear that Moore's professional reputation similarly would be harmed if she failed to fulfill her fiduciary obligations. To my mind, this is quite a close call. Perhaps the balance could have been tipped by additional, more detailed allegations about the closeness or nature of the friendship, details of the business and social interactions between the two, or allegations raising additional considerations that might inappropriately affect Moore's ability to impartially consider pursuit of a lawsuit against Stewart. On the facts pled, however, I cannot say that I have a reasonable doubt of Moore's ability to properly consider demand.

No particular felicity is alleged to exist between Stewart and Seligman. The amended complaint reports in ominous tones, however, that Seligman, who is a director both for MSO and for JWS, contacted JWS' chief executive officer about an unflattering biography of Stewart slated for publication. From this, the Court is asked to infer that Seligman acted in a way that preferred the protection of Stewart over her fiduciary duties to one or both of these companies. Without details about the nature of the contact, other than Seligman's wish to "express concern," it is impossible reasonably to make this inference. Stewart's public image, as plaintiff persistently asserts, is critical to the fortunes of MSO and its shareholders. As a fiduciary of MSO, Seligman may have felt obligated to express concern and seek additional information about the publication before its release. As a fiduciary of JWS, she could well have anticipated some risk of liability if any of the unflattering characterizations of Stewart proved to be insufficiently researched or made carelessly. There is no allegation that Seligman made any inappropriate attempt to prevent the publication of the biography. Nor does the amended complaint indicate whether the biography was ultimately published and, if so, whether Seligman's inquiry is believed to have resulted in any changes to the content of the book. As alleged, this matter does not serve to raise a reasonable doubt of Seligman's independence or ability to consider demand on Count I.

In sum, plaintiff offers various theories to suggest reasons that the outside directors might be inappropriately swayed by Stewart's wishes or interests, but fails to plead sufficient facts that could permit the Court reasonably to infer that one or more of the theories could be accurate. Evidence to support (or refute) any of the theories might have been uncovered by an examination of the corporate books and records, to which the plaintiff would have been entitled for this purpose. n64 Board minutes or voting records, for example, could reveal if the outside directors have in the past challenged Stewart's proposals, or not, voted in line with Stewart, or in opposition to her, and shown on which issues the outside directors have been more or less likely to go along with Stewart's wishes. Armed with such information, plaintiff (and this Court) would be in a much better position to evaluate whether there exists a reasonable doubt of the outside directors' resolve to act independently of Stewart. It appears, however, that plaintiff made no such investigation, instead relying largely, if not solely, on information from media reports to support the assertion that demand would be futile.

It is troubling to this Court that, notwithstanding repeated suggestions, encouragement, and downright admonitions over the years both by this Court and by the Delaware Supreme Court, litigants continue to bring derivative complaints pleading demand futility on the basis of precious little investigation beyond perusal of the morning newspapers. This failure properly to investigate whether a majority of directors fairly can evaluate demand may lead to either (or both) of two equally appalling results. If there is no reasonable doubt that the board could respond to demand in the proper fashion, failure to make demand and filing the derivative action results in a waste of the resources of the litigants, including the corporation in question, as well as those of this Court. If the facts to support reasonable doubt could have been ascertained through more careful pre-litigation investigation, the failure to discover and plead those facts still results in a waste of resources of the litigants and the Court and, in addition, ties the hands of this Court to protect the interests of shareholders where the board is unable or unwilling to do so. This results in the dismissal of what otherwise may have been meritorious claims, fails to provide relief to the company's shareholders, and further erodes public confidence in the legal protections afforded to investors.

Moreover, the Supreme Court's admonition to allow "the benefit of reasonable inferences from well-pleaded factual allegations," *White II* at 550, is not inconsistent with declining to infer "the existence of other facts that would have been proved or disproven by a further pre-suit investigation." *White I* at 364. The reason for this consistency is straightforward: if a complaint is devoid of facts that could have been proved (if they existed) by use of §220, it is not "well-pleaded," and to infer the existence of those facts, when they could easily have been proved by the use of §220, is not "reasonable." . . .

The course of the litigation in *In re Walt Disney Co. Derivative Litigation* is instructive on this point. In that case the shareholder-plaintiffs alleged that the director-defendants breached their fiduciary duty when they approved an employment contract with a very large severance package for president, Michael Ovitz, and when the directors granted Ovitz a non-fault termination under that contract upon his departure from Disney's employ just over a year later. In October 1998, this Court granted the defendants motion to dismiss under Rule 23.1. The Court determined that the amended complaint had failed to raise a reasonable doubt of whether Michael Eisner, Disney's CEO and Ovitz's longtime friend, was disinterested in the challenged transactions or of whether a majority of the directors approving either the contract or the non-fault termination was independent of Eisner. In addition, the Court determined that "Plaintiffs [had] failed to plead facts giving rise to a reasonable doubt that the Board, as a matter of law, was reasonably informed" when approving Ovitz's contract. The complaint also failed to plead adequately that the approval of the contract amounted to waste, and "there [was] no allegation that the Board did not consider the pertinent issues surrounding Ovitz's termination."

On appeal, the Supreme Court largely affirmed the Court of Chancery decision to grant the motion to dismiss. Although troubled by the lavish compensation awarded to Ovitz in exchange for meager benefits deriving to Disney and by the "casual, if not sloppy and perfunctory" manner in which the directors addressed Ovitz's hiring and termination, the Court agreed that the amended complaint was "so inartfully drafted that it was properly dismissed under our pleading standards for derivative suits." The Supreme Court, however, determined that the plaintiffs should be given an opportunity to replead (1) whether reliance on the advice of compensation expert Graef Crystal should afford the board protection against claims of breach of the duty of care and (2) whether granting Ovitz a non-fault termination constituted waste.

The plaintiffs then used a books and records request to investigate possible wrongdoing in relation to Ovitz's hiring and termination. The second amended complaint adequately pled demand futility because the facts, which were uncovered through examination of the corporate records and documents, showed a lack of oversight so egregious that it called into question the directors' good faith exercise of their fiduciary duties.

It would be inappropriate to speculate on the merits of the underlying claims in any case, including this one, on a motion to dismiss under Rule 23.1. Therefore I have and express no opinion regarding the merits of Count I as may have been determined had it survived for trial. I would be remiss, though, if I failed to point out that with a bit more detail about the "relationships," "friendships," and "inter-connections" among Stewart and the other defendants or with some additional arguments as to why there may be a reasonable doubt of the directors' incentives when evaluating demand with respect to Count I, there may have been a reasonable doubt as to one or all of the outside directors disinterest, independence, or ability to consider and respond to demand free from improper extraneous influences. Nevertheless, on this pleading, no such doubt is raised. The defendants' motions to dismiss the amended complaint for failure adequately to plead demand futility are granted with respect to Count I. . . .

# Chapter 12
# Fundamental Transactions

## 12.8  The Appraisal Remedy

### 12.8.4  The Nature of "Fair Value"

*§12.8.4, page 459: Insert the following material at the end of the section:*

#### NOTE ON *IN RE EMERGING COMMUNICATIONS, INC.,* *SHAREHOLDERS LITIGATION*

*In re Emerging Communications, Inc., Shareholders Litigation* is an appraisal and freezeout merger opinion with a clear discussion of valuation issues. Of particular interest in this case is the enormous difference between the appraised value of the company and both merger price and the market price of company stock prior to the merger.

## 12.10  Controlling Shareholder Fiduciary Duty on the First Step of a Two-Step Tender Offer

### 12.10.3  Special Committees of Independent Directors in Controlled Mergers

*§12.10.3, page 483: Insert the following material at the end of the section:*

*In re Emerging Communications, Inc., Shareholders Litigation* is a combined appraisal and freezeout merger opinion. While other portions of the opinion are of interest at other points in the casebook, the most challenging and instructive portion of *Emerging Communications* deals with its analysis of the independence and potential liability of the directors who approved a grotesquely lopsided freezeout merger transaction. Note the close scrutiny that the court gives the ties of directors to the controlling shareholder. The obvious parallel in the Chancery

Court caselaw is the scrutiny given to the independence of the Special Litigation Committee in the different context of a derivative suit, in *In re Oracle Corp., Derivative Litigation, supra.*

## IN RE EMERGING COMMUNICATIONS, INC. SHAREHOLDERS LITIGATION
### *2004 Del. Ch. LEXIS 70 (2004)*

JACOBS, Justice

Addressed in this Opinion are the merits of consolidated statutory appraisal and class actions for breach of fiduciary duty. These actions all arise out of the two-step "going-private" acquisition of the publicly owned shares of Emerging Communications, Inc. ("ECM"), by Innovative Communications Corporation, L.L.C. ("Innovative"), ECM's majority stockholder. The first step tender offer was commenced on August 18, 1998 by Innovative for 29% of ECM's outstanding shares at a price of $10.25 per share. The balance of ECM's publicly held shares were acquired in a second-step cash-out merger of ECM into an Innovative subsidiary, at the same price, on October 19, 1998.

At the time of this two-step transaction (the "Privatization"), 52% of the outstanding shares of ECM, and 100% of the outstanding shares of Innovative, were owned by Innovative Communication Company, LLC ("ICC"). ICC, in turn, was wholly owned by ECM's Chairman and Chief Executive Officer, Jeffrey J. Prosser ("Prosser"). Thus, Prosser had voting control of both of the parties to the Privatization transaction.

In June 1998, shortly after the Privatization proposal was announced, a fiduciary duty class action was brought on behalf of the former public shareholders of ECM by Brickell Partners, an ECM shareholder. On February 10, 1999, four months after the Privatization was consummated, an appraisal action was filed by Greenlight Capital, L.P. and certain of its affiliates (collectively, "Greenlight").... [T]he Brickell fiduciary duty action and the Greenlight appraisal and fiduciary duty actions were consolidated, and were tried on the merits between September 17, 2001 and November 6, 2001....

This is the decision of the Court, after trial, on the merits of the consolidated fiduciary and appraisal actions.

## I.  THE FACTS

. . .

The plaintiffs, as noted are Brickell Partners, which represents a class of persons who owned shares in ECM between May 29, 1998 and October 19, 1998; and Greenlight, which comprises three investment funds that focus on special situation value investments....

There are two groups of defendants: (1) the "ECM defendants," which consist of ECM, ICC, and Innovative; and (2) the "Board defendants," who were ECM's directors at the time of the Privatization. In addition to Jeffrey Prosser, who was also ECM's Chairman and Chief Executive Officer, ECM's directors were Richard Goodwin; John Raynor; Sir Shridath Ramphal; Salvatore Muoio; John Vondras; and Terrence Todman. Each of the board defendants served as an ECM director at Prosser's request.

. . . At the time of the October 1998 Privatization, ECM's principal business was the Virgin Islands Telephone Co. ("Vitelco"), which was the exclusive provider of local wired telephone services in the USVI. Vitelco represented the largest portion of ECM's business, and accounted for approximately 88% of its revenues. . . .

The Board Defendants, and their respective backgrounds, are described at this point.

Richard Goodwin, a member of the Massachusetts Bar, is a noted author of books on American history, government, and politics. In 1959, Mr. Goodwin served as a law clerk to United States Supreme Court Justice Felix Frankfurter, and during the 1960's, he served as Assistant Special Counsel to President John F. Kennedy. . . .

Sir Shridath S. Ramphal ("Ramphal"), a native of Guyana, is a Barrister at Law who has held numerous prestigious government and academic positions. . . .

. . . Ramphal served as a director of, and a paid consultant to, ATN (ECM's corporate predecessor) in 1992, 1993, 1994, and 1995, during which years he was paid (respectively), $20,000, $140,000, $140,000, and $120,000.

John G. Vondras ("Vondras"), is a professional engineer, with over 25 years of independent experience in the telecommunications industry. . . . In 1986, Vondras spent two weeks in the USVI assisting Prosser on technical due diligence in Prosser's purchase of Vitelco. . . .

Salvatore Muoio ("Muoio"), is a principal and general partner of S. Muoio and Co., LLC, an investment advising firm, with significant experience in finance and the telecommunications sector. . . .

Terrence Todman, ("Todman"), a USVI native, is a former United States ambassador to Argentina, Denmark, Spain, Costa Rica, Guinea, and Chad, and has served as special advisor to the Governor of the USVI. . . .

John P. Raynor, ("Raynor"), a practicing attorney, was a partner of an Omaha, Nebraska law firm, and served as Prosser's personal attorney as well as ECM's counsel. Raynor was also a business associate of Mr. Prosser, had been a director of ATN, and acted as Prosser's advisor in formulating the terms of the Privatization transaction.

B. BACKGROUND LEADING TO THE FORMATION OF ECM

ECM's corporate predecessor, Atlantic TeleNetwork, Inc. ("ATN"), was a company that Prosser and a partner, Cornelius Prior, formed in 1987 to acquire the Virgin Islands Telephone Corporation ("Vitelco").

Vitelco, which was ATN's (and later ECM's) principal subsidiary, was (and still is) the exclusive provider of local wired telephone service in the USVI, ... Vitelco was an extremely valuable asset, for several reasons. At the time of the Privatization, Vitelco faced no competition in the foreseeable future, and was guaranteed an 11.5% rate of return on the rate base for local telephone service by the Virgin Islands Public Service Commission. Vitelco's business, which is essentially non-cyclical and not materially affected by recession or inflation, was enhanced by its membership in the Rural Telephone Finance Cooperative ("RTFC"), a non-profit lending cooperative that provided Vitelco with capital at below-market interest rates. Prosser and his entities had access to RTFC financing only because of their affiliation with Vitelco.

Moreover, Vitelco had been essentially free from taxation. In May 1997, Vitelco was granted by the USVI Industrial Development Commission ("IDC") a five year tax abatement from 90% of income taxes and 100% of gross receipts, property and excise taxes (running from October 1998 through October 2003). . . .

On December 31, 1997, ECM began trading as a public company on the American Stock Exchange. Shortly after Prosser obtained control of ECM, he appointed his long-time ATN directors, Raynor and Ramphal, to the ECM board. Prosser also appointed Messrs. Goodwin, Muoio and Vondras to the ECM board. . . .

ECM's life as a public company was short — only ten and one half months. . . . On January 20, 1998, ECM hired Prudential to advise it on the fairness of a potential merger of Innovative into ECM's subsidiary ATNCo. (the "Proposed Merger"). During the next month, Prosser formulated the terms of the Proposed Merger, assisted by Prudential, the law firm of Cahill, Gordon and Reindel, ECM's legal advisors ("Cahill Gordon"), and director John Raynor.

On February 27, 1998, Prosser sent to each ECM director an outline of the terms of the Proposed Merger, a draft merger agreement, and proposed resolutions creating a special board committee that would consist of Messrs. Raynor, Goodwin, and Ramphal. . . .

Whether or not the First Special Committee actively considered the Proposed Merger is a heavily disputed issue. . . .

During the third week of May 1998, Prosser began having significant reservations about the Proposed Merger, because the low market interest in ECM's common stock had caused that stock to be undervalued.[7] On May 21, 1998, Prosser, together with Raynor, met with representatives of Prudential and Cahill

---

7. Prosser Dep. June 7, 2000, at 67-69. On the first day ECM stock was traded, its high and low sales prices were $8.25 and $7.875, respectively. During the second calendar quarter of 1997 (April 1–June 30), ECM shares traded at prices ranging from a high of $8.9375 to a low of $6.25 per share. On the last trading day before the public announcement of the Privatization, the reported closing price was $7.00 per share. JX 155 at SC4133. Prosser informed the ECM board that the ECM stock price had failed to reach the desired appreciation as a result of the small public float and the fact that the stock was not followed by Wall Street analysts. JX 155 at SC 4111.

Gordon to discuss the feasibility of Innovative acquiring all of the outstanding stock of ECM. By that point, Prosser had decided (in Raynor's words) to "flip the transaction." ... Having concluded that the market was not recognizing ECM's intrinsic value, Prosser switched from being a seller of ECM stock to becoming a buyer of that stock. Although Prosser had placed a value of $13.25 per share on ECM for purposes of the Split Off that had occurred only 5 months before, as a buyer of that same stock he was now proposing to pay only $9.125 per share.

... On May 28, Raynor, Prosser and Thomas Minnich, ECM's Chief Operating Officer, informed the RTFC that they had decided to abandon the Proposed Merger and to take ECM private. The next day, Prosser delivered to the ECM board a letter withdrawing the Proposed Merger and proposing instead that Innovative acquire all the ECM shares it did not already own. The proposed Privatization was structured as a first-step cash tender offer for ECM's publicly traded shares at $9.125 per share, to be followed by a second-step cash-out merger at the same price....

Prosser's May 29th letter was the first occasion that the ECM board and the First Special Committee (other than Raynor) learned of the abandonment of the Proposed Merger in favor of the Privatization. Those directors were never told of the roles played by Prudential, Cahill and Raynor — all supposedly retained to represent the interest of the ECM minority stockholders — in formulating the terms of the newly-substituted going private transaction.[10] ...

At the May 29 ECM directors' meeting, the board formed another special committee (the "Second Special Committee") to review the fairness of the proposed Privatization. The directors selected to serve as members of this Second Special Committee were Messrs. Richard Goodwin, John Vondras, and Shridath Ramphal....

Because one of the Second Special Committee members lived in Indonesia and the other lived in England, practicality dictated that Goodwin would be the Committee chair. In that capacity, Goodwin was designated to — and did — take the lead role in negotiating with Prosser and in selecting the Committee's legal and financial advisors. Mr. Goodwin interviewed William Schwitter of Paul, Hastings, Janofsky & Walker LLP ("Paul Hastings"), as a potential legal advisor to the Second Special Committee, and on June 5, 1998, the Committee retained the Paul Hastings Firm as its legal counsel. Later, after meeting with representatives of J.P. Morgan and Houlihan Lokey Howard & Zukin ("Houlihan") at his home in Massachusetts, Goodwin recommended that the Committee retain Houlihan as its financial advisor, and in mid-July, 1998, the Second Special Committee retained Houlihan in that capacity....

---

10. The $9.125 per share merger price was arrived at by Prosser in consultation with Prudential, and no one else had a significant role in that decision. Prosser Dep. June 7, 2000 at 73-74. The First Special Committee members (other than Raynor) were not told of the ongoing plans to change the transaction until May 29, 1998....

As part of its pre-financial analysis investigation of ECM, Houlihan conducted (among other things) a review of ECM's financial information. That information included financial projections for ECM, dated March 25, 1998 (the "March projections"), that had been prepared by James Heying, ECM's then–Chief Financial Officer and Executive Vice President of Acquisitions.... What Houlihan was *not* provided, however, were financial projections dated June 22, 1998 (the "June projections")... that Prosser had caused Heying to prepare as part of Prosser's and ICC's application to the RTFC to finance the acquisition of ECM's minority shares.

The June projections forecasted substantially higher growth than did the March projections. Based on the June projections, as modified by the RFTC, the RFTC concluded in July 1998 that ECM was worth (for loan approval purposes) approximately $28 per share.... Recognizing that the Privatization gave Prosser "the opportunity to retain control at a price below the true market value of the company,"... the RTFC approved financing that would enable Prosser to offer up to $11.40 per share.... That suggests, and Prosser later confirmed, that he always planned (and gave himself sufficient elbow room) to increase his initial offer by some amount.... Moreover, the $60 million RTFC loan represented the amount Prosser had asked for, not the limit of what the RTFC would have allowed him to borrow....

Although Prosser made the June projections available to his legal advisor (Cahill), his financial advisor (Prudential), and his lender (the RTFC), the June projections were never provided to the Second Special Committee, Houlihan, or the ECM board. Instead, Prosser directed Heying to send Houlihan the March projections, even though the June projections were available by that point. As a result, the Committee and its advisors believed — mistakenly — that the March projections were the most recent projections available....

On August 4, 1998, the Committee met with Houlihan to discuss Houlihan's preliminary analysis, which had been furnished to the Committee members in the form of a draft presentation booklet. After explaining in detail his firm's assumptions and methodologies, Houlihan's representative informed the Committee that it was not prepared to opine that $9.125 was a price that was fair to the minority stockholders. After further discussion, the Second Special Committee agreed that $9.125 would not provide adequate compensation to the ECM minority....

[Eventually,] Prosser raised his offer to $10.25 per share, but told Goodwin that $10.25 was his final offer. Because the price had been going up in roughly quarter point increments, Goodwin countered by asking for $10.50 per share. Prosser rejected that request, pointing out that $10.25 was already "straining the limits of [his] financing" for the transaction.... At that point, Goodwin made a judgment that the Committee "had reached the limits of how far we could push...,"... and informed the other Committee members — Ramphal and Vondras — of his conclusion. Ramphal and Vondras agreed to stop the negotiations at that point....

The Committee having obtained what they believed was the highest available price, the question then became whether that price was fair. On August 12, 1998, Goodwin and Vondras had a telephonic meeting with Houlihan and Paul Hastings to review Prosser's $10.25 offer. Having updated its financial analysis, Houlihan concluded that the revised offer price of $10.25 was fair to ECM's public shareholders from a financial point of view. Goodwin and Vondras thereafter voted to recommend that the full ECM board approve the Privatization....

A telephonic meeting of the ECM board to consider Prosser's revised offer to buy all of ECM's publicly held stock for $10.25 per share, was held on August 13, 1998, the following day....

... After discussion, the board determined to approve the Privatization, but only if a majority of the shares held by the minority stockholders were tendered in the first-step tender offer....

... At the time of the Tender Offer, there were 10,959,131 outstanding ECM shares, of which 5,606,873 shares were owned by Prosser through ICC, and the remaining 5,352,258 were held by the public. As of September 25, 1998, 3,206,844 of those shares (*i.e.,* a majority of the minority shares) had been tendered....

## II. THE PARTIES' CONTENTIONS AND THE ISSUES PRESENTED

As earlier noted, the plaintiffs have brought and litigated two separate actions — a statutory appraisal action and a class action asserting claims that the Privatization was not entirely fair to ECM's minority shareholders. In a statutory appraisal action, the Court must determine the "fair value" of the corporation whose stock is being appraised.... Plaintiff Greenlight claims that the statutory fair value of ECM at the time of the merger was $41.16 per share, plus the value of certain corporate opportunities that Prosser is claimed to have usurped (valued at $3.79 per share), for a total fair value of $44.95 per share.

In a class action seeking to invalidate a "going private" acquisition of a corporation's minority stock by its majority stockholder, the standard under which this Court reviews the validity of the transaction and the liability of the fiduciaries charged with breach of duty, is entire fairness.... That standard of review has two aspects: fair dealing and fair price....

In the fiduciary duty class action, the basic issues are whether the defendants dealt fairly with the ECM minority and whether the $10.25 per share transaction price was fair. Because the plaintiffs' class action damages claim is identical (dollar-wise) to their statutory appraisal claim, the fiduciary "fair price," and statutory "fair value," contentions converge and are addressed in connection with the statutory appraisal claim....

## III. THE FAIR PRICE AND FAIR VALUE OF ECM

Although each side's experts valued ECM using both the comparable company and DCF approaches, ... [t]his Court views the parties' virtual non-treatment of the comparable company valuation as a tacit concession that that [it is] of no material significance. . . .

Both sides agree, and our case law recognizes, that a DCF valuation is based upon three inputs: (a) the projections of free cash flow for a specified number of years, (b) the estimated terminal value of the firm at the end of the "projection period," and (c) the discount rate. . . . Although the parties raise a plethora of DCF-related issues, those disputes center around four pivotal questions: (1) which projections (March or June) provide the more appropriate free cash flow input to the DCF model; (2) what is the appropriate discount rate for ECM; (3) how much weight (if any) should the market value of ECM's stock be given in the valuation; and (4) should the value resulting from the DCF method be increased by the value of the businesses that are claimed to be corporate opportunities of ECM? The issues that fall within these four groupings are addressed in this Part of the Opinion.

A. WHICH SET OF ECM'S PROJECTIONS — MARCH OR JUNE — IS MORE RELIABLE
   FOR PURPOSES OF A DCF VALUATION ON THE MERGER DATE?

Critical to any DCF valuation are the projected revenues, expenses. reserves, and other charges of the firm being valued. . . . [A]t Prosser's direction, Heying prepared two sets of management projections, contemporaneously and in the normal course of business. The first set was prepared on March 25, 1998; the second, on June 22, 1998. Plaintiffs' expert, Prof. Zmijewski, used the June projections to derive his projected cash flow inputs, whereas defendants' expert, Duff & Phelps (Bayston) used the March projections, but modified them in significant respects. The issue is what set of projections is the more reliable for purposes of appraising ECM as of the merger date. . . .

[A]s a general proposition (with which defendants' expert, Gilbert Matthews, agreed), "an appraiser should rely on a company's most recent contemporaneous management forecasts unless there are compelling reasons to the contrary." . . . Here, the facts compellingly point to reliance on the June projections which, unlike the March projections, incorporated ECM's first quarter of actual results as a stand-alone company. . . .

B. WHAT IS THE APPROPRIATE DISCOUNT RATE?

The second major group of issues concerns the appropriate rate for discounting the projected free cash flows. Both Prof. Zmijewski and Mr. Bayston determined their discount rate(s) using the Weighted Average Cost of Capital ("WACC") and the Capital Asset Pricing Model ("CAPM") formulas. Prof. Zmijewski used the WACC formula, without adjustment, to calculate a discount rate of 8.8% during the 1998–2002 period when ECM's tax abatement would be in effect, and 8.5% thereafter, assuming that ECM's tax abatement would not be renewed. Mr. Bayston also used the WACC model, but modified the formula and the inputs to that formula by adding various premiums, substituting new debt costs, and using a different debt-to-equity weighting, to arrive at a discount rate of 11.5%.

To understand the significance of the disputes that arise under this heading, it is useful to explain how the discount rate is determined under the WACC model. Under WACC, the discount rate is calculated based upon the subject company's cost of capital. WACC is the sum of: (1) the percentage of the company's capital structure that is financed with equity, multiplied by the company's cost of equity capital, plus (2) the percentage of the company's capital structure that is financed with debt, multiplied by its after-tax cost of debt....

$$\textbf{WACC} = \text{(Leveraged Cost of Equity} \times \text{Equity \% of Capital)}$$
$$+ \text{(Cost of Long Term Debt} \times (1 - \text{tax rate)}$$
$$\times \text{Debt \% of Capital)}.$$

...

[...T]he Court accepts Prof. Zmijewski's 6.3% cost of debt input, and rejects Mr. Bayston's 8% cost-of-debt assumption, the effect of which was to increase Bayston's calculated WACC from 10.9% to 11.16%....

Both Prof. Zmijewski and Mr. Bayston used the CAPM formula to calculate ECM's cost of equity. Using that standard approach, Zmijewski derived a cost of equity of 10.4% (for the years when the tax abatement would be in effect), and 10.3% (when the current tax abatement expires). Bayston's initial cost of equity was somewhat lower—9.9%—but Bayston then increased it to 14% by adding "premiums" totaling 4.1%.... More specifically, Bayston added a "small stock premium" of 1.7% and a "company-specific premium" of 2.4%, the latter consisting of a 1 to 1.5% "super-small stock premium" and a .9 to 1.4% hurricane risk premium."... Those "premiums" account for most of the difference between these two experts' cost of equity inputs. Accordingly, the issue becomes whether either of these premiums is appropriate in these circumstances....

[T]he Court determines that the correct cost of equity for ECM at the merger date was 11.6% (Bayston's initial 9.9% plus a 1.7% small firm/small stock premium). That cost of equity figure does not include a premium for hurricane damage risk....

For the reasons previously discussed, the Court cannot accept in its entirety the DCF valuation of either side's expert.... Based upon the Court's findings, the appropriate discount rate [ED.: combining the costs of debt and equity] is determined to be 8.69%, and the value of ECM as of the merger date is determined to be $38.05 per share....

C. WHAT WEIGHT SHOULD BE ACCORDED TO ECM'S MARKET PRICE AS EVIDENCE OF FAIR VALUE?

To support their claim that the fair value of ECM on the merger date was no more than $10.38 per share, the defendants urge that "where, as here, the market for a publicly traded security is an active and efficient one, the market price [of ECM's common stock] is, at the least, important corroborative evidence of value..." ... For that argument, the defendants rely upon the expert testimony of Professor Burton Malkiel of Princeton University. Prof. Malkiel opined that ECM's stock "was traded in an efficient market with enough volume and a low enough bid-asked spread, and that it reflected news without delay; and the-se...indicators led [Prof. Malkiel] to conclude that ECM was traded in an efficient market and that the [$7.00 per share] market price of ECM common stock prior to the buyout...was a reasonable reflection of its value." ... Intending no disrespect to Professor Malkiel, the Court is unable to accept his conclusion in this specific case. However sound Professor Malkiel's market price-based theory may be in other circumstances, that theory is inapplicable to these facts because its premise is not supported by either the trial record or Delaware law....

... [T]he Court rejects the defendants' argument that the market price of ECM stock corroborates the $10.25 price as the fair or intrinsic value of ECM on the date of the merger. In this case, ECM's unaffected stock market price merits little or no weight....

### E.   THE FAIR VALUE OF ECM AND THE UNFAIRNESS OF THE MERGER PRICE

As a consequence of the foregoing determinations, the fair value of ECM on the merger date is found to be $416,996,000, or $38.05 per share.... Under *8 Del. C. §262*, Greenlight, as the single appraisal claimant, is entitled to recover that per share amount, multiplied by the 750,300 shares for which it seeks appraisal, plus interest as determined in Part III F, *infra*, of this Opinion.

From that fair value finding it further follows that the $10.25 per share merger price was not a "fair price" within the meaning of the Delaware fiduciary duty case law beginning with *Weinberger v. UOP, Inc.*... Although that, without more, is dispositive, the unfairness of the merger price rests upon more than that one bit of simple deductive logic. The overwhelming weight of the credible evidence of record also compels that conclusion....

## IV.   WAS THE TRANSACTION THE PRODUCT OF FAIR DEALING?

. . .

In this case, this Court's determination of ECM's "fair value" disposes of both Greenlight's appraisal action and the "fair price" aspect of the plaintiffs' fiduciary duty claim. The determination that price is not fair raises a preliminary, threshold question of whether in this case any "fair dealing" analysis need be undertaken at all. It is arguable that where (as here) the merger price is found to be unfair, it would be difficult, if not impossible, for the merger to be found "entirely fair" even if the process leading up to the merger involved fair dealing.... That supposition, if correct, would lead to the result that where the merger price is found not to be fair, that finding establishes, *ipso facto,* the unfairness of the merger, thereby obviating the need for any analysis of the process oriented issues. The Supreme Court has not yet addressed that question, however.

What the Supreme Court has decided is that where an interested merger is found to be unfair and the corporation's charter has a *Section 102(b)(7)* exculpatory provision, this Court must then proceed to "identify the breach or breaches of fiduciary duty upon which liability [for damages] will be predicated in the *ratio decidendi* of its determination that entire fairness has not been established."... That is, "when entire fairness is the applicable standard of judicial review, a determination that the director defendants are exculpated from paying monetary damages can be made only *after the basis* for their liability has been decided."...

That mandate, I find, is applicable here. In this case the defendants have raised a *§102(b)(7)* exculpatory defense. In determining that the merger price was not fair, this Court did not address whether the unfairness was the product of a breach of fiduciary duty or if so, the nature or character of that duty. Accordingly, a "fair dealing" analysis is required in this case, if only to enable the Court to determine the "basis for the [defendants'] liability" for *§102(b)(7)* exculpation purposes....

### (c) *The Burden of Proof Issue*

The final threshold issue is which side has the burden of proof. Both sides agree that because the Privatization is a self-dealing transaction of which the majority stockholder stands on both sides, entire fairness is the standard of review *ab initio*.... The only question is whether the burden of proof, which normally falls upon the defendants, has shifted to the plaintiffs in this particular case.

The defendants argue that the burden of establishing that the merger was not entirely fair has shifted to the plaintiffs, because the merger was approved by both an informed independent committee of disinterested directors and an informed majority of minority stockholders.... The short answer is that the merger was not approved by a committee of independent directors who were properly informed or independent of Prosser, nor was it approved by an informed vote of a majority of ECM's minority stockholders....

### B. FAIR DEALING ANALYZED

A fair dealing analysis requires the Court to address "issues of when the transaction was timed, how it was initiated, structured, negotiated, and disclosed to the board, and how director and shareholder approval was obtained."...

### 1. *Timing, Initiation and Structure*

Our courts have recognized that a freeze-out merger of the minority proposed by the majority stockholder is inherently coercive.... Where, as here, the freeze-out merger is initiated by the majority stockholder, that fact, even though [not] dispositive, is evidence of unfair dealing.

Another circumstance that evidences the absence of fair dealing is where the transaction is timed in a manner that is financially disadvantageous to the stockholders and that enables the majority stockholder to gain correspondingly.... Here, the evidence of unfair time could not be more persuasive. Prosser's initial proposal was to merge Innovative into a wholly owned subsidiary of ECM. That would have benefited ECM stockholders and enabled them to remain as investors in a larger merged company. Because ECM's stock price was depressed, Prosser abandoned that proposal at the eleventh hour and "flipped" the deal for his sole personal benefit to take advantage of the temporarily and artificially depressed stock price. That stock price then became the "floor" for the equally depressed and unfair Privatization price, and benefited Prosser to the same extent that it disadvantaged the minority stockholders who were now being squeezed out of the enterprise.

... [T]he transaction was also unfairly structured, in that Prudential and Cahill, the firms that had been retained as advisors to ECM in the initially Proposed (but later abandoned) Merger, were co-opted by Prosser to serve as his advisors.... Prudential and Cahill were in the best position to represent the interests of the ECM minority. Those same advisers were now switching sides to represent interests that were adverse to that same minority....

### 2.  *The Adequacy of the Minority Shareholders' Representation*

A critical aspect of any fair dealing analysis is the adequacy of the representation of the minority stockholders' interests. In this case, that issue is critical, because a majority of the ECM board members were not independent of Prosser, making it necessary to appoint a Special Committee to negotiate on the minority stockholders' behalf. Unfortunately, a majority of the Special Committee members also lacked independence, and the one Committee member who arguably was independent did not function effectively as a champion of the minority's interests.

Besides Prosser, the ECM board had six members, all of whom Prosser had directly appointed: Raynor, Ramphal, Muoio, Goodwin, Vondras, and Todman. It is undisputed that Prosser, whose wholly-owned entity was the acquirer of ECM's minority interest, was conflicted. But, most of the remaining directors also had disabling conflicts because they were economically beholden to Prosser. Directors who "through personal or other relationships are beholden to the controlling person[]" lack independence from that person....

Raynor, who was Prosser's long time lawyer, was clearly conflicted. In 1996, 1997, and 1998, virtually one hundred percent of the legal fees that Raynor generated for his law firm were attributable to work he performed for Prosser and Prosser-owned entities....

If further evidence of non-independence were needed, in July 1998 — during ECM's consideration of the Privatization proposal — Prosser agreed to pay

Raynor $2.4 million over a five year period as compensation for his past services. There was no negotiation over that fee — Raynor requested $2.4 million and Prosser agreed to it. Nor was the $2.4 million compensation arrangement ever disclosed to the ECM board, Compensation Committee or the Special Committee, yet Raynor voted as an ECM director to approve the Privatization.... For Raynor to have participated in the board's Privatization deliberations and vote as an ECM director without disclosing this contemporaneously negotiated compensation arrangement, was highly misleading to Raynor's fellow directors and a breach of his fiduciary duty owed to them and to ECM.

Ramphal was similarly beholden to Prosser. Ramphal was originally introduced to Prosser by his son-in-law, Sir Ronald Sanders, who had a consulting arrangement with Prosser at that time. Like Sanders, Ramphal also fell into a lucrative consultancy with Prosser. In 1993 and 1994, Ramphal was paid consulting fees of $140,000 in both years, and in 1995 he was paid $120,000. On average, those amounts represented 22.5% of Ramphal's total income for that period.... Those amounts were in addition to the $30,000 directors' fee that Ramphal received annually.... Moreover, in 1998, Ramphal received $115,000 for his service on the ECM Board and special committees....

Muoio was also a consultant to a Prosser entity and beholden to Prosser. As of mid-1997, Muoio was on an annual $200,000 retainer for providing banking/financial advisory services,... and he viewed Prosser as a source of additional future lucrative consulting fees. In March 1998, Muoio sought up to an additional $2 million for serving as financial adviser on a potential acquisition by ECM of CoreComm Inc. That effort was unsuccessful only because the acquisition ultimately never took place....

Lastly, Goodwin, Vondras and Todman received annual directors' fees of $100,000, a generous amount given that ECM's board met only three or four times in 1998.... Goodwin and Vondras each also received $50,000 and $15,000 for their service on the Special Committee.... The $115,000 Vondras received in 1998 for serving on ECM's board and Special Committee represented approximately 10% of his income for that year....

Although the directors' fees received by Goodwin, Vondras and Todman would not, without more, necessarily constitute a disabling financial interest,... the record shows that all three of these directors — indeed, all the board defendants — expected to continue as directors of Prosser entities and benefit from the substantial compensation which accompanied that status. In fact, all of ECM's directors except Muoio were appointed to the Innovative board after the Privatization. That expectation, coupled with the fact that his director and committee fees represented a sizeable portion of his income, was sufficient to vitiate Vondras' independence for purposes of considering objectively whether the Privatization was fair to the minority stockholders....

In summary, the Court finds that a majority of the full board of ECM (Prosser, Raynor, Ramphal, Vondras, and Muoio) were beholden to Prosser and, thus, were not independent of him. The Court further finds that a majority of the Special

Committee (Ramphal and Vondras) were beholden to, and therefore not independent of, Prosser, leaving Goodwin as the only arguably independent Committee
member and Todman as the only arguably, independent non-Committee director.
As previously found, Goodwin, as Committee chair, did almost all of the Committee's work himself. Unfortunately, the work that Goodwin performed in that
role, including his negotiations with Prosser, were fatally compromised and,
consequently, inadequate to represent the interests of ECM's minority shareholders effectively....

There are several reasons why Mr. Goodwin's efforts as the Special Committee's chairman, and as its sole functioning member, were doomed to failure.

The first is that Prosser withheld the June projections, and knowledge of their
existence, from the Committee and its advisors, Houlihan and Paul Hastings....

Second, Prosser misled Goodwin by falsely representing that $10.25 per share
was already straining the limits of the financing available to him. In fact, Prosser's
financing would have enabled him to increase his offer to $11.40 per share, and
the record evidence indicates that the RTFC was willing to lend him more, based
on its implied valuation of ECM as conservatively worth at least $27 per share.
n163 There is no evidence that Goodwin knew of Prosser's financing arrange-
ments or the RTFC's valuation (for merger financing purposes) of ECM.

Third, and finally, Goodwin was careless, if not reckless, by routing all of his
communications with the other Special Committee members through Eling
Joseph, Prosser's secretary. The result was to give Prosser access to the Committee's confidential deliberations and strategy. That inexplicable method of chan-
neling communications to Goodwin's fellow Committee members further
confirms the severe information imbalance that existed between the two "bargaining" sides....

### 3.  The Adequacy of the Board And Shareholder Approvals

The ... final aspect of fair dealing concerns the adequacy of the board and
shareholder approvals of the challenged transaction. In this case, those approvals
were uninformed and, accordingly, of no legal consequence....

The approval of the transaction by a majority of the minority shareholders
was ... legally ineffective, because the misdisclosures and omissions in the disclosure documents sent to shareholders in connection with the Privatization rendered that vote uninformed. Those mis-disclosures and omissions also violated
the fiduciary duty of disclosure owed by ECM's majority stockholder and by the
ECM directors who were responsible for the accuracy of those documents....

First, the Proxy Statement omitted to disclose to the minority shareholders the
existence of the June projections and the fact that those projections had been
furnished to Prudential and the RTFC, but were withheld from the Special Committee and its advisors....

Second, the disclosure documents misled minority stockholders about the
Special Committee's and the board's independence from Prosser. The Schedule

14D-9, which was disseminated in connection with the first-step tender offer, disclosed the members of the Special Committee and their compensation, but not their consulting relationships or retainer agreements with other Prosser entities....

For all these reasons, the Court finds that the Privatization transaction, and the $10.25 per share merger price that has been adjudicated as unfair, were the product of unfair dealing. Accordingly, the Court concludes that the Privatization was not entirely fair to the minority stockholders of ECM. Having so found, the Court must now determine the liability consequences of that determination.

## V. THE DEFENDANTS' FIDUCIARY DUTY BREACHES AND LIABILITY THEREFOR

Having concluded that the Privatization was not entirely fair, the Court must next determine the nature of the fiduciary duty violation — whether of care, loyalty, or good faith — that resulted in the unfair transaction.... Under *Emerald Partners v. Berlin*, ... that is necessary to enable the Court to adjudicate which (if any) of the director defendants is liable for money damages, because ECM's *§102(b)(7)* charter provision exculpates those directors found to have violated *solely* their duty of care from liability for money damages....

By its terms, [EMC's charter exculpation] does not apply to fiduciaries other than directors. Thus, Article Seventh does not apply to Prosser in his capacity as ECM's controlling stockholder, or to ICC or Innovative, the entities that Prosser controlled and through which he effected the Privatization. Prosser, as majority stockholder, breached his duty of loyalty to Greenlight and the plaintiff shareholder class, by eliminating ECM's minority stockholders for an unfair price in an unfair transaction that afforded the minority no procedural protections. For that breach of duty Prosser is liable to Greenlight and the shareholder class. So also are the two Prosser-controlled entity defendants, Innovative and ICC, which were the mechanisms through which Prosser accomplished the Privatization. Those entities are liable for having aided and abetted Prosser's breach of fiduciary duty....

The liability of the directors must be determined on an individual basis because the nature of their breach of duty (if any), and whether they are exculpated from liability for that breach, could vary for each director.

Prosser clearly is liable in his capacity as a director for breach of his duty of loyalty, conduct that is not exculpated under Article Seventh. Prosser is also liable on the basis that he "derived an improper personal benefit" from the Privatization transaction....

Raynor also is liable for breaching his fiduciary duty of loyalty — conduct that is excluded from the exculpatory shield of [EMC's §102(b)(7) charter provision]. Raynor did not personally and directly benefit from the unfair transaction (as did Prosser), but he actively assisted Prosser in carrying out the Privatization, and he acted to further Prosser's interests in that transaction, which were antithetical to the interests of ECM's minority stockholders.

Raynor acted in concert with Prosser, who was the source of Raynor's liveli-
hood, to "flip" the transaction from a merger of Innovative into ATNCo., to a
going private merger of ECM into Innovative.... Raynor also assisted Prosser
and Innovative in obtaining RTFC financing for the Privatization ... at the time
when Raynor was still serving on the First Special Committee, ostensibly to
safeguard the interests of ECM's minority stockholders.... After the Second
Special Committee was formed, Raynor attended a meeting with Prosser and
two ECM officers and the RTFC to discuss issues relating to the structuring of
the revised deal.... Finally, on July 20, 1998, Opus Capital Partners ("Opus")
sent a letter to Goodwin, complaining that the initial $9.125 price was too low and
should be around $30.... This letter was somehow "leaked" to Cahill, Pruden-
tial, and Raynor, ... and Raynor reported its contents of the Opus letter to the
RTFC, editorializing that "Opus — biggest [shareholder with] dissenting opinion
on buy back bought in @ $6 or $7/share [but] believes should be valued @ $30 per
share." ...

Although Raynor did not benefit directly from the transactions, his loyalties ran
solely to Prosser, because his economic interests were tied solely to Prosser and he
acted to further those economic interests. Accordingly, Raynor is liable to Greenlight and the shareholder class for breaching his fiduciary duty of loyalty and/or
good faith....

The Court also concludes, albeit with reluctance, that Muoio is similarly
liable....

Muoio is culpable because he voted to approve the transaction even though he
knew, or at the very least had strong reasons to believe, that the $10.25 per share
merger price was unfair. Muoio was in a unique position to know that. He was a
principal and general partner of an investment advising firm, with significant
experience in finance and the telecommunications sector....

... Muoio's conduct is explainable in terms of only one of two possible mindsets.
The first is that Muoio made a deliberate judgment that to further his personal
business interests, it was of paramount importance for him to exhibit his primary
loyalty to Prosser. The second was that Muoio, for whatever reason, "consciously
and intentionally disregarded" his responsibility to safeguard the minority stockholders from the risk, of which he had unique knowledge, that the transaction was
unfair.... If motivated by either of those mindsets, Muoio's conduct would have
amounted to a violation of his duty of loyalty and/or good faith.... That leaves
the four remaining directors — Goodwin, Ramphal, Todman, and Vondras — whose
conduct, while also highly troublesome, is far more problematic from a liability
standpoint than that of Prosser, Raynor, and Muoio. Like Raynor and Muoio,
those four directors were not independent of Prosser, they all voted for the Privatization, and none had a personal conflicting financial interest in, or derived a personal
benefit from, that transaction to the exclusion of the minority stockholders.

The conduct of these four directors differs from that of Raynor and Muoio, in
that there is no evidence that any of those four affirmatively colluded with Prosser
to effectuate the Privatization, or that they otherwise deliberately engaged in

conduct disloyal to the minority stockholders' interests. Nor have the plaintiffs shown that any of those directors knew or had reason to believe, that the merger price was unfair. . . .

It is correct (and this Court has found) that none of the Committee members was independent of Prosser, that viewed with perfect hindsight the magnitude of the negotiated price increase was negligible, and that Goodwin permitted his communications with Ramphal and Vondras to be routed through Prosser's secretary. In quite different circumstances that might establish a violation of the duties of good faith and/or loyalty, especially since the burden of establishing their entitlement falls upon the directors seeking exculpation. But here that procedural burden does not help the plaintiffs, because the evidence, viewed as a whole, fails to establish a *prima facie* case of bad faith or disloyalty that these directors would be called upon to negate or disprove.

More specifically, although Goodwin, Ramphal and Vondras, because of their non-independent relationship to Prosser, might have been motivated to aid Prosser in his scheme to force out ECM's minority at an unfair price, there is no evidence that they actually engaged in such improperly motivated conduct, or otherwise acted with disloyal intent. . . .

## VI. CONCLUSION

For the reasons set forth above:

(1) In the appraisal action, Innovative, as the surviving corporation, is liable to Greenlight in the amount of $38.05 per share for each of the 750,300 shares that are subject to the appraisal, plus interest at the rate of 6.27%, compounded monthly, from the date of the merger to the date of the judgment.

(2) In the fiduciary duty action, defendants Innovative, ICC, Prosser, Raynor and Muoio are jointly and severally liable to the plaintiff class and to Greenlight (in its capacity as holder of litigation rights assigned by former ECM shareholders) in an amount equal to $27.80 per share.[193] . . .

*§12.10.4, page 495: Insert the following material at the end of the section:*

## A FURTHER NOTE ON THE DELAWARE LAW OF GOING-PRIVATE MERGERS

In his opinion *In Re Cox Communications, Inc., Shareholder Litigation* (Del. Ch. June 6 2005), Vice Chancellor Strine took the trouble to write a short and

---

193. $27.80 per share is equal to the difference between the fair value of ECM on the merger date ($38.05 per share) and the merger price paid to the ECM minority shareholders ($10.25 per share).

customarily intelligent commentary on the practical effects of the Delaware Supreme Court holding in *Kahn v. Lynch Communications*. *Cox Communications* dealt with an application to settle class actions brought on the very announcement of a cash-out merger plan that the controlling family had proposed to an independent negotiating committee of the board. The committee had negotiated an increase in the proposed price as well as a provision mandating that the merger be contingent upon majority approval of the company's public shareholders. While the shareholders' counsel had not participated in these negotiations, the settlement agreement between them and the controlling defendants provided that the pendency of the class actions had had some causative effect on the deal negotiations. Such provisions are customary in agreements of this type.

## IN RE COX COMMUNICATIONS, INC., SHAREHOLDER LITIGATION
### (Del. Ch. June 6 2005)

V.C. STRINE,

. . .

It would not be much of a stretch to say that the central idea of Delaware's approach to corporation law is the empowerment of centralized management, in the form of boards of directors and the subordinate officers they choose, to make disinterested business decisions. The business judgment rule exemplifies and animates this idea.

But this idea also presents to corporate law makers — of both the statutory and common law variety — a correlative challenge . . . : how to regulate transactions between corporations and their own directors, officers, or controlling stockholders. And, with the later emergence of a vibrant market for corporate control, came the need to address the extent to which certain corporate transactions with, or defensive reactions towards, third parties sufficiently implicate the self-interest of directors and officers as to cast doubt on their ability to pursue their corporations' best interests with unconflicted fidelity. In other words, for the law of corporations, much of the hard thinking has been what to do about business decisions in which directors have non-stockholder interests that might bias their judgment.

By the enactment of the comprehensive revision of the Delaware General Corporation Law in 1967, the Delaware law of corporations had long accepted the notion that it was unwise to ban interested transactions altogether. Consistent with that premise, the revised DGCL addressed interested transactions by crafting a legal incentive system for vesting decision-making authority over such transactions in those who were not burdened with a conflict. To that end, §144 of the DGCL says that a transaction between a corporation and an officer or director is not per se voidable so long as the transaction is approved, after full disclosure, either by: 1) a majority of the disinterested directors; or 2) a good faith vote of the stockholders. By those methods, respect for the business judgment of the board can be maintained with integrity, because the law has taken into account the conflict and required that the business judgment be either proposed by the disinterested directors or ratified by the stockholders it affects. In the absence of those protections, the transaction is presumed voidable absent a demonstration, by the interested party, that the transaction is fair.

Lest I be chastened by learned commentators on our law, I must hasten to add that §144 has been interpreted as dealing solely with the problem of per se invalidity; that is, as addressing only the common law principle that interested transactions were entirely invalid and providing a road map for transactional planners to avoid that fate. The somewhat different question of when an interested transaction might give rise to a claim for breach of fiduciary duty — i.e., to a claim in equity — was left to the common law of corporations to answer. Mere compliance with §144 did not necessarily suffice.

But the common law of corporations also was centered on the idea of the business judgment rule and its approach to interested transactions looked much like that codified in §144. The approval by a majority of the disinterested directors of an interested transaction was held to invoke the business judgment rule standard of review, and to relieve the proponents of the burden to show that the transaction was entirely fair to the corporation. But a good example of the distinction between §144 and the common law of corporations is their disparate approach to stockholder ratification. By its own terms, §144 alleviates the possibility of per se invalidity by a vote of stockholders, without any explicit requirement that a majority of the disinterested stockholders approve. The common law, by contrast, only gives ratification effect to approval of the interested transaction by a majority of the disinterested stockholders.[20]

This example helps make another point, which is the continuing struggle in our law to determine how to balance the goals of respecting business judgments made by boards and protecting stockholders from abuse from self-interested fiduciaries. In the 1980s, much of what was most compelling and urgent in corporation law, was the judiciary's articulation of the freedom that directors had to address hostile takeover bids. At least in our law, what emerged were common law rules that encouraged boards to invest decision-making primacy in outside directors rather than insiders, because it was presumed that outside directors, as opposed to CEOs and CFOs who had their primary jobs at stake, would be less likely to resist a takeover simply to remain directors of a public company. When independent directors were given substantial authority, the law was more willing to conclude that the board's actions in resisting a takeover were permissible. But even then, the "omnipresent specter that a board may be acting in its own interest, rather than those of the corporation and its shareholders" subjected defensive

---

20. E.g., *Harbor Finance Partners v. Huizenga*, 751 A.2d 879, 900-01 (Del. Ch.1999).

actions to heightened scrutiny, under a reasonableness form of review that was tighter than the bare rationality test of the business judgment rule.[21]

For present purposes, what is most critical is how the Delaware Supreme Court addressed the standard of review that would apply to a very particular type of interested transaction: a merger in which a controlling stockholder acquires the rest of the shares it did not control. Within the Court of Chancery, there was some doctrinal debate about whether a merger with a controlling stockholder could be structured in a manner that would invoke the business judgment rule standard of review. In *In re Trans World Airlines, Inc. Shareholders Litigation,* Chancellor Allen suggested that if the merger was negotiated and approved by a special committee of independent directors, then the business judgment rule standard of review should apply. By contrast, in *Citron v. E.I. DuPont De Nemours & Co.,* Vice Chancellor Jacobs held that even if the merger was approved by a fully informed majority of the minority vote, the entire fairness standard would still apply because of the implicit coercion that the electorate would feel in voting.[24] Their fear that the controller would retaliate against a negative vote, Vice Chancellor Jacobs suggested, rendered a Minority Approval Condition an insufficient guarantee of fairness in this unique transactional context to give that vote ratification effect.

In the important case of *Kahn v. Lynch Communications, Inc.,* the Delaware Supreme Court resolved this doctrinal debate. In its decision, the Supreme Court held that regardless of the procedural protections employed, a merger with a controlling stockholder would always be subject to the entire fairness standard. Even if the transaction was 1) negotiated and approved by a special committee of independent directors; and 2) subject to approval by a majority of the disinterested shares (i.e., those shares not held by the controller or its affiliates), the best that could be achieved was a shift of the burden of persuasion on the issue of fairness from the defendants to the plaintiffs. In reaching this decision, the Supreme Court expressly relied on *Citron's* reasoning about the implicit coercion thought to be felt by minority stockholders in this transactional context. Less clear is why the Supreme Court refused to give weight to independent director approval, given that *Aronson v. Lewis* had held that independent directors were presumed to be capable of exercising a disinterested business judgment in deciding whether to cause the company to sue a controlling stockholder. In part, *Lynch's* decision on this score seemed to turn on a vestigial concept from a discarded body of case law; namely,

---

21. *Unocal Corp. v. Mesa Petroleum Co.,* 493 A.2d 946, 954 (Del .1985); *see also Revlon, Inc. v. MacAndrews & Forbes Holdings, Inc.,* 506 A.2d 173, 180 (Del.1986).

24. From a close reading of the *Citron* decision, one discerns that Vice Chancellor Jacobs felt the *Weinberger v. UOP, Inc.,* 457 A.2d 701 (Del.1983) and *Rosenblatt v. Getty Oil Co.,* 493 A.2d 929, 937 (Del.1985) had already decided the key question and that he was bound to that determination. *Citron,* 584 A.2d at 500-01. He therefore attempted to craft a rationale for what he perceived to be the Supreme Court's binding refusal to give business judgment rule treatment to a merger subject to a Minority Approval Condition. *Id.* at 502.

that because there no longer needed to be a "business purpose" for a merger with a controlling stockholder,[29] it was somehow not a "business judgment" for independent directors to conclude that a merger was in the best interests of the minority stockholders.

That is an odd and unsatisfying rationale, which, if taken seriously, would have implications for all decisions by directors who agree to cash mergers. All in all, it is perhaps fairest and more sensible to read *Lynch* as being premised on a sincere concern that mergers with controlling stockholders involve an extraordinary potential for the exploitation by powerful insiders of their informational advantages and their voting clout. Facing the proverbial 800 pound gorilla who wants the rest of the bananas all for himself, chimpanzees like independent directors and disinterested stockholders could not be expected to make sure that the gorilla paid a fair price.[31] Therefore, the residual protection of an unavoidable review of the financial fairness whenever plaintiffs could raise a genuine dispute of fact about that issue was thought to be a necessary final protection. But, in order to encourage the use of procedural devices such as special committees and Minority Approval Conditions that tended to encourage fair pricing, the Court did give transactional proponents a modest procedural benefit — the shifting of the burden of persuasion on the ultimate issue of fairness to the plaintiffs — if the transaction proponents proved, in a factually intensive way, that the procedural devices had, in fact, operated with integrity. In the case of a special committee, later case law held that the defendants would only be relieved of the burden of proving fairness if it first proved that "the committee function[ed] in a manner which indicates that the controlling shareholder did not dictate the terms of the transaction and that the committee exercised real bargaining power."[33] In the case of a Minority Approval Condition, the defendants had the usual ratification burden — to show that all material facts had been disclosed and the absence of coercive threats. But in either event, or in the exceedingly rare case in which both protections were employed in advance of, and not as part of a negotiated settlement, the most the defendants could get was a burden shift.

Although it is an undeniable reality that *Lynch* stated that any merger with a controlling stockholder, however structured, was subject to a fairness review, it would be unfair not to make explicit another reality. No defendant in *Lynch*, and no defendant since, has argued that the use of an independent special committee *and* a Minority Approval Condition sufficiently alleviates any implicit coercion

---

29. *Weinberger* eliminated this requirement, which was the rule of *Singer v. Magnavox Co.*, 380 A.2d 969 (Del.1977). See *Weinberger*, 457 A.2d at 715.

31. See *Pure Resources*, 808 A.2d 421, 436 (Del. Ch.2002); Leo E. Strine, Jr., *The Inescapably Empirical Foundation of the Common Law of Corporations*, 27 DEL. J. CORP. L. 499, 509 (2002) (both describing the evolution of this thinking).

33. *Kahn v. Tremont Corp.*, 694 A.2d 422, 429 (Del.1997); see also *In re Cysive, Inc. Shareholders Litig.*, 836 A.2d 531, 548-49 (Del. Ch.2003) (explaining why this approach makes the question of burden-shifting conflate with the question of procedural fairness).

as to justify invocation of the business judgment rule. For this reason, it is important not to assume that the Supreme Court has already rejected this more precisely
focused contention.

## QUESTIONS

What are the costs and benefits of a rule that would give business judgment rule
review to a going-private merger that satisfied the two-part procedural protections
that the court describes in this excerpt, and what are the costs and benefits of the
rule of *Kahn v. Lynch Communications*?

Which rule do you think better advances the goals of the corporation law, and
do we agree what those are?

## NOTE: MORE ON GOING-PRIVATE MERGERS

Vice Chancellor Strine continued in the *In Re Cox Communications* opinion to
elucidate the effects of the Lynch rule in the context of objectors at the settlement
hearing who took the position that the class action plaintiffs had added no value
and should their application for an attorney's fee should not be granted:

V.C. STRINE:

The incentive effects created by *Lynch* are largely what inspire the objectors'
position. Rather than describe the objectors' position with same fervor with which
they articulate it, I will instead describe the more reasonable aspects of their
arguments as I distill them, drawing on the record the parties have presented
and the many other settlements of this kind that have been presented to the
Court of Chancery. . . .

Initially, it cannot be ignored that *Lynch* created a strong incentive for the use of
special negotiating committees in addressing mergers with controlling stockholders. This is a very useful incentive. In the main, the experience with such committees has been a positive one. Independent directors have increasingly understood
and aggressively undertaken the burdens of acting as a guarantor of the minority's
interest, by undertaking a deep examination of the economics of the transactions
they confront and developing effective negotiation strategies to extract value for the
minority from the controller. Critical to the effectiveness of the special committee
process has been the selection of experienced financial and legal advisors, who can
help the special committee overcome the lack of managerial expertise at their
disposal. When it works well, the combination of a special committee, with general
business acumen and a fair amount of company specific knowledge, with wily
advisors who know how to pull the levers in merger transactions in order to extract
economic advantage, is a potent one of large benefit to minority stockholders.

But *Lynch* also created other unintended and unanticipated incentive effects
which the objectors point out. For starters, the absence of any additional standard

of review-affecting benefit for a Minority Approval Condition, has made the use of that independent, and functionally distinct, mechanism less prevalent.[34] From a controller's standpoint, accepting this condition from the inception of the negotiating process added an element of transactional risk without much liability-insulating compensation in exchange. Therefore, controllers were unlikely to accept a Minority Approval Condition as an initial requirement, and would, at most, agree to such a Condition at the insistence of a special committee and/or as a way to settle with the plaintiffs.

As a result, *Lynch* did not tend to make prevalent the transactional structure that most clearly mirrors an arms' length merger. In an arms' length merger, the DGCL requires two independent approvals, which it is fair to say serve independent integrity-enforcing functions. The first approval is by the board. In a third-party merger, it is presumed that the board is disinterested and used to full advantage the capability of centralized management to act as an expert bargaining agent. The active agency of centralized management to test the market and bargain is not something that the stockholders can do for themselves. But in a third-party merger, the stockholders are also given an important role. They get to hold their bargaining agent's feet to the fire by wielding the power at the ballot box to either ratify or reject their agent's work product. By this method, the principals (i.e., the stockholders) get to protect themselves by voting no if they believe that their bargaining agent has done a poor job, for whatever reason. Operating to give this approval step real meaning are legal requirements prohibiting coercion in the voting process and requiring the disclosure of all material facts bearing on the approval decision.[37]

These steps are in important ways complements and not substitutes. A good board is best positioned to extract a price at the highest possible level because it does not suffer from the collective action problem of disaggregated stockholders. But boards are rarely comprised of independent directors whose own financial futures depend importantly on getting the best price and, history shows, are sometimes timid, inept, or . . . , well, let's just say worse. Although stockholders are not well positioned to use the voting process to get the last nickel out of a purchaser, they are well positioned to police bad deals in which the board did not at least obtain something in the amorphous "range" of financial fairness.

In the context of a merger with controlling stockholder, the complementary role of disinterested director and disinterested stockholder approval is difficult to

---

34. The plaintiffs' own well-respected expert agrees that this is a negative aspect of *Lynch*. Guhan Subramanian, *Post-Siliconix Freeze-outs: Theory and Evidence* (Harvard Law School Olin Series Discussion Paper # 472, August 2004) at 19; see also Guhan Subramanian, *Fixing Freezeouts,* — YALE L.J. — — (forthcoming 2005) (Harvard Law School Olin Series Discussion Paper # 501, December 2004) at 46-48.

37. *E.g., Williams v. Geier,* 671 A.2d 1368, 1382-83 (Del.1996) (actual or structural coercion of voters is improper and can void a transaction); *Zirn v. VLI Corp.,* 621 A.2d 773 (Del.1993) (all material facts bearing on a merger decision must be disclosed by the board).

conceive of as less important. For a variety of obvious reasons (e.g., informational asymmetries, the possibility that the outside directors might be more independent in appearance than in substance, or might lack the savvy to effectively counter the controller), the integrity-enforcing utility of a Minority Approval Condition seems hard to dispute. And, with increasingly active institutional investors and easier information flows, stockholders have never been better positioned to make a judgment as to whether a special committee has done its job. At the same time, the ability of disaggregated stockholders to reject by a binary up or down vote obviously "unfair" deals does not translate into their ability to do what an effective special committee can do, which is to negotiate effectively and strike a bargain much higher in the range of fairness. As a practical matter, however, the effect of *Lynch* in the real world of transactions was to generate the use of special committees alone.

The incentive system that *Lynch* created for plaintiffs' lawyers is its most problematic feature, however, and the consequence that motivates the objectors' contentions here. After *Lynch,* there arose a pattern of which this case is simply one of the latest examples.

Unlike any other transaction one can imagine — even a *Revlon* deal — it was impossible after *Lynch* to structure a merger with a controlling stockholder in a way that permitted the defendants to obtain a dismissal of the case on the pleadings. Imagine, for example, a controlled company on the board of which sat Bill Gates and Warren Buffett. Each owned 5% of the company and had no other business dealings with the controller. The controller announced that it was offering a 25% premium to market to buy the rest of the shares. The controlled company's board meets and appoints Gates and Buffett as a special committee. The board also resolves that it will not agree to a merger unless the special committee recommends it and unless the merger is conditioned on approval by two-thirds of the disinterested stockholders. The special committee hires a top five investment bank and top five law firm and negotiates the price up to a 38% premium. The special committee then votes to approve the deal and the full board accepts their recommendation. The disinterested stockholders vote to approve the deal by a huge margin that satisfies the two-thirds Minority Approval Condition.

After that occurs, a lawsuit is filed alleging that the price paid is unfair. The filing party can satisfy Rule 11 as to that allegation because financial fairness is a debatable issue and the plaintiff has at least a colorable position. The controller and the special committee go to their respective legal advisors and ask them to get this frivolous lawsuit dismissed. What they will be told is this, "We cannot get the case dismissed. We can attempt to show the plaintiffs that we are willing to beat them on this and persuade them to drop it voluntarily because they will, after great expense, lose. But if they want to fight a motion to dismiss, they will win, see *Lynch.* At the very least, therefore, if the plaintiffs are willing to fight, it would be rational for you to pay an amount to settle the case that reflects not only the actual out-of-pocket costs of defense to get the case to the summary judgment stage, but the (real but harder to quantify) costs of managerial and directorial time in responding to discovery over a past transaction.''

For both the proponents of mergers with controlling stockholders (i.e., controllers and the directors involved in the transactions, all of whom become defendants in lawsuits attacking those transactions) and the plaintiffs' lawyers who file suits, this incentive effect of *Lynch* manifested itself in a unique approach to "litigation." Instead of suing once a controller actually signs up a merger agreement with a special committee of independent directors, plaintiffs sue as soon as there is a public announcement of the controller's intention to propose a merger.

This case is typical of that phenomenon because the plaintiffs sued the same day that the Family announced it was prepared to buy the rest of the Cox shares. The suits were filed despite the express indication that the Family was going to negotiate its $32 per share opening bid with a special committee of independent directors and the absence of any attempt to coerce that committee or to rush it in its work.

In this regard, this case is paradigmatic. And that is what bothers the objectors.

To understand why, one must grasp what typically happens in these suits attacking a proposal to negotiate a transaction. After the suits are filed, the special committee gets down to its work. The litigation meanwhile remains dormant for the obvious reason that there is no agreed-upon transaction to challenge, by way of injunction or otherwise.

After the special committee completes its analysis of value and is ready to negotiate price and conditions, the activity heats up and the special committee begins bargaining — the so-called "first track." At some point in the negotiation process, the defendants — usually through the controller — open up a "second track" of negotiations with the plaintiffs' counsel. Increasingly, in this second track, the plaintiffs engage a financial advisor of their own, whose work is shared with the defendants in an effort to show that the controller's original offer was unfair and that a higher price should be paid in order to avoid a lawsuit. This second track proceeds in partial isolation from the first track in the sense that the plaintiffs' counsel is not made privy to all of the back and forth of the first track.

Indeed, the artistry of defense counsel is to bring the first and second tracks to the same destination at the same time. At some point towards the very end of the first track, the controller frames the negotiation with the special committee in a manner so that it can assure itself that the special committee is likely to accept a particular price subject to the negotiation of an acceptable merger agreement and the delivery of a final fairness opinion from the special committee's financial advisor. When that price is known but before there is a definitive deal, defense counsel (who by now has a sense of the plaintiffs' bargaining position) makes its "final and best offer" to plaintiffs' counsel. The plaintiffs' counsel then accepts via an MOU that is subject to confirmatory discovery.

As the objectors point out and this court has often noted in settlement hearings regarding these kind of cases in the past, the ritualistic nature of a process almost invariably resulting in the simultaneous bliss of three parties — the plaintiffs'

lawyers, the special committee, and the controlling stockholders — is a jurisprudential triumph of an odd form of tantra. I say invariably because the record
contains a shocking omission — the inability of the plaintiffs, despite their pro-
duction of expert affidavits, to point to one instance in the precise context of a case
of this kind (i.e., cases started by attacks on negotiable going-private proposals) of
the plaintiffs' lawyers refusing to settle once a special committee has agreed on
price with a controller.

That bears repeating. In no instance has there been a situation when the controller's lawyer told the plaintiffs' lawyer this is my best and final offer and
received the answer, "sign up your deal with the special committee, and we'll
meet you in the Chancellor's office for the scheduling conference on our motion
to expedite." Rather, in every instance, the plaintiffs' lawyers have concluded
that the price obtained by the special committee was sufficiently attractive, that
the acceptance of a settlement at that price was warranted.[39]

The objectors use this admittedly material fact to buttress another argument
they make about *Lynch*. That argument, which is again something members of this
court have grasped for some time, rests in the ease for the plaintiffs' lawyers of
achieving "success" in this ritual. When a controlling stockholder announces a
"proposal" to negotiate a going-private merger, the controller is, like any bidder,
very unlikely to present his full reserve price as its opening bid. Moreover, given
the nature of *Lynch* and its progeny, and their emphasis on the effectiveness of the
special committee as a bargaining agent, the controller knows, and special committee members will demand, that real price negotiations proceed after the opening bid, and that those negotiations will almost certainly result in any
consummated deal occurring at a higher price.

For plaintiffs' lawyers, the incentives are obvious. By suing on the proposal, the
plaintiffs' lawyers can claim that they are responsible, in part, for price increases
in a deal context in which price increases are overwhelmingly likely to occur.
Added to this incentive is the fact that the plaintiffs' lawyers know that the *Lynch*
standard gives them the ability, on bare satisfaction of notice pleading standards
and Rule 11, to defeat a motion to dismiss addressed to any complaint challenging
an actual merger agreement with a special committee, even one conditioned on
Minority Approval. Because of this ability, the plaintiffs' claims always have
settlement value because of the costs of discovery and time to the defendants.
Add to this another important ingredient, which is that once a special committee
has negotiated a material price increase with the aid of well-regarded financial
and legal advisors, the plaintiffs' lawyers can contend with a straight-face that it
was better to help get the price up to where it ended than to risk that the controller
would abandon the deal. Abandonment of the deal, the plaintiffs' lawyers will
say with accuracy, will result in the company's stock price falling back to its

---

39. *See* Elliott J. Weiss & Lawrence J. White, *File Early, Then Free Ride: How Delaware Law
(Mis)Shapes Shareholder Class Actions*, 57 VAND. L. REV. 1797, 1820 & n. 84, 1833-34 (2004); Weiss
Aff ¶ 15.

pre-proposal level, which is always materially lower as it does not reflect the anticipation of a premium-generating going private transaction. . . .

In seeking fees in these cases, the plaintiffs' lawyers have been pragmatic. Recognizing that they, at best, can claim "shared credit" with the special committee, the plaintiffs' lawyers have tempered their fee requests and have asked for relatively small percentage of the "benefit" — i.e., the difference between the price of the controller's opening bid and the final merger price agreed to by the special committee. But, at the same time, the rewards that they reap are substantial, especially when measured on an hourly basis and against the relative lack of risk that this kind of litigation entails. With the incentive that *Lynch* provides to defense counsel to settle the case and put the threat of continued litigation behind them, the plaintiffs' bar knows that the defendants will be willing to concede that the price increase was due in some material way to their desire to settle the litigation. Furthermore, the plaintiffs know that this court had been modest in awarding fees in this context, so that defendants do not fear that a settlement would result in demands for huge fees that would either draw objectors or cause the controller (if it agrees to pay the fee, as is almost always the case) to bear too much additional pain. All in all, this is a story that the objectors regard as indicative of a broken element of our system of representative litigation.

### C.   SILICONIX: ANOTHER ROAD TO GOING PRIVATE IS PAVED

Of course, things cannot be quite that simple. And they are not. To describe why, I must add more jurisprudential context and then bring in the arguments raised by the plaintiffs' experts.

Under Delaware law, the doctrine of independent legal significance exists. That doctrine permits corporations to take, if the DGCL permits it, a variety of transactional routes to the same destination. For years, there had existed a strand of Delaware law that stated that a controlling stockholder who made a tender offer — as opposed to a merger proposal — to acquire the rest of the controlled company's shares had no duty to offer a fair price. So long as the controller did not actually coerce the minority stockholders or commit a disclosure violation, its tender offer was immune from equitable intervention for breach of fiduciary duty. . . .

The opportunity that the tender offer line of cases presented for transactional planners interested in deal certainty was tempered, however, by the unsettled nature of a related question. By their very nature, going private transactions involve the desire by a controlling stockholder to acquire all of the company and to avoid the costs that come with having other equity holders. In most tender offers, at least some percentage of the shares will not tender, not necessarily because the offer was too low, but for other reasons (lack of focus, administrative failures by brokers, etc.). At the controller's disposal was the short-form merger technique, which permitted a controller, without a formal process, to merge out the remaining stockholders if the controller's ownership had increased to 90%

through the tender offer. But the uncertainty was whether the short-form merger would be subject to the *Lynch* standard. In *In re Unocal Exploration Corp. Shareholders Litigation,* that uncertainty was resolved, with the Court of Chancery, and then the Supreme Court, holding that the short-form merger statute specifically contemplated the absence of any negotiation process and that to impose the entire fairness standard on such mergers would therefore intrude on the transactional freedom authorized by §253. In that transactional context, stockholders who believed that the price was unfair had an exclusive remedy: appraisal.

After *Unocal Exploration* was decided by this court, transactional lawyers put together the *Solomon* strand of authority with that new certainty and generated a new, and less negotiation- and litigation-intensive route to going private: a front tender offer designed to get the controller 90% of the shares, coupled with a back-end short form merger. In subsequent cases in this Court, it was held that this method of transaction — which came to be known by the first written decision addressing it — *In re Siliconix Inc. Shareholders Litigation* — did not trigger entire fairness review so long as the offer was not actually coercive and there was full disclosure. In the later case of *Pure Resources,* this Court held that the mere fact that the controller had taken the *Siliconix* route did not relieve it of fiduciary duties. Although those duties did not include a duty to pay a fair price, the court held that a *Siliconix* transaction could be subject to fairness review to protect the minority unless:

(i)    the offer is subject to a nonwaivable majority of the minority tender condition,

(ii)   the controlling shareholder commits to consummate a short-form merger promptly after increasing its holdings above ninety percent,

(iii)  the controlling shareholder "has made no retributive threats," and

(iv)   the independent directors are given complete discretion and sufficient time "to react to the tender offer, by (at the very least) hiring their own advisors," providing a recommendation to the non-controlling shareholders, and disclosing adequate information to allow the non-controlling shareholders an opportunity for informed decision making.[50]

In *Pure Resources,* the relationship between the *Lynch* and *Siliconix* forms of transactions was explored in depth and the logical tension between our common law's disparate approach to the form of equitable review for those forms was acknowledged. Rather than subject the *Siliconix* form to the rigid *Lynch* standard, this court decided that it was better to formulate protective standards that were more flexible, with the hope that at a later stage the two strands could be made coherent, in a manner that addressed not only the need to protect minority

---

50. Ronald J. Gilson & Jeffrey N. Gordon, *Controlling Controlling Stockholders,* 152 U. PA. L.REV. 785, 827-28 (2003) (paraphrasing and distilling the holdings of *Pure Resources,* 808 A.2d at 445).

stockholders but also the utility of providing a non-litigious route to effecting transactions that often were economically efficient both for the minority who received a premium and in the sense of creating more rationally organized corporations.[51]

Since *Siliconix* was decided, controllers have therefore had two different transactional methods to choose between in attempting to go private. One can imagine various reasons why a controller might prefer one route or the other, depending on variables like the controller's ownership stake, the extent of the public float, the presence of big holders, the desire for certainty and closure, and which route might yield the best price for it. For example, the further a controller was from 90% to begin with, the more attractive the merger route might be, and vice versa, simply for efficiency reasons in both cases.

### D. THE PLAINTIFFS' EXPERT COUNTER ATTACK

For present purposes, however, what is relevant is the empirical evidence that the plaintiffs have submitted to counter the objectors' position. To confront the scholarly work of Weiss and White, who are of the view that litigation of this kind is of no material benefit to minority stockholders, the plaintiffs have submitted an affidavit from Professor Guhan Subramanian of the Harvard Law School.

Subramanian makes two major arguments. First, Subramanian cites to his own recent scholarly studies to support his view that the *Lynch* form of transaction results, on average, in going private transactions that pay the minority a higher premium in comparison to the pre-announcement market price than do *Siliconix* deals. Second, Subramanian attempts to show that the filing of lawsuits under *Lynch* challenging going private merger proposals by controlling stockholders are a material factor in producing these more favorable results.

I will now explain in summary form Subramanian's arguments and explain why I conclude that the first of his arguments is his strongest, and that his other point is less convincing.

### 1. Lynch Transactions Versus Siliconix Transactions

In recent work, Professor Subramanian studied the prices at which going-private transactions occurred since *Siliconix*, breaking them down between merger, or *Lynch*, transactions and tender offer, or *Siliconix*, transactions. Subramanian finds that the final premium paid over the pre-announcement market price was on average higher in *Lynch* deals than *Siliconix* deals, and that the difference was statistically significant. Likewise, he finds that controllers, on average, increase their opening bids more when pursuing a *Lynch* merger than a *Siliconix* tender offer and that the difference is statistically significant. Subramanian,

---

51. 808 A.2d at 434-35, 443-44; *see also Cysive*, 836 A.2d 531, 549-51 (Del. Ch.2003)

after controlling for other possible factors, concludes that these outcomes differ primarily because of the stronger bargaining hand given to the special committee in the *Lynch* context versus the *Siliconix* context. Because the *Lynch* transaction can only proceed with the special committee's approval unless the controller wants to take on the affirmative burden to prove fairness and because a merger transaction presupposes a negotiated price and a tender offer does not, Subramanian believes that minority stockholders do better in *Lynch* deals.

The active bargaining agency of the special committee is, Subramanian concludes, the critically absent feature in *Siliconix* deals. In those deals, the special committee is usually making, at most, a recommendation rather than acting as a necessary approving force and the (disaggregated) minority stockholders are required to make a binary choice between accepting or rejecting the tender offer, without a prior process of negotiation by a bargaining agent on their behalf. Subramanian posits that even when any structural coercion is removed, the stockholders are poorly positioned to extract the controllers' best price. . . .

Recognizing, however, that the higher premiums he finds in *Lynch* deals could be solely or almost entirely due to the stronger hand the merger form gives to special committees, Subramanian has performed additional work in order to try to show that the filing of lawsuits like this one is in material part responsible for the higher premiums he finds in *Lynch* deals.

In his affidavits, Subramanian posits that the better results are due to two related factors, which both operate in the same direction. First, in the *Lynch* context, the special committee's refusal to agree to the merger stops the transaction in its tracks, absent the controller's willingness to use its control of the board to force the merger through over the committee's objection and thereby take up the burden of proving fairness. The second, related factor is the plaintiffs' ability to wield the *Lynch* fairness standard, thus giving them a non-dismissible claim that always has settlement value. By contrast, in *Siliconix,* the controller, under *Pure Resources,* may escape fairness review even if the special committee recommends not to tender, and the plaintiffs may face dismissal so long as the complaint cannot plead non-compliance with the conditions outlined in *Pure Resources.* Subramanian infers that the controller can pay a lower price in the *Siliconix* context because the weaker hand of the special committee and plaintiffs, *combined,* will enable controllers to keep more nickels in their pockets and still close deals. For that reason, Subramanian thinks *Lynch,* and the role that it provides to plaintiffs as a watchdog, "polices the worst control shareholder deals, and benefits target company shareholders. . . . "

To convince the court that he is right, Professor Subramanian tries to . . . show empirically that the efforts of litigating plaintiffs, and not just the work of special committees, are good for minority stockholders in the larger going-private context. . . .

First, Subramanian divided his going private sample into two categories: transactions with monetary settlements and transactions without monetary settlements. In the first category, he included all settlements in which it was agreed that the plaintiffs' efforts helped increase the price. In the second category, he included all transactions in which there was no litigation, litigation that resulted in a dismissal (seemingly all voluntarily dismissed without prejudice), or litigation that was settled without monetary consideration. Next, comparing these two categories, he finds that the category of cases in which the litigation produced a monetary settlement resulted in a higher average premium, 51.7%, than the other catch-all category, 31.3%. Subramanian believes this is evidence that litigation stipulated to have created a monetary benefit tends to produce a higher premium than in transactions when no such benefit has been stipulated to exist.

Frankly, I am not persuaded . . . [Subramanian's] sample is very small and the record does not reveal what percentage of each category is comprised of *Lynch* versus *Siliconix* deals. Nor does the record reveal any case-specific reasons explaining why certain lawsuits fell within one category or the other. For example, one can imagine a situation when there has been a lengthy non-public bargaining process with a special committee leading to an announced agreement, and the filing of a *Lynch* complaint focused mostly on disclosures but with a non-dismissible claim of financial unfairness. In those situations, the controllers might have been more than willing to disclose more information about the good process involved, and to use that as a basis to get rid of a suit that had, because of the *Lynch* standard, settlement value. Ditto for situations when tardy suits were filed and controllers told the plaintiffs to go litigate, only for the plaintiffs to punk out and dismiss their claims without prejudice.

As a trial judge, putting suits of that kind in a bucket together with cases with no litigation at all skews the analysis from the start. There is absolutely no reason in the record to suspect that the plaintiffs' firms who settled cases with no monetary benefit or who dismissed cases without prejudice were different from those who settled cases with a monetary benefit. Unless there is a basis to suspect that there was some different group of firms bringing the cases in his two categories — and there is none — Subramanian overestimates how much his small data set says about the potential efficacy of lawsuits attacking going private proposals. And it does even less to show the actual efficacy of litigation to produce good results for stockholders.

Why? Because comparing cases ending with a stipulation that the litigation caused a monetary benefit with cases that did not result in a monetary benefit does not demonstrate the efficacy of litigation, any more than comparing Barry Bonds' at-bats in which he got a hit to those in which he did not would prove Barry Bonds' overall worth as a hitter. We know Barry Bonds is a good hitter precisely because we can see that the results he produces on average from all the instances when he gets to bat are superior to almost anyone else's. By comparing litigation that is stipulated to have created monetary value with other similar litigation that did not result in such value, we do nothing to show what effect litigation has in general. Rather, we show that in those cases in which litigation was stipulated to have influenced a monetary result on a going private, the result was more favorable (in the narrow sense of having resulted in a higher final premium to market) than in cases when the litigation was not stipulated to have created a monetary result increasing the price of the going private's effectuation. Because both types of cases were actually litigated, doesn't that actually suggest that whatever differences resulted might have had to do primarily with factors unrelated to the litigation itself, such as the specific business circumstances of the target companies involved in the going-private transactions?

Relatedly, if it is the same lawyers who bring both categories of cases, Subramanian lacks a good explanation why the lawyers, like the litigation they bring, are so erratically effective. That is, again, isn't it possible that the category of cases resolved with no "monetary benefit" involved situations when it was implausible not just for the plaintiffs, but for the special committees, to argue for a greater price than was ultimately paid — a case specific variation? Even if that is not the case, if the same plaintiffs' lawyers are willing to settle for less of a premium in certain transactions than they do in others, isn't it also possible that they invariably settle at the same level as the special committee and will not risk pressing a fairness challenge in any instance, even if that means dismissing a case without prejudice? If so, how does this data distinguish between the value of litigation and the value of a special committee? Similarly, if the difference in outcomes relates to the fact that more of the deals in the first category were *Lynch* deals, and more of the deals in the second category were *Siliconix* deals, something I cannot tell from the record, Subramanian is again back to his original problem — the inability to determine whether it is the stronger hand that special committees have in merger transactions than in tender offers that virtually alone drives the results, or whether the greater potential litigation threat in the *Lynch* context is also a materially important contributing factor.

Because there are no good examples of situations when a plaintiff's attack on a going private *proposal* has, by actual litigation, added actual value, Subramanian and the plaintiffs are left relying on a more general premise. Reduced to its essence, the message of the plaintiffs, . . . is that the objectors come wielding a solution in search of a problem. The pragmatic way that Delaware is now handling going-private transactions works well when viewed from a broad perspective, they say, and there is no reason to believe it malfunctioned here. Although the way that cases like this proceed is untraditional in the sense that they rarely, if ever, involve any actual prosecution of legal claims, the resulting sausage is savory for all affected constituencies. Even if suits like this are prematurely filed, the overall data tends to support the conclusion that this court's tolerance of "shared credit" settlements in this context has been wise. By promoting the use of special committees as bargaining agents, and permitting suits upon the announcement of a proposed going-private merger, the current *Lynch* transaction/litigation structure must enhance the effectiveness of special committees to some extent. The precise degree to which this litigation helps is difficult, if not impossible, to determine, but so what: the end product is what matters.

# Chapter 13

# Public Contests for Corporate Control

## 13.1 Introduction

*§13.1, page 500: Insert the following material at the end of the section:*

### NOTE ON THE EUROPEAN UNION TAKEOVER DIRECTIVE

Controversy over the regulation of hostile takeovers in general — and of management defensive tactics in particular — is by no means limited to the United States. The European Union promulgated its long-awaited Takeover Directive in December 2003, after fourteen years of negotiation. The Directive was adopted only after the E.U. Member States reached the radical compromise of making its two most important provisions optional — a decision that naturally limits the extent to which the Directive can impose uniformity on takeover policy in the E.U.

The first of these key provisions is Article 9 of the Directive, which prohibits target companies from taking defensive actions to defeat hostile bids without a shareholder vote. This rule of managerial passivity in the face of a hostile takeover reflects the policy of the UK City Code. It is a rule of shareholder choice rather than board decision making, which is precisely the reverse of the approach that Delaware courts seem to have adopted. However, at this point it appears that Germany, Scandinavian countries, and perhaps France as well will opt out of Article 9 of the Directive to give corporate boards more discretion to defend against hostile offers.

The second key provision of the Takeover Directive is the so-called breakthrough rule embodied in Article 11. Under the breakthrough rule, a hostile acquirer that obtains more than 75 percent of voting equity of a target company *in economic value* could remove the board of directors, regardless of any restrictions on the voting rights in the charter (including differential voting rights among multiple classes of stock) and any restrictions on the transfer of securities. All shares vote equally on charter amendments proposed by such an acquirer. In addition, multiple voting class structures and restrictions on shareholder votes are unenforceable under Article 11 against the bidder in a takeover, and do not apply to target shareholders who must vote on defensive measures.

Again, it appears that (at least) the Scandinavian countries and Germany will opt out of Article 11, and France may do so as well.

## 13.5   *Pulling Together* Unocal *and* Revlon

*§13.5, page 548: Add the following material at the end of the carryover paragraph:*

### NOTE: DEVELOPMENTS IN LOCK-UPS AND FIDUCIARY OUTS

The Notes on Deal Protections and Fiduciary Outs in the text (pp. 544–549) suggest that at the end of the day, the law must sensibly accord to directors the ability to make a deliberate and informed business decision, in good faith, without fear of being second-guessed, whether or not a transaction constitutes a "change in control." When the transaction does constitute a "change in control," judicial deference will be expressed in some form of heightened scrutiny (reasonableness in relation to something); when the transaction is not a "Revlon" transaction, that deference may indeed be expressed in the language of the business judgment rule. That is, the text reflects the view that the corporation law — or the Delaware courts in construing it — does not mandate specific terms of merger agreements, but requires a process that is informed and honestly pursued in the interests of the corporation and its shareholders.

The 2003 opinion excised below presents an interesting factual context in which this issue is discussed and is warmly disagreed upon by members of the Delaware Supreme Court.

### OMNICARE, INC. v. NCS HEALTHCARE, INC.
818 A.2d 914 (Del. 2003)

Before Veasey, C.J. Walsh, Holland, Berger and Steele, Justices, constituting the Court en Banc.

Holland, Justice, for the majority:

NCS Healthcare, Inc. ("NCS"), a Delaware corporation, was the object of competing acquisition bids, one by Genesis Health Ventures, Inc. ("Genesis"), a Pennsylvania corporation, and the other by Omnicare, Inc. ("Omnicare"), a Delaware corporation. The proceedings before this Court were expedited due to exigent circumstances, including the pendency of the stockholders' meeting to consider the NCS/Genesis merger agreement. The determinations of this Court were set forth in a summary manner following oral argument to provide clarity and certainty to the parties going forward. Those determinations are explicated in this opinion.

*Overview of Opinion:* The board of directors of NCS, an insolvent publicly traded Delaware corporation, agreed to the terms of a merger with Genesis. Pursuant to that agreement, all of the NCS creditors would be paid in full and the corporation's stockholders would exchange their shares for the shares of Genesis, a publicly traded Pennsylvania corporation.

Several months after approving the merger agreement, but before the stockholder vote was scheduled, the NCS board of directors withdrew its prior recommendation in favor of the Genesis merger. In fact, the NCS board recommended that the stockholders reject the Genesis transaction after deciding that a competing proposal from Omnicare was a superior transaction. The competing Omnicare bid offered the NCS stockholders an amount of cash equal to more than twice the then current market value of the shares to be received in the Genesis merger. The transaction offered by Omnicare also treated the NCS corporation's other stakeholders on equal terms with the Genesis agreement.

The merger agreement between Genesis and NCS contained a provision authorized by Section 251(c) of Delaware's corporation law. It required that the Genesis agreement be placed before the corporation's stockholders for a vote, even if the NCS board of directors no longer recommended it.

At the insistence of Genesis, the NCS board also agreed to omit any effective fiduciary clause from the merger agreement. In connection with the Genesis merger agreement, two stockholders of NCS, who held a majority of the voting power, agreed unconditionally to vote all of their shares in favor of the Genesis merger. Thus, the combined terms of the voting agreements and merger agreement guaranteed, ab initio, that the transaction proposed by Genesis would obtain NCS stockholder's approval.

The Court of Chancery ruled that the voting agreements, when coupled with the provision in the Genesis merger agreement requiring that it be presented to the stockholders for a vote pursuant to 8 Del. C. §251(c), constituted defensive measures within the meaning of *Unocal Corp. v. Mesa Petroleum Co.* After applying the *Unocal* standard of enhanced judicial scrutiny, the Court of Chancery held that those defensive measures were reasonable. We have concluded that, in the absence of an effective fiduciary out clause, those defensive measures are both preclusive and coercive. Therefore, we hold that those defensive measures are invalid and unenforceable.

*The Parties:* The defendant, NCS, is a Delaware corporation headquartered in Beachwood, Ohio. NCS is a leading independent provider of pharmacy services to long-term care institutions including skilled nursing facilities, assisted living facilities and other institutional healthcare facilities.

NCS common stock consists of Class A shares and Class B shares. The Class B shares are entitled to ten votes per share and the Class A shares are entitled to one vote per share. The shares are virtually identical in every other respect.

The defendant Jon H. Outcalt is Chairman of the NCS board of directors. Outcalt owns 202,063 shares of NCS Class A common stock and 3,476,086 shares of Class B common stock. The defendant Kevin B. Shaw is President, CEO and a director of NCS. At the time the merger agreement at issue in this dispute was executed with Genesis, Shaw owned 28,905 shares of NCS Class A common stock and 1,141,134 shares of Class B common stock.

The NCS board has two other members, defendants Boake A. Sells and Richard L. Osborne. Sells is a graduate of the Harvard Business School. He was Chairman and CEO at Revco Drugstores in Cleveland, Ohio from 1987 to 1992, when he was replaced by new owners. Sells currently sits on the boards of both public and private companies. Osborne is a full-time professor at the Weatherhead School of Management at Case Western Reserve University. He has been at the university for over thirty years. Osborne currently sits on at least seven corporate boards other than NCS.

The defendant Genesis is a Pennsylvania corporation with its principal place of business in Kennett Square, Pennsylvania. It is a leading provider of healthcare and support services to the elderly. The defendant Geneva Sub, Inc., a wholly owned subsidiary of Genesis, is a Delaware corporation formed by Genesis to acquire NCS.

The plaintiffs in the class action own an unspecified number of shares of NCS Class A common stock. They represent a class consisting of all holders of Class A common stock. As of July 28, 2002, NCS had 18,461,599 Class A shares and 5,255,210 Class B shares outstanding.

Omnicare is a Delaware corporation with its principal place of business in Covington, Kentucky. Omnicare is in the institutional pharmacy business, with annual sales in excess of $2.1 billion during its last fiscal year. Omnicare purchased 1000 shares of NCS Class A common stock on July 30, 2002. . . .

FACTUAL BACKGROUND

. . . Beginning in late 1999, changes in the timing and level of reimbursements by government and third-party providers adversely affected market conditions in the health care industry. As a result, NCS began to experience greater difficulty in collecting accounts receivables, which led to a precipitous decline in the market value of its stock. NCS common shares that traded above $20 in January 1999 were worth as little as $5 at the end of that year. By early 2001, NCS was in default on approximately $350 million in debt, including $206 million in senior bank debt and $102 million of its 5¾% Convertible Subordinated Debentures (the "Notes"). After these defaults, NCS common stock traded in a range of $0.09 to $0.50 per share until days before the announcement of the transaction at issue in this case.

NCS began to explore strategic alternatives. . . . NCS retained UBS Warburg, L.L.C. . . . UBS Warburg contacted over fifty different entities to solicit their interest in a variety of transactions with NCS. . . . By October 2000, NCS had only received one non-binding indication of interest valued at $190 million, substantially less than the face value of NCS's senior debt. This proposal was reduced by 20% after the offeror conducted its due diligence review. . . .

In April 2001, NCS received a formal notice of default and acceleration from the trustee for holders of the Notes. As NCS's financial condition worsened, the Noteholders formed a committee to represent their financial interests (the "Ad Hoc Committee"). At about that time, NCS began discussions with various investor groups regarding a restructuring in a "pre-packaged" bankruptcy. NCS did not receive any proposal that it believed provided adequate consideration for its stakeholders. At that time, full recovery for NCS's creditors was a remote prospect, and any recovery for NCS stockholders seemed impossible.

On July 20, Joel Gemunder, Omnicare's President and CEO, sent Shaw a written proposal to acquire NCS in a bankruptcy sale under Section 363 of the Bankruptcy Code. This proposal was for $225 million subject to satisfactory completion of due diligence. NCS asked Omnicare to execute a confidentiality agreement so that more detailed discussions could take place.[3]

In August 2001, Omnicare increased its bid to $270 million, but still proposed to structure the deal as an asset sale in bankruptcy. Even at $270 million, Omnicare's proposal was substantially lower than the face value of NCS's outstanding debt. It would have provided only a small recovery for Omnicare's Noteholders and no recovery for its stockholders. In October 2001, NCS sent Glen Pollack of Brown Gibbons [a new banker representing NCS] to meet with Omnicare's financial advisor, Merrill Lynch, to discuss Omnicare's interest in NCS. Omnicare responded that it was not interested in any transaction other than an asset sale in bankruptcy.

There was no further contact between Omnicare and NCS between November 2001 and January 2002. Instead, Omnicare began secret discussions with Judy K. Mencher, a representative of the Ad Hoc Committee. In these discussions, Omnicare continued to pursue a transaction structured as a sale of assets in bankruptcy. In February 2002, the Ad Hoc Committee notified the NCS board that Omnicare had proposed an asset sale in bankruptcy for $313,750,000.

In January 2002, Genesis was contacted by members of the Ad Hoc Committee concerning a possible transaction with NCS. Genesis executed NCS's standard confidentiality agreement and began a due diligence review. Genesis had recently emerged from bankruptcy because, like NCS, it was suffering from dwindling government reimbursements.

Genesis [had] previously lost a bidding war to Omnicare in a different transaction. This led to bitter feelings between the principals of both companies. More importantly, this bitter experience for Genesis led to its insistence on exclusivity agreements and lock-ups in any potential transaction with NCS.

3. Discovery had revealed that, at the same time, Omnicare was attempting to lure away NCS's customers through what it characterized as the "NCS Blitz." The "NCS Blitz" was an effort by Omnicare to target NCS's customers. Omnicare has engaged in an "NCS Blitz" a number of times, most recently while NCS and Omnicare were in discussions in July and August 2001.

NCS's [financial] performance improved. The NCS directors began to believe that it might be possible for NCS to enter into a transaction that would provide some recovery for NCS stockholders.... In March 2002, NCS ... formed an independent [board] committee ... the Independent Committee"). The NCS board thought this was necessary because, due to NCS's precarious financial condition, it felt that fiduciary duties were owed to the enterprise as a whole rather than solely to NCS stockholders. Sells and Osborne were selected as the members of the committee, and given authority to consider and negotiate possible transactions for NCS. The entire four member NCS board, however, retained authority to approve any transaction. The Independent Committee retained the same legal and financial counsel as the NCS board.

The Independent Committee met for the first time on May 14, 2002. At that meeting Pollack suggested that NCS seek a "stalking-horse merger partner" to obtain the highest possible value in any transaction. The Independent Committee agreed with the suggestion.

Two days later, on May 16, 2002, Scott Berlin of Brown Gibbons, Glen Pollack and Boake Sells met with George Hager, CFO of Genesis, and Michael Walker, who was Genesis's CEO. At that meeting, Genesis made it clear that if it were going to engage in any negotiations with NCS, it would not do so as a "stalking horse." As one of its advisors testified, "We didn't want to be someone who set forth a valuation for NCS which would only result in that valuation ... being publicly disclosed, and thereby creating an environment where Omnicare felt to maintain its competitive monopolistic positions, that they had to match and exceed that level." Thus, Genesis "wanted a degree of certainty that to the extent [it] w[as] willing to pursue a negotiated merger agreement ..., [it] would be able to consummate the transaction [it] negotiated and executed."

In June 2002, Genesis proposed a transaction that would take place outside the bankruptcy context. Although it did not provide full recovery for NCS's Noteholders, it provided the possibility that NCS stockholders would be able to recover something for their investment. As discussions continued, the terms proposed by Genesis continued to improve. On June 25, the economic terms of the Genesis proposal included repayment of the NCS senior debt in full, full assumption of trade credit obligations, an exchange offer or direct purchase of the NCS Notes providing NCS Noteholders with a combination of cash and Genesis common stock equal to the par value of the NCS Notes (not including accrued interest), and $20 million in value for the NCS common stock. Structurally, the Genesis proposal continued to include consents from a significant majority of the Noteholders as well as support agreements from stockholders owning a majority of the NCS voting power.

NCS's financial advisors and legal counsel met again with Genesis and its legal counsel on June 26, 2002, to discuss a number of transaction-related issues. At this meeting, Pollack asked Genesis to increase its offer to NCS stockholders.... Genesis agreed to offer a total of $24 million in consideration for the NCS common stock, or an additional $4 million, in the form of Genesis common stock.

At the June 26 meeting, Genesis's representatives demanded that, before any further negotiations take place, NCS agree to enter into an exclusivity agreement with it. As Hager from Genesis explained it: "[I]f they wished us to continue to try to move this process to a definitive agreement, that they would need to do it on an exclusive basis with us. We were going to, and already had incurred significant expense, but we would incur additional expenses . . . , both internal and external, to bring this transaction to a definitive signing. We wanted them to work with us on an exclusive basis for a short period of time to see if we could reach agreement." On June 27, 2002, Genesis's legal counsel delivered a draft form of exclusivity agreement for review and consideration by NCS's legal counsel.

The Independent Committee met on July 3, 2002, to consider the proposed exclusivity agreement. Pollack presented a summary of the terms of a possible Genesis merger, which had continued to improve. The then-current Genesis proposal included (1) repayment of the NCS senior debt in full, (2) payment of par value for the Notes (without accrued interest) in the form of a combination of cash and Genesis stock, (3) payment to NCS stockholders in the form of $24 million in Genesis stock, plus (4) the assumption, because the transaction was to be structured as a merger, of additional liabilities to trade and other unsecured creditors.

NCS director Sells testified [that] Pollack told the Independent Committee at a July 3, 2002 meeting that Genesis wanted the Exclusivity Agreement to be the first step towards a completely locked up transaction that would preclude a higher bid from Omnicare:

A.   [Pollack] explained that Genesis felt that they had suffered at the hands of Omnicare and others. I guess maybe just Omnicare. I don't know much about Genesis [*sic*] acquisition history. But they had suffered before at the 11:59:59 and that they wanted to have a pretty much bulletproof deal or they were not going to go forward.

Q.   When you say they suffered at the hands of Omnicare, what do you mean?

A.   Well, my expression is that that was related to — a deal that was related to me or explained to me that they, Genesis, had tried to acquire, I suppose, an institutional pharmacy, I don't remember the name of it. Thought they had a deal and then at the last minute, Omnicare outbid them for the company in a like 11:59 kind of thing, and that they were unhappy about that. And once burned, twice shy.

After NCS executed the exclusivity agreement, Genesis provided NCS with a draft merger agreement, a draft Noteholders' support agreement, and draft voting agreements for Outcalt and Shaw, who together held a majority of the voting power of the NCS common stock.

Genesis and NCS negotiated the terms of the merger agreement over the next three weeks. During those negotiations, the Independent Committee and the Ad Hoc Committee persuaded Genesis to improve the terms of its merger.

The parties were still negotiating by July 19, and the exclusivity period was automatically extended to July 26. At that point, NCS and Genesis were close to executing a merger agreement and related voting agreements. Genesis proposed a short extension of the exclusivity agreement so a deal could be finalized. On the morning of July 26, 2002, the Independent Committee authorized an extension of the exclusivity period through July 31.

By late July 2002, Omnicare came to believe that NCS was negotiating a transaction, possibly with Genesis or another of Omnicare's competitors, that would potentially present a competitive threat to Omnicare. Omnicare also came to believe, in light of a run-up in the price of NCS common stock, that whatever transaction NCS was negotiating probably included a payment for its stock. Thus, the Omnicare board of directors met on the morning of July 26 and, on the recommendation of its management, authorized a proposal to acquire NCS that did not involve a sale of assets in bankruptcy.

On the afternoon of July 26, 2002, Omnicare faxed to NCS a letter outlining a proposed acquisition. The letter suggested a transaction in which Omnicare would retire NCS's senior and subordinated debt at par plus accrued interest, and pay the NCS stockholders $3 cash for their shares. Omnicare's proposal, however, was expressly conditioned on negotiating a merger agreement, obtaining certain third party consents, and completing its due diligence.

Mencher saw the July 26 Omnicare letter and realized that, while its economic terms were attractive, the "due diligence" condition substantially undercut its strength. In an effort to get a better proposal from Omnicare, Mencher telephoned Gemunder and told him that Omnicare was unlikely to succeed in its bid unless it dropped the "due diligence outs." She explained this was the only way a bid at the last minute would be able to succeed. Gemunder considered Mencher's warning "very real," and followed up with his advisors. They, however, insisted that he retain the due diligence condition "to protect [him] from doing something foolish." Taking this advice to heart, Gemunder decided not to drop the due diligence condition.

Late in the afternoon of July 26, 2002, NCS representatives received voicemail messages from Omnicare asking to discuss the letter. The exclusivity agreement prevented NCS from returning those calls. In relevant part, that agreement precluded NCS from "engag[ing] or particpat[ing] in any discussions or negotiations with respect to a Competing Transaction or a proposal for one." The July 26 letter from Omnicare met the definition of a "Competing Transaction."

Despite the exclusivity agreement, the Independent Committee met to consider a response to Omnicare. It concluded that discussions with Omnicare about its July 26 letter presented an unacceptable risk that Genesis would abandon merger discussions. The Independent Committee believed that, given Omnicare's past bankruptcy proposals and unwillingness to consider a merger, as well as its decision to negotiate exclusively with the Ad Hoc Committee, the risk of losing the Genesis proposal was too substantial. Nevertheless, the Independent Committee instructed Pollack to use Omnicare's letter to negotiate for improved terms with Genesis.

On July 27, Genesis proposed substantially improved terms. First, it proposed to retire the Notes in accordance with the terms of the indenture, thus eliminating the need for Noteholders to consent to the transaction. This change involved paying all accrued interest plus a small redemption premium. Second, Genesis increased the exchange ratio for NCS common stock to one-tenth of a Genesis common share for each NCS common share, an 80% increase. Third, it agreed to lower the proposed termination fee in the merger agreement from $10 million to $6 million. In return for these concessions, Genesis stipulated that the transaction had to be approved by midnight the next day, July 28, or else Genesis would terminate discussions and withdraw its offer.

The Independent Committee and the NCS board both scheduled meetings for July 28. The committee met first. Although that meeting lasted less than an hour, the Court of Chancery determined the minutes reflect that the directors were fully informed of all material facts relating to the proposed transaction. After concluding that Genesis was sincere in establishing the midnight deadline, the committee voted unanimously to recommend the transaction to the full board.

The full board met thereafter. After receiving similar reports and advice from its legal and financial advisors, the board concluded that "balancing the potential loss of the Genesis deal against the uncertainty of Omnicare's letter, results in the conclusion that the only reasonable alternative for the Board of Directors is to approve the Genesis transaction."

The board first voted to authorize the voting agreements with Outcalt and Shaw, for purposes of Section 203 of the Delaware General Corporation Law ("DGCL"). The board was advised by its legal counsel that "under the terms of the merger agreement and because NCS shareholders representing in excess of 50% of the outstanding voting power would be required by Genesis to enter into stockholder voting agreements contemporaneously with the signing of the merger agreement, and would agree to vote their shares in favor of the merger agreement, shareholder approval of the merger would be assured even if the NCS Board were to withdraw or change its recommendation. These facts would prevent NCS from engaging in any alternative or superior transaction in the future." (emphasis added).

After listening to a summary of the merger terms, the board then resolved that the merger agreement and the transactions contemplated thereby were advisable and fair and in the best interests of all the NCS stakeholders. The NCS board further resolved to recommend the transactions to the stockholders for their approval and adoption. A definitive merger agreement between NCS and Genesis and the stockholder voting agreements were executed later that day.

The Court of Chancery held that it was not a per se breach of fiduciary duty that the NCS board never read the NCS/Genesis merger agreement word for word.

Among other things, the NCS/Genesis merger agreement provided the following:

- NCS stockholders would receive 1 share of Genesis common stock in exchange for every 10 shares of NCS common stock held;
- NCS stockholders could exercise appraisal rights under 8 Del. C. §262;

- NCS would redeem NCS's Notes in accordance with their terms;
- NCS would submit the merger agreement to NCS stockholders regardless of whether the NCS board continued to recommend the merger;
- NCS would not enter into discussions with third parties concerning an alternative acquisition of NCS, or provide non-public information to such parties, unless (1) the third party provided an unsolicited, bona fide written proposal documenting the terms of the acquisition; (2) the NCS board believed in good faith that the proposal was or was likely to result in an acquisition on terms superior to those contemplated by the NCS/Genesis merger agreement; and (3) before providing non-public information to that third party, the third party would execute a confidentiality agreement at least as restrictive as the one in place between NCS and Genesis; and
- If the merger agreement were to be terminated, under certain circumstances NCS would be required to pay Genesis a $6 million termination fee and/or Genesis's documented expenses, up to $5 million.

Voting Agreements: Outcalt and Shaw, in their capacity as NCS stockholders, entered into voting agreements with Genesis. NCS was also required to be a party to the voting agreements by Genesis.

Those agreements provided, among other things, that:

- Outcalt and Shaw were acting in their capacity as NCS stockholders in executing the agreements, not in their capacity as NCS directors or officers;
- Neither Outcalt nor Shaw would transfer their shares prior to the stockholder vote on the merger agreement;
- Outcalt and Shaw agreed to vote all of their shares in favor of the merger agreement; and
- Outcalt and Shaw granted to Genesis an irrevocable proxy to vote their shares in favor of the merger agreement.
- The voting agreement was specifically enforceable by Genesis.

. . .

Omnicare's Superior Proposal: On July 29, 2002, hours after the NCS/Genesis transaction was executed, Omnicare faxed a letter to NCS restating its conditional proposal and attaching a draft merger agreement. Later that morning, Omnicare issued a press release publicly disclosing the proposal.

On August 1, 2002, Omnicare filed a lawsuit attempting to enjoin the NCS/Genesis merger, and announced that it intended to launch a tender offer for NCS's shares at a price of $3.50 per share. On August 8, 2002, Omnicare began its tender offer. By letter dated that same day, Omnicare expressed a desire to discuss the terms of the offer with NCS. Omnicare's letter continued to condition its proposal on satisfactory completion of a due diligence investigation of NCS.

On August 8, 2002, and again on August 19, 2002, the NCS Independent Committee and full board of directors met separately to consider the Omnicare tender offer in light of the Genesis merger agreement. NCS's outside legal counsel and NCS's financial advisor attended both meetings. The board was unable to determine that Omnicare's expressions of interest were likely to lead to a "Superior Proposal," as the term was defined in the NCS/Genesis merger agreement.

On September 10, 2002, NCS requested and received a waiver from Genesis allowing NCS to enter into discussions with Omnicare without first having to determine that Omnicare's proposal was a "Superior Proposal."

On October 6, 2002, Omnicare irrevocably committed itself to a transaction with NCS. Pursuant to the terms of its proposal, Omnicare agreed to acquire all the outstanding NCS Class A and Class B shares at a price of $3.50 per share in cash. As a result of this irrevocable offer, on October 21, 2002, the NCS board withdrew its recommendation that the stockholders vote in favor of the NCS/Genesis merger agreement. NCS's financial advisor withdrew its fairness opinion of the NCS/Genesis merger agreement as well.

Genesis Rejection Impossible: The Genesis merger agreement permits the NCS directors to furnish non-public information to, or enter into discussions with, "any Person in connection with an unsolicited bona fide written Acquisition Proposal by such person" that the board deems likely to constitute a "Superior Proposal." That provision has absolutely no effect on the Genesis merger agreement. Even if the NCS board "changes, withdraws or modifies" its ecommendation, as it did, it must still submit the merger to a stockholder vote.

A subsequent filing with the Securities and Exchange Commission ("SEC") states: "the NCS independent committee and the NCS board of directors have determined to withdraw their recommendations of the Genesis merger agreement and recommend that the NCS stockholders vote against the approval and adoption of the Genesis merger." In that same SEC filing, however, the NCS board explained why the success of the Genesis merger had already been predetermined. "Notwithstanding the foregoing, the NCS independent committee and the NCS board of directors recognize that (1) the existing contractual obligations to Genesis currently prevent NCS from accepting the Omnicare irrevocable merger proposal; and (2) the existence of the voting agreements entered into by Messrs. Outcalt and Shaw, whereby Messrs. Outcalt and Shaw agreed to vote their shares of NCS Class A common stock and NCS Class B common stock in favor of the Genesis merger, ensure NCS stockholder approval of the Genesis merger."

This litigation was commenced to prevent the consummation of the inferior Genesis transaction.

LEGAL ANALYSIS

. . .

The Court of Chancery concluded that, because the stock-for-stock merger between Genesis and NCS did not result in a change of control, the NCS directors' duties under *Revlon* were not triggered by the decision to merge with Genesis. The Court of Chancery also recognized, however, that *Revlon* duties are imposed "when a corporation initiates an active bidding process seeking to sell itself." The Court of Chancery then concluded, alternatively, that Revlon duties had not been triggered because NCS did not start an active bidding process, and the NCS board "abandoned" its efforts to sell the company when it entered into an exclusivity agreement with Genesis.

After concluding that the Revlon standard of enhanced judicial review was completely inapplicable, the Court of Chancery then held that it would examine the decision of the NCS board of directors to approve the Genesis merger pursuant to the business judgment rule standard. After completing its business judgment rule review, the Court of Chancery held that the NCS board of directors had not breached their duty of care by entering into the exclusivity and merger agreements with Genesis. The Court of Chancery also held, however, that "even applying the more exacting *Revlon* standard, the directors acted in conformity with their fiduciary duties in seeking to achieve the highest and best transaction that was reasonably available to [the stockholders]." . . .

The Court of Chancery's decision to review the NCS board's decision to merge with Genesis under the business judgment rule rather than the enhanced scrutiny standard of *Revlon* is not outcome determinative for the purposes of deciding this appeal. We have assumed arguendo that the business judgment rule applied to the decision by the NCS board to merge with Genesis. We have also assumed arguendo that the NCS board exercised due care when it: abandoned the Independent Committee's recommendation to pursue a stalking horse strategy . . . ; executed an exclusivity agreement with Genesis; acceded to Genesis' twenty-four hour ultimatum for making a final merger decision; and executed a merger agreement that was summarized but never completely read by the NCS board of directors.

Deal Protection Devices Require Enhanced Scrutiny: The dispositive issues in this appeal involve the defensive devices that protected the Genesis merger agreement. The Delaware corporation statute provides that the board's management decision to enter into and recommend a merger transaction can become final only when ownership action is taken by a vote of the stockholders. Thus, the Delaware corporation law expressly provides for a balance of power between boards and stockholders which makes merger transactions a shared enterprise and ownership decision. Consequently, a board of directors' decision to adopt defensive devices to protect a merger agreement may implicate the stockholders' right to effectively vote contrary to the initial recommendation of the board in favor of the transaction. . . .

In *QVC*, we explained that the application of an enhanced judicial scrutiny test involves a judicial "review of the reasonableness of the substantive merits of the board's actions." In applying that standard, we held that "a court should not ignore the complexity of the directors' task" in the context in which action was taken.

Accordingly, we concluded that a court applying enhanced judicial scrutiny should not decide whether the directors made a perfect decision but instead should decide whether "the directors' decision was, on balance, within a range of reasonableness."

Genesis' One Day Ultimatum: The record reflects that two of the four NCS board members, Shaw and Outcalt, were also the same two NCS stockholders who combined to control a majority of the stockholder voting power. Genesis gave the four person NCS board less than twenty-four hours to vote in favor of its proposed merger agreement. Genesis insisted the merger agreement include a Section 251(c) clause, mandating its submission for a stockholder vote even if the board's recommendation was withdrawn. Genesis further insisted that the merger agreement omit any effective fiduciary out clause.

Genesis also gave the two stockholder members of the NCS board, Shaw and Outcalt, the same accelerated time table to personally sign the proposed voting agreements. These voting agreements committed them irrevocably to vote their majority power in favor of the merger and further provided in Section 6 that the voting agreements be specifically enforceable. Genesis also required that NCS execute the voting agreements.

Genesis' twenty-four hour ultimatum was that, unless both the merger agreement and the voting agreements were signed with the terms it requested, its offer was going to be withdrawn. According to Genesis' attorneys, these "were unalterable conditions to Genesis' willingness to proceed."

Genesis insisted on the execution of the interlocking voting rights and merger agreements because it feared that Omnicare would make a superior merger proposal. The NCS board signed the voting rights and merger agreements, without any effective fiduciary out clause, to expressly guarantee that the Genesis merger would be approved, even if a superior merger transaction was presented from Omnicare or any other entity.

*Deal Protection Devices.* Defensive devices, as that term is used in this opinion, is a synonym for what are frequently referred to as "deal protection devices." Both terms are used interchangeably to describe any measure or combination of measures that are intended to protect the consummation of a merger transaction. Defensive devices can be economic, structural, or both.

Deal protection devices need not all be in the merger agreement itself. In this case, for example, the Section 251(c) provision in the merger agreement was combined with the separate voting agreements to provide a structural defense for the Genesis merger agreement against any subsequent superior transaction. Genesis made the NCS board's defense of its transaction absolute by insisting on the omission of any effective fiduciary out clause in the NCS merger agreement. . . .

In this case, the stockholder voting agreements were inextricably intertwined with the defensive aspects of the Genesis merger agreement. In fact, the voting agreements with Shaw and Outcalt were the linchpin of Genesis' proposed tripartite defense. Therefore, Genesis made the execution of those voting agreements a non-negotiable condition precedent to its execution of the merger agreement.... [T]he Court of Chancery held that the acts which locked-up the Genesis transaction were the Section 251(c) provision and "the execution of the voting agreement by Outcalt and Shaw."

With the assurance that Outcalt and Shaw would irrevocably agree to exercise their majority voting power in favor of its transaction, Genesis insisted that the merger agreement reflect the other two aspects of its concerted defense, i.e., the inclusion of a Section 251(c) provision and the omission of any effective fiduciary out clause. Those dual aspects of the merger agreement would not have provided Genesis with a complete defense in the absence of the voting agreements with Shaw and Outcalt.

*These Deal Protection Devices Unenforceable:* In this case, the Court of Chancery correctly held that the NCS directors' decision to adopt defensive devices to completely "lock up" the Genesis merger mandated "special scrutiny" under the two-part test set forth in *Unocal....* The record does not, however, support the Court of Chancery's conclusion that the defensive devices adopted by the NCS board to protect the Genesis merger were reasonable and proportionate to the threat that NCS perceived from the potential loss of the Genesis transaction.

Pursuant to the judicial scrutiny required under *Unocal*'s two-stage analysis, the NCS directors must first demonstrate "that they had reasonable grounds for believing that a danger to corporate policy and effectiveness existed...." To satisfy that burden, the NCS directors are required to show they acted in good faith after conducting a reasonable investigation. The threat identified by the NCS board was the possibility of losing the Genesis offer and being left with no comparable alternative transaction.

The second stage of the *Unocal* test requires the NCS directors to demonstrate that their defensive response was "reasonable in relation to the threat posed." This inquiry involves a two-step analysis. The NCS directors must first establish that the merger deal protection devices adopted in response to the threat were not "coercive" or "preclusive," and then demonstrate that their response was within a "range of reasonable responses" to the threat perceived. A response is "preclusive" if it deprives stockholders of the right to receive all tender offers or precludes a bidder from seeking control by fundamentally restricting proxy contests or otherwise. This aspect of the *Unocal* standard provides for a disjunctive analysis. If defensive measures are either preclusive or coercive they are draconian and impermissible. In this case, the deal protection devices of the NCS board were both preclusive and coercive....

In this case, the Court of Chancery did not expressly address the issue of "coercion" in its *Unocal* analysis. It did find as a fact, however, that NCS's public stockholders (who owned 80% of NCS and overwhelmingly supported Omnicare's offer) will be forced to accept the Genesis merger because of the structural defenses approved by the NCS board.

Consequently, the record reflects that any stockholder vote would have been robbed of its effectiveness by the impermissible coercion that predetermined the outcome of the merger without regard to the merits of the Genesis transaction at the time the vote was scheduled to be taken. Deal protection devices that result in such coercion cannot withstand *Unocal*'s enhanced judicial scrutiny standard of review because they are not within the range of reasonableness....

*Effective Fiduciary Out Required:* The defensive measures that protected the merger transaction are unenforceable not only because they are preclusive and coercive but, alternatively, they are unenforceable because they are invalid as they operate in this case. Given the specifically enforceable irrevocable voting agreements, the provision in the merger agreement requiring the board to submit the transaction for a stockholder vote and the omission of a fiduciary out clause in the merger agreement completely prevented the board from discharging its fiduciary responsibilities to the minority stockholders when Omnicare presented its superior transaction. "To the extent that a [merger] contract, or a provision thereof, purports to require a board to act or not act in such a fashion as to limit the exercise of fiduciary duties, it is invalid and unenforceable."[74]...

Under the circumstances presented in this case, where a cohesive group of stockholders with majority voting power was irrevocably committed to the merger transaction, "[e]ffective representation of the financial interests of the minority shareholders imposed upon the [NCS board] an affirmative responsibility to protect those minority shareholders' interests." The NCS board could not abdicate its fiduciary duties to the minority by leaving it to the stockholders alone to approve or disapprove the merger agreement because two stockholders had already combined to establish a majority of the voting power that made the outcome of the stockholder vote a foregone conclusion.

The Court of Chancery noted that Section 251(c) of the Delaware General Corporation Law now permits boards to agree to submit a merger agreement for a stockholder vote, even if the Board later withdraws its support for that agreement and recommends that the stockholders reject it. The Court of Chancery also noted that stockholder voting agreements are permitted by Delaware law. In refusing to certify this interlocutory appeal, the Court of Chancery stated "it is simply nonsensical to say that a board of directors abdicates its duties to manage the 'business and affairs' of a corporation under Section 141(a) of the DGCL by agreeing to the inclusion in a merger agreement of a term authorized by §251(c) of the same statute."[80]

---

74. [Paramount Communications Inc. v. QVC Network Inc., 637 A.2d 34, 51 (Del.1993) (citation omitted). Restatement (Second) of Contracts §193 explicitly provides that a "promise by a fiduciary to violate his fiduciary duty or a promise that tends to induce such a violation is unenforceable on grounds of public policy." The comments to that section indicate that "[d]irectors and other officials of a corporation act in a fiduciary capacity and are subject to the rule stated in this Section." Restatement (Second) of Contracts §193 (1981)

80. [Section 251(c) was amended in 1998 to allow for the inclusion in a merger agreement of a term requiring that the agreement be put to a vote of stockholders whether or not their directors continue to recommend the transaction. Before this amendment, Section 251 was interpreted as precluding a stockholder vote if the board of directors, after approving the merger agreement but before the stockholder vote, decided no longer to recommend it. See *Smith v. Van Gorkom*, 488 A.2d 858, 887-88 (Del.1985).

Taking action that is otherwise legally possible, however, does not ipso facto comport with the fiduciary responsibilities of directors in all circumstances.

Genesis admits that when the NCS board agreed to its merger conditions, the NCS board was seeking to assure that the NCS creditors were paid in full and that the NCS stockholders received the highest value available for their stock. In fact, Genesis defends its "bulletproof" merger agreement on that basis. We hold that the NCS board did not have authority to accede to the Genesis demand for an absolute "lock-up."

The directors of a Delaware corporation have a continuing obligation to discharge their fiduciary responsibilities, as future circumstances develop, after a merger agreement is announced. Genesis anticipated the likelihood of a superior offer after its merger agreement was announced and demanded defensive measures from the NCS board that completely protected its transaction.

Instead of agreeing to the absolute defense of the Genesis merger from a superior offer, however, the NCS board was required to negotiate a fiduciary out clause to protect the NCS stockholders if the Genesis transaction became an inferior offer. By acceding to Genesis' ultimatum for complete protection in futuro, the NCS board disabled itself from exercising its own fiduciary obligations at a time when the board's own judgment is most important, i.e. receipt of a subsequent superior offer.

Any board has authority to give the proponent of a recommended merger agreement reasonable structural and economic defenses, incentives, and fair compensation if the transaction is not completed. To the extent that defensive measures are economic and reasonable, they may become an increased cost to the proponent of any subsequent transaction. Just as defensive measures cannot be draconian, however, they cannot limit or circumscribe the directors' fiduciary duties. Notwithstanding the corporation's insolvent condition, the NCS board had no authority to execute a merger agreement that subsequently prevented it from effectively discharging its ongoing fiduciary responsibilities. . . .

The NCS board was required to contract for an effective fiduciary out clause to exercise its continuing fiduciary responsibilities to the minority stockholders. . . .

In the context of this preclusive and coercive lock up case, the protection of Genesis' contractual expectations must yield to the supervening responsibility of the directors to discharge their fiduciary duties on a continuing basis. The merger agreement and voting agreements, as they were combined to operate in concert in this case, are inconsistent with the NCS directors' fiduciary duties. To that extent, we hold that they are invalid and unenforceable.

VEASEY, Chief Justice, with whom STEELE, Justice, joins dissenting.
. . .

The process by which this merger agreement came about involved a joint decision by the controlling stockholders and the board of directors to secure what appeared to be the only value-enhancing transaction available for a company on the brink of bankruptcy. The Majority adopts a new rule of law that imposes a prohibition on the NCS board's ability to act in concert with controlling stockholders to lock up this merger. The Majority reaches this conclusion by analyzing the challenged deal protection measures as isolated board actions. The Majority concludes that the board owed a duty to the NCS minority stockholders to refrain from acceding to the Genesis demand for an irrevocable lock-up notwithstanding the compelling circumstances confronting the board and the board's disinterested, informed, good faith exercise of its business judgment.

Because we believe this Court must respect the reasoned judgment of the board of directors and give effect to the wishes of the controlling stockholders, we respectfully disagree with the Majority's reasoning that results in a holding that the confluence of board and stockholder action constitutes a breach of fiduciary duty. The essential fact that must always be remembered is that this agreement and the voting commitments of Outcalt and Shaw concluded a lengthy search and intense negotiation process in the context of insolvency and creditor pressure where no other viable bid had emerged. Accordingly, we endorse the Vice Chancellor's well-reasoned analysis that the NCS board's action before the hostile bid emerged was within the bounds of its fiduciary duties under these facts.

We share with the Majority and the independent NCS board of directors the motivation to serve carefully and in good faith the best interests of the corporate enterprise and, thereby, the stockholders of NCS. It is now known, of course, after the case is over, that the stockholders of NCS will receive substantially more by tendering their shares into the topping bid of Omnicare than they would have received in the Genesis merger, as a result of the post-agreement Omnicare bid and the injunctive relief ordered by the Majority of this Court. Our jurisprudence cannot, however, be seen as turning on such ex post felicitous results. Rather, the NCS board's good faith decision must be subject to a real-time review of the board action before the NCS-Genesis merger agreement was entered into.

AN ANALYSIS OF THE PROCESS LEADING TO THE LOCK-UP REFLECTS A QUINTESSENTIAL, DISINTERESTED AND INFORMED BOARD DECISION REACHED IN GOOD FAITH

The Majority has adopted the Vice Chancellor's findings and has assumed arguendo that the NCS board fulfilled its duties of care, loyalty, and good faith by entering into the Genesis merger agreement. Indeed, this conclusion is indisputable on this record. The problem is that the Majority has removed from their proper context the contractual merger protection provisions. The lock-ups here cannot be reviewed in a vacuum. A court should review the entire bidding process to determine whether the independent board's actions permitted the directors to inform themselves of their available options and whether they acted in good faith.

Going into negotiations with Genesis, the NCS directors knew that, up until that time, NCS had found only one potential bidder, Omnicare. Omnicare had refused to buy NCS except at a fire sale price through an asset sale in bankruptcy. Omnicare's best proposal at that stage would not have paid off all creditors and would have provided nothing for stockholders. The Noteholders, represented by the Ad

Hoc Committee, were willing to oblige Omnicare and force NCS into bankruptcy if Omnicare would pay in full the NCS debt. Through the NCS board's efforts, Genesis expressed interest that became increasingly attractive.

Negotiations with Genesis led to an offer paying creditors off and conferring on NCS stockholders $24 million — an amount infinitely superior to the prior Omnicare proposals.

But there was, understandably, a sine qua non. In exchange for offering the NCS stockholders a return on their equity and creditor payment, Genesis demanded certainty that the merger would close. If the NCS board would not have acceded to the Section 251(c) provision, if Outcalt and Shaw had not agreed to the voting agreements and if NCS had insisted on a fiduciary out, there would have been no Genesis deal! Thus, the only value-enhancing transaction available would have disappeared. NCS knew that Omnicare had spoiled a Genesis acquisition in the past, and it is not disputed by the Majority that the NCS directors made a reasoned decision to accept as real the Genesis threat to walk away. Based on Genesis's prior dealings with Omnicare, NCS had good reason to take the Genesis ultimatum seriously.

When Omnicare submitted its conditional eleventh-hour bid, the NCS board had to weigh the economic terms of the proposal against the uncertainty of completing a deal with Omnicare. Importantly, because Omnicare's bid was conditioned on its satisfactorily completing its due diligence review of NCS, the NCS board saw this as a crippling condition, as did the Ad Hoc Committee. As a matter of business judgment, the risk of negotiating with Omnicare and losing Genesis at that point outweighed the possible benefits. [FN96] The lock-up was indisputably a sine qua non to any deal with Genesis.

A lock-up permits a target board and a bidder to "exchange certainties." (Citing *Rand v. Western Airlines* Del. Ch. 1994 WL 89006 (Del.Ch.) *aff'd* 659 A.2d 228 (Del.1995). . . . Certainty itself has value. The acquirer may pay a higher price for the target if the acquirer is assured consummation of the transaction. The target company also benefits from the certainty of completing a transaction with a bidder because losing an acquirer creates the perception that a target is damaged goods, thus reducing its value. *Network, Inc.*, 637 A.2d at 51.

[In *Rand v. Western Airlines* a stock lock-up on 30% of the outstanding shares, the] Court recognized that the lock-up agreement "foreclose[d] further bidding," but noted that the board had canvassed the market, found only one party willing to acquire Western, and made a decision calculated to maximize stockholder value by pursuing "the only viable prospect that remained." The Court also noted that, in return for the lock-up, the acquirer agreed to limit its own "outs" that would prevent consummation of the merger. The merging parties, then, "exchanged certainties" by locking up the deal, which was approved by the Court of Chancery and affirmed by this Court.[101]

---

101. *Western* opinion at *6 ("Western gained a substantial benefit for its stockholders by keeping the only party expressing any interest at the table while achieving its own assurances that the transaction would be consummated.").

While the present case does not involve an attempt to hold on to only one interested bidder, the NCS board was equally concerned about "exchanging certainties" with Genesis. If the creditors decided to force NCS into bankruptcy, which could have happened at any time as NCS was unable to service its obligations, the stockholders would have received nothing. The NCS board also did not know if the NCS business prospects would have declined again, leaving NCS less attractive to other bidders, including Omnicare, which could have changed its mind and again insisted on an asset sale in bankruptcy.

Situations will arise where business realities demand a lock-up so that wealth-enhancing transactions may go forward. Accordingly, any bright-line rule prohibiting lock-ups could, in circumstances such as these, chill otherwise permissible conduct.

### OUR JURISPRUDENCE DOES NOT COMPEL THIS COURT TO INVALIDATE THE JOINT ACTION OF THE BOARD AND THE CONTROLLING STOCKHOLDERS

The Majority invalidates the NCS board's action by announcing a new rule that represents an extension of our jurisprudence. That new rule can be narrowly stated as follows: A merger agreement entered into after a market search, before any prospect of a topping bid has emerged, which locks up stockholder approval and does not contain a "fiduciary out" provision, is per se invalid when a later significant topping bid emerges. As we have noted, this bright-line, per se rule would apply regardless of (1) the circumstances leading up to the agreement and (2) the fact that stockholders who control voting power had irrevocably committed themselves, as stockholders, to vote for the merger. Narrowly stated, this new rule is a judicially-created "third rail" that now becomes one of the given "rules of the game," to be taken into account by the negotiators and drafters of merger agreements. In our view, this new rule is an unwise extension of existing precedent.

Although it is debatable whether *Unocal* applies — and we believe that the better rule in this situation is that the business judgment rule should apply[102] — we will, nevertheless, assume arguendo — as the Vice Chancellor did — that *Unocal* applies. Therefore, under *Unocal* the NCS directors had the burden of going forward with the evidence to show that there was a threat to corporate policy and effectiveness and that their actions were reasonable in response to that threat. The Vice Chancellor correctly found that they reasonably perceived the threat that NCS did not have a viable offer from Omnicare — or anyone else — to pay off its creditors, cure its insolvency and provide some payment to stockholders. The NCS board's actions — as the Vice Chancellor correctly held — were reasonable in relation to the threat because the Genesis deal was the "only game in town," the NCS directors got the best deal they could

---

102. The basis for the Unocal doctrine is the "omnipresent specter" of the board's self-interest to entrench itself in office. *Unocal Corp. v. Mesa Petroleum Co.*, 493 A.2d 946, 954 (Del.1985). NCS was not plagued with a specter of self-interest. Unlike the Unocal situation, a hostile offer did not arise here until after the market search and the locked-up deal with Genesis.

from Genesis and — but-for the emergence of Genesis on the scene — there would have been no viable deal. . . .

In our view, the Majority misapplies the *Unitrin* concept of "coercive and preclusive" measures to preempt a proper proportionality balancing. Thus, the Majority asserts that "in applying enhanced judicial scrutiny to defensive devices designed to protect a merger agreement, . . . a court must . . . determine that those measures are not preclusive or coercive. . . . Here, the deal protection measures were not adopted unilaterally by the board to fend off an existing hostile offer that threatened the corporate policy and effectiveness of NCS. They were adopted because Genesis — the "only game in town" — would not save NCS, its creditors and its stockholders without these provisions.

The Majority — incorrectly, in our view — relies on *Unitrin* to advance its analysis. The discussion of "draconian" measures in *Unitrin* dealt with unilateral board action, a repurchase program, designed to fend off an existing hostile offer by American General. In *Unitrin* we recognized the need to police preclusive and coercive actions initiated by the board to delay or retard an existing hostile bid so as to ensure that the stockholders can benefit from the board's negotiations with the bidder or others and to exercise effectively the franchise as the ultimate check on board action. *Unitrin* polices the effect of board action on existing tender offers and proxy contests to ensure that the board cannot permanently impose its will on the stockholders, leaving the stockholders no recourse to their voting rights.

The very measures the Majority cites as "coercive" were approved by Shaw and Outcalt through the lens of their independent assessment of the merits of the transaction. The proper inquiry in this case is whether the NCS board had taken actions that "have the effect of causing the stockholders to vote in favor of the proposed transaction for some reason other than the merits of that transaction."

Outcalt and Shaw were fully informed stockholders. As the NCS controlling stockholders, they made an informed choice to commit their voting power to the merger. The minority stockholders were deemed to know that when controlling stockholders have 65% of the vote they can approve a merger without the need for the minority votes.

Moreover, to the extent a minority stockholder may have felt "coerced" to vote for the merger, which was already a fait accompli, it was a meaningless coercion — or no coercion at all — because the controlling votes, those of Outcalt and Shaw, were already "cast." Although the fact that the controlling votes were committed to the merger "precluded" an overriding vote against the merger by the Class A stockholders, the pejorative "preclusive" label applicable in a Unitrin fact situation has no application here.

Therefore, there was no meaningful minority stockholder voting decision to coerce.

In applying *Unocal* scrutiny, we believe the Majority incorrectly preempted the proportionality inquiry. In our view, the proportionality inquiry must account for the reality that the contractual measures protecting this merger agreement were necessary to obtain the Genesis deal. The Majority has not demonstrated that the director action was a disproportionate response to the threat posed. Indeed, it is clear to us that the board action to negotiate the best deal reasonably available with the only viable merger partner (Genesis) who could satisfy the creditors and benefit the stockholders, was reasonable in relation to the threat, by any practical yardstick.

## An Absolute Lock-up Is Not a Per Se Violation of Fiduciary Duty

We respectfully disagree with the Majority's conclusion that the NCS board breached its fiduciary duties to the Class A stockholders by failing to negotiate a "fiduciary out" in the Genesis merger agreement. What is the practical import of a "fiduciary out?" It is a contractual provision, articulated in a manner to be negotiated, that would permit the board of the corporation being acquired to exit without breaching the merger agreement in the event of a superior offer.

In this case, Genesis made it abundantly clear early on that it was willing to negotiate a deal with NCS but only on the condition that it would not be a "stalking horse." Thus, it wanted to be certain that a third party could not use its deal with NCS as a floor against which to begin a bidding war.

As a result of this negotiating position, a "fiduciary out" was not acceptable to Genesis. The Majority Opinion holds that such a negotiating position, if implemented in the agreement, is invalid per se where there is an absolute lock-up. We know of no authority in our jurisprudence supporting this new rule, and we believe it is unwise and unwarranted. . . .

One hopes that the Majority rule announced here — though clearly erroneous in our view — will be interpreted narrowly and will be seen as sui generis. By deterring bidders from engaging in negotiations like those present here and requiring that there must always be a fiduciary out, the universe of potential bidders who could reasonably be expected to benefit stockholders could shrink or disappear.

Nevertheless, if the holding is confined to these unique facts, negotiators may be able to navigate around this new hazard.

Accordingly, we respectfully dissent.

STEELE, Justice, dissenting.

I respectfully dissent from the majority opinion, join the Chief Justice's dissent in all respects and dissent separately in order to crystallize the central focus of my objection to the majority view.

I would affirm the Vice Chancellor's holding denying injunctive relief.

Here the board of directors acted selflessly pursuant to a careful, fair process and determined in good faith that the benefits to the stockholders and corporation flowing from a merger agreement containing reasonable deal protection provisions outweigh any speculative benefits that might result from entertaining a putative higher offer. A court asked to examine the decision making process of the board should decline to interfere with the consummation and execution of an otherwise valid contract.

In my view, the Vice Chancellor's unimpeachable factual findings preclude further judicial scrutiny of the NCS board's business judgment that the hotly negotiated terms of its merger agreement were necessary in order to save the company from financial collapse, repay creditors and provide some benefits to NCS stockholders. . . .

In my opinion, Delaware law mandates deference under the business judgment rule to a board of directors' decision that is free from self interest, made with due care and in good faith.

Under Delaware law, the business judgment rule is the offspring of the fundamental principle, codified in §141(a), that the business and affairs of a Delaware corporation are managed by or under its board of directors. . . . The business judgment rule exists to protect and promote the full and free exercise of the managerial power granted to Delaware directors.

Importantly, *Smith v. Van Gorkom*, correctly casts the focus on any court review of board action challenged for alleged breach of the fiduciary duty of care "only upon the basis of the information then reasonably available to the directors and relevant to their decision. . . ." Though criticized particularly for the imposition of personal liability on directors for a breach of the duty of care, *Van Gorkom* still stands for the importance of recognizing the limited circumstances for court intervention and the importance of focusing on the timing of the decision attacked. . . .

In the factual context of this case, the NCS board had thoroughly canvassed the market in an attempt to find an acquirer, save the company, repay creditors and provide some financial benefit to stockholders. They did so in the face of silence, tepid interest to outright hostility from Omnicare. The only bona fide, credible merger partner NCS could find during an exhaustive process was Genesis, a company that had experienced less than desirable relations with Omnicare in the past. Small wonder NCS' only viable merger partner made demands and concessions to acquire contract terms that enhanced assurance that the merger would close. The NCS board agreed to lock up the merger with contractual protection provisions in order to avoid the prospect of Genesis walking away from the deal leaving NCS in the woefully undesirable position of negotiating with a company that had worked for months against NCS' interests by negotiating with NCS' creditors. Those negotiations suggested no regard for NCS' stockholders' interests, and held out only the hope of structuring a purchase of NCS in a bankruptcy environment.

The contract terms that NCS' board agreed to included no insidious, camouflaged side deals for the directors or the majority stockholders nor transparent provisions for entrenchment or control premiums. At the time the NCS board and the majority stockholders agreed to a voting lockup, the terms were the best reasonably available for all the stockholders, balanced against a genuine risk of no deal at all. The cost benefit analysis entered into by an independent committee of the board, approved by the full board and independently agreed to by the majority stockholders cannot be second guessed by courts with no business expertise that would qualify them to substitute their judgment for that of a careful, selfless board or for majority stockholders who had the most significant economic stake in the outcome.

We should not encourage proscriptive rules that invalidate or render unenforceable precommitment strategies negotiated between two parties to a contract who will presumably, in the absence of conflicted interest, bargain intensely over every meaningful provision of a contract after a careful cost benefit analysis. Where could this plain common sense approach be more wisely invoked than where a board, free of conflict, fully informed, supported by the equally conflict-free holders of the largest economic interest in the transaction, reaches the conclusion that a voting lockup strategy is the best course to obtain the most benefit for all stockholders?

This fundamental principle of Delaware law so eloquently put in the Chief Justice's dissent, is particularly applicable here where the NCS board had no alternative if the company were to be saved. If attorneys counseling well motivated, careful, and well-advised boards cannot be assured that their clients' decision — sound at the time but later less economically beneficial only because of post-decision, unforeseeable events — will be respected by the courts, Delaware law, and the courts that expound it, may well be questioned. I would not shame the NCS board, which acted in accordance with every fine instinct that we wish to encourage, by invalidating their action approving the Genesis merger because they failed to insist upon a fiduciary out. I use "shame" here because the majority finds no breach of loyalty or care but nonetheless sanctions these directors for their failure to insist upon a fiduciary out as if those directors had no regard for the effect of their otherwise disinterested, careful decision on others....

Delaware corporate citizens now face the prospect that in every circumstance, boards must obtain the highest price, even if that requires breaching a contract entered into at a time when no one could have reasonably foreseen a truly "Superior Proposal." The majority's proscriptive rule limits the scope of a board's cost benefit analysis by taking the bargaining chip of foregoing a fiduciary out "off the table" in all circumstances. For that new principle to arise from the context of this case, when Omnicare, after striving to buy NCS on the cheap by buying off its creditors, slinked back into the fray, reversed its historic antagonistic strategy and offered a conditional "Superior Proposal" seems entirely counterintuitive.

The majority declares that a fairly negotiated exchange of consideration is invalid and unenforceable on the theory that its terms preclude minority stockholders from accepting a superior alternative or that it coerces them into accepting an inferior deal while presupposing that the objectionable terms of NCS' agreement with Genesis are "defensive measures." The majority equates those contract provisions with measures affirmatively adopted to prevent a third party bidder from frustrating a deal with an acquirer with which management may choose to deal without being fully informed or for their own self interest. . . .

I believe that the absence of a suggestion of self-interest or lack of care compels a court to defer to what is a business judgment that a court is not qualified to second guess.

However, I recognize that another judge might prefer to view the reasonableness of the board's action through the *Unocal* prism before deferring. Some flexible, readily discernable standard of review must be applied no matter what it may be called. Here, one deferring or one applying *Unocal* scrutiny would reach the same conclusion.

When a board agrees rationally, in good faith, without conflict and with reasonable care to include provisions in a contract to preserve a deal in the absence of a better one, their business judgment should not be second-guessed in order to invalidate or declare unenforceable an otherwise valid merger agreement. The fact that majority stockholders free of conflicts have a choice and every incentive to get the best available deal and then make a rational judgment to do so as well neither unfairly impinges upon minority shareholder choice or the concept of a shareholder "democracy" nor has it any independent significance bearing on the reasonableness of the board's separate and distinct exercise of judgment. Therefore, I respectfully dissent.

## QUESTIONS

1. On July 28, 2002 the NCS Board voted to approve the enhanced terms of the Genesis offer, which included its agreement to commit (without a fiduciary out) to call a shareholder meeting to vote on the deal knowing that an irrevocable proxy was being given by the controlling block of shares. According to Vice Chancellor Lamb, below, the Board was well informed of its options and the risks that it faced at that time. The board understood that in approving the proposal it was "locking up" the transaction at that time after a long process in which it sought the best deal. Even the majority opinion in the Supreme Court reports that the board concluded that "balancing the potential loss of the Genesis deal against the uncertainty of Omnicare's letter, results in the conclusion that the only reasonable alternative for the Board of Directors is to approve the Genesis transaction." In your opinion in reaching its result in this case, does the majority conclude that the board breached a duty of care? Of loyalty or good faith? What did it do that was wrong?

2. Applying a *Unocal/Unitrin* analysis to the execution of the Genesis agreement, what would you identify as the risk that the Board sought to protect against?

What in the view of the majority makes its choice "unreasonable"? Does the majority opinion in effect hold that *the law required the board to accept the business risk* that Genesis would walk if it did not get the deal protections it sought? How can you support this result from a policy perspective?

3. Should the law always require that shareholders should have available the best price at the time of the vote? (Of course, in most cases this is the practical state of affairs already since shareholders will rarely if ever vote for a lower price if a (materially) higher price is available.) The problem here arises from the willingness of the control shareholders to give irrevocable proxies in order to induce Genesis to make a higher offer. That, of course is what makes the shareholders meeting a mere ritual and makes so important the absence of a fiduciary out in the merger provision requiring the board to call a meeting.

4. To what extent do you think the majority's analysis was affected by the fact that the controlling shareholders did not represent a majority of the equity capital? (The Court notes that the public shareholders represented 80 percent of the equity and that, according to the court, they wanted the Omincare deal. Is this a legitimate consideration in your opinion?

5. Did Genesis have any obligation *not* to ask for the controller's irrevocable proxy, or for the merger term mandating the calling of a shareholders meeting at which the merger would be voted upon (authorized by §251[c]) or to refrain from giving the seller a twenty-four-hour deadline? If these positions did not violate a duty of any sort, what is the significance to the majority of its taking these positions?

6. In holding that a fiduciary out must be included in the merger agreements undertaking to call a meeting, the majority quotes the Restatement (Second) of Contracts §193: "The Restatement explicitly provides that a "promise by a fiduciary to violate his fiduciary duty or a promise that tends to induce such a violation is unenforceable on grounds of public policy." The comments to that section indicate that "[d]irectors and other officials of a corporation act in a fiduciary capacity and are subject to the rule stated in this Section." Back to question 1: what duty did the members of the board violate [or promise to violate] on July 28?

7. The majority opinion holds: "Under the circumstances presented in this case, where a cohesive group of stockholders with majority voting power was irrevocably committed to the merger transaction, "[e]ffective representation of the financial interests of the minority shareholders imposed upon the [NCS board] an affirmative responsibility to protect those minority shareholders' interests." Is not the court *assuming* just what the protecting the interests of the minority required on July 28? Is this not the same question that the Board was asking itself on that day?

8. What is your evaluation of the arguments of the dissents?

9. What effects can we expect this case to have in the sale of corporations with controlling shareholders. See also *Mcmullen v. Beran*, 765 A.2d 910 (Del. 2000).

## 13.7  Proxy Contests for Corporate Control

## 13.7.2  Manipulation of the Proxy Contest

*§13.7.2, page 564: Insert the following material before* Unitrin.

*In re MONY Group Inc., Shareholder Litigation* provides useful insight into the reach of the *Blasius* doctrine and the standard of review when the board postpones a planned shareholder meeting and record date — and counts old proxies obtained in the original meeting — in order to enhance the prospect that a board-endorsed merger will succeed.

IN RE THE MONY GROUP, INC.
SHAREHOLDER LITIGATION
2004 Del. Ch. LEXIS 35 (As revised April 14, 2004)

LAMB, Vice Chancellor.

On February 17, 2004, the court granted a preliminary injunction against a stockholder vote on a proposed merger agreement pending supplemental disclosures concerning payments under officer change-in-control agreements. A week later, the defendant directors postponed until May 18, 2004 the stockholder meeting at which the vote was scheduled to take place and established a new record date of April 8, 2004. The plaintiffs now allege that in doing so, the defendant board deliberately acted to frustrate the stockholder franchise. The plaintiffs also allege that certain disclosures in the supplemental proxy statement are misleading and that the MONY defendants' plan to vote proxies received before the February 17 decision is both unauthorized and inequitable. The majority of these "old" cards were voted in favor of the merger.

The plaintiffs seek an injunction sterilizing the defendants' votes (which constitute approximately 7% of the outstanding shares), requiring the defendants to make corrective disclosures, and invalidating all old proxies.... After carefully considering the record before it, the court finds that a disinterested and independent majority of the defendant directors acted in accordance with their fiduciary duties when they postponed the meeting and set a new record date. Because that decision is not the product of any inequity or unfairness, but rather is one that permits a full and fair vote, the court will review it under the business judgment rule.

The court determines that, as a matter of law, the "old" proxies empower the proxy holders to vote at the postponed meeting. Because the record is incomplete, however, the court is unable to reach any conclusion about the equitable challenges to the use of those proxies at this time, other than to deny an injunction on that basis. Finally, the court concludes that the claims attacking the disclosure in the revised proxy statement lack merit, as they are either factually unsupported or would improperly require the defendant directors to characterize their actions and decisions. . . .

## A. THE PARTIES

Defendant MONY is a publicly traded Delaware corporation engaged in the life insurance business. Defendants Tom H. Barrett, David L. Call, G. Robert Durham, Robert Holland, Jr., James L. Johnson, Robert R. Kiley, Jane C. Pfeiffer, Thomas C. Theobald, Frederick W. Kanner, David M. Thomas, and Margaret M. Foran are outside directors of MONY (the "Outside Directors"). Defendants Michael I. Roth, Samuel J. Foti, and Kenneth M. Levine are inside directors (the "Inside Directors," together with the Outside Directors, the "Board"). Roth is the Chairman and CEO of MONY, Foti is MONY's President and Chief Operating Officer, and Levine is Executive Vice President and Chief Investment Officer of MONY.

Defendant AXA is a Delaware corporation also engaged in the insurance industry. AXA is a wholly owned subsidiary of AXA, S.A., a French corporation. AIMA Acquisition Co. is a wholly owned Delaware subsidiary of AXA created solely to affect the proposed merger.

The plaintiffs, who seek to act as class representatives for all holders of MONY common stock other than the defendants, are MONY common stockholders who have continuously owned MONY common stock during the relevant period. The plaintiffs are E.M. Capital, Inc., Elm Realty, Inc., Congregate Investors, Ltd., Abbot Hill Partners, L.P., Alan Martin, Amanda Kahn-Kirby, The Jewish Foundation for Education of Women, Edward Cantor, and Jerome Muskal.

## B. MONY/AXA MERGER AND ITS FINANCING

On September 17, 2003, MONY and AXA executed and publicly announced a merger agreement. Under certain change-in-control agreements ("CICs"), management of MONY stood to gain approximately $79 million if the merger consummated, of which amounts the three Inside Directors would receive about $47 million.

The agreement provided for a $31 per share all cash acquisition of MONY by AXA. In order to finance this transaction, AXA issued convertible debt securities known as "ORANs" to its stockholders. . . . These ORANs will convert into AXA shares on completion of the acquisition. The ORANs were issued at £12.75, which was a 23% discount to AXA's closing price on September 17, 2003. Should the acquisition not be completed by December 21, 2004, the ORANS will be redeemed at face value plus interest at 2.4% per annum. Since the ORANS were issued, the market price of AXA stock has increased. Thus, persons who hold long positions in ORANs stand to gain a large profit on that investment if the MONY/AXA merger is consummated. Conversely, arbitrageurs who sell ORANs short stand to gain if that same merger is not completed.

... In a February 17, 2004 opinion (the "Opinion"), ... the court held, on the basis of the preliminary record before it, that the Board did indeed meet all of its obligations under *Revlon,* and that its decision that the merger proposal was the best proposal reasonably available was a valid decision within the discretion of the Board. The court did, however, grant a limited injunction, relating solely to proxy statement disclosures concerning payments under the CICs held by officers of MONY....

### D.   INCREASE IN TRADING VOLUME AND ITS EFFECT ON THE VOTE

MONY has approximately 50 million shares of stock outstanding.... In the nine trading days of September 2003 following the announcement of the merger agreement, the average daily trading volume for MONY shares was 1,797,078 shares. In the remaining three months of 2003, the average daily trading volume declined to 326, 535; 175, 741; and 131, 832, respectively....

For reasons not completely explained in the record, trading activity in MONY shares increased dramatically after the original January 2, 2004 record date. Between the beginning of the year and February 13, 2004, the average daily trading volume jumped to 426,050. During the five-day period beginning February 17, 2004, nearly 15 million shares were traded.... All told, trading in MONY shares after the record date, up until February 20, 2004, amounted to approximately 52% of the total number of MONY common shares outstanding....

This pattern of heavy trading gave rise to increasing concern on the part of MONY's proxy solicitor, D.F. King & Co., that MONY would be unable to secure the votes necessary to approve the merger. There are several reasons for this, as explained in the Affidavit of Peter C. Harkins, King's President and CEO. First, when shares trade in the market, they generally trade without a proxy, so that the person acquiring the shares does not obtain the right to vote those shares on the merger. Instead, the power to vote remains with the seller who was the record date holder. Second, persons who sell shares frequently do not vote them. Indeed, many institutional stockholders have a policy against voting shares they no longer own. Thus, the unusually heavy trading volume beginning immediately after the original record date was likely to reduce the pool of potential voters. This, in turn, led to an increase in the percentage of votes *actually cast* that would have to be in favor of the AXA merger in order to obtain the requisite absolute majority of shares outstanding as of the record date....

The plaintiff's claim that the "defendants knew that an anomalous increase in trading in MONY shares was due to holders of ORANs who were purchasing MONY stock at a premium specifically to vote for the merger and obtain a huge return on their ORAN investment at the expense of MONY shareholders....

While the speculative purchase of MONY stock by those long in ORANs is undoubtedly *one* reason for the increase in trading volume of MONY shares, it is not *the sole* reason. Other likely reasons for an increase in trading include the Opinion enjoining the stockholder vote, a downgrade in MONY's credit rating by S&P, ... a change of review status of MONY by A.M. Best, ... the disclosure in the Opinion of the Lincoln Financial Group letters, AXA's February 17 announcement that it would not raise its offer for MONY, and certain institutional voting advisory firm announcements recommending against a vote for the merger.

Moreover, it is not clear that those long ORANs were the only ORAN holders involved in trading MONY stock. As noted by various media services, Schwartz, ... and CSFB, the Board's independent financial advisor, ... those who are short ORANs are incentivized to acquire MONY shares in order to impede the AXA/MONY transaction. Indeed, Highfields, a hedge fund that publicly filed a letter with this court urging it to enjoin MONY from changing the record date (presumably to ensure that the merger was not approved) has an equity stake just short of 5% in MONY, and has a large short position in ORANs. ...

On February 22, 2004, the Board met to discuss the circumstances surrounding the merger. At this meeting, the Board received presentations from CSFB, D.F. King, and outside legal counsel.... Lawyers from Dewey Ballantine and Richards, Layton & Finger, MONY's outside counsel, reviewed the legal principles applicable to the Board's meeting and the status of litigation in this court.... CSFB's presentation again indicated it would issue a fairness opinion in regard to the merger....

King's presentation, made by Harkins, discussed the effect of the increased trading and recommended establishing April 8, 2004 as the new record date and May 18, 2004 as the new date for the special stockholder meeting.... During this presentation, the Board discussed who might buy MONY shares in the time period between the announcement of the new record date and the date itself. Harkins discussed the effect of arbitrageurs' trading in, and accumulation of, MONY shares, specifically those long and *short* ORANs....

Having received the reports, the Board discussed the likely effect on shareholder value based on several hypotheticals proposed by Theobald, an outside director.... The Board discussed options if the merger was not approved: (1) firing senior management and bringing in a new team; (2) keeping the current management team and engaging in further cost-cutting actions; or (3) selling the Company in pieces. The Board then compared estimated stockholder value under these alternatives with the value of the merger.... Following discussions with executive management and CSFB, the Board concluded that none of those possibilities would be likely to result in stockholder value approaching the value that the MONY stockholders would receive in the proposed merger.... The Board thus determined that the revised merger was in the best interests of the MONY stockholders and proceeded to approve it.

The Board then considered whether or not to change the record date. While the Board was partially driven by a desire to enfranchise MONY's current stockholders (who are undoubtedly quite a different group from MONY's stockholders as of the old record date) in the face of a stale record date, . . . it is abundantly clear that the Board made its decision with an eye on approval of the merger. . . .

The Board believed that changing the record date would increase the possibility of the merger getting approved in two ways. First, it would likely increase the percentage of votes cast, thus decreasing the percentage of "yes" votes needed from that group to achieve a majority. Second, the Board surmised that the stockholders of record as of the new record date would be more inclined to vote in favor of the merger than the stockholders of record as of the old record date. . . .

### H.  USE OF OLD PROXIES

On March 30, 2004, MONY filed revised proxy materials with the SEC. These materials indicate that MONY intends to vote proxies received for the cancelled February 24, 2004 special stockholders' meeting at the May 18, 2004 special stockholders' meeting. . . . Fifty-eight percent of the proxies in hand were voted in favor of the original merger agreement. . . .

This action has been challenged by the plaintiffs both on the technical ground that the previously submitted proxies do not allow their use at the May 18, 2004 meeting and on the ground that such use would be inequitable. The record does not reflect that the Board was informed of, or considered, this decision.

## IV.

The shareholder franchise occupies a special place in Delaware corporation law, and our courts are vigilant in policing fiduciary misconduct that has the effect of impeding or interfering with the effectiveness of a stockholder vote. . . . This is particularly the case in matters relating to the election of directors or involving issues of directorial control. . . . In other matters in which directors submit proposals to a stockholder vote, the courts maintain vigilance to ensure that the voting process, which is largely controlled by the board of directors, allows the stockholders a full and fair opportunity to vote. . . .

*Blasius* involved a contest to elect a new board majority and draws its strong doctrinal justification from that context. It is in that context that the pivotal question that Chancellor Allen identified — "the question who, as between the principal and the agent, has authority with respect to a matter of internal corporate governance"[49] — is most heavily implicated. . . .

[W]hen the matter to be voted on does not touch on issues of directorial control, courts will apply the exacting *Blasius* standard sparingly, and only in circumstances in which self-interested or faithless fiduciaries act to deprive stockholders

---

49. *Blasius Indus., Inc., 564 A.2d at 660.*

of a full and fair opportunity to participate in the matter and to thwart what appears to be the will of a majority of the stockholders, as in *State of Wisconsin Investment Board v. Peerless Systems Corporation.*[51] Where such circumstances are not present, the business judgment rule will ordinarily apply in recognition of the fact that directors must continue to manage the business and affairs of the corporation, even with respect to matters that they have placed before the stockholders for a vote.... This notion also recognizes the fact that in the context of a stockholder vote a board of directors must perform a myriad of ministerial functions in order to ensure an orderly voting process which all, in some way, indirectly affect the vote. For example, scheduling the meeting and record dates, deciding on a location for the meeting, choosing inspectors of elections, or retaining proxy solicitors are all decisions that directors are often called upon to make that could be seen as affecting the shareholder vote....

[S]etting a new meeting and record date, by itself, does not fall within this category of [acts prohibited by equity]. The board owes its fiduciary duties to the corporation and its stockholders, not merely to a set of stockholders as of a certain record date. While actions such as coercing stockholders preclude a "full and fair opportunity to vote," ... setting a new meeting date and record date, by itself, does not do so. Instead, in the proper circumstances, doing so can provide for a vote that is, for lack of a better term, fuller and fairer, in that more stockholders having a direct interest in the outcome of the vote are likely to vote. This is

---

51. *2000 Del. Ch. LEXIS 170 (Sept. 27, 2000).* In *Peerless* the board of directors made a proposal to increase by 1,000,000 the number of shares available for issuance though the company's existing option plan. This proposal was included in the proxy statement for the company's annual meeting. A large institutional stockholder, SWIB, opposed this proposal and wrote to the other stockholders urging them to vote against it. When the annual meeting was convened, the vote was running against this proposal, although the overall turnout on this issue was lower than on the other, noncontroversial issues before the meeting. Acting on his own, as chairman of the meeting, the CEO (who was presumably eligible for grants under the plan) closed the polls as to the other matters but left the polls open on the controversial proposal and adjourned the meeting for 30 days. While he later claimed to have discussed doing so with the other directors, the board as a whole did not consider the matter. The company did not publicize these actions and did not even inform SWIB until 12 days later. During the adjournment, the company continued to solicit votes in favor of the proposal as well as revocations of previously submitted votes against it. When the meeting was reconvened, the proposal passed by a slim margin.

Although *Peerless* does not involve issues touching on control, the court applied the *Blasius* standard because it perceived that the self-interested CEO's actions were taken to interfere with the stockholder vote, *which at the time was running against the proposal.* The Chancellor recognized that the corporation could have simply reproposed the matter at another meeting. Nevertheless, he viewed the totality of the actions taken in connection with the adjournment as evidencing an improper purpose. Thus, he cast on the defendants the burden of showing a compelling justification for their actions.

*Blasius* is not easily or readily applied outside the context of matters touching on directorial control, as its demanding standard could unduly limit the legitimate exercise of directorial power and discretion in other contexts. Nevertheless, in any voting context, actions taken for the purpose of interfering with a full and fair exercise of the stockholder franchise will run afoul of basic equitable limitations found in our law. *Schnell, 285 A.2d 437.*

especially true in this case where a clear majority of shareholders who have voted before the postponement expressed approval of the merger. . . .

Viewed in its entirety, the record suggests no circumstances requiring application of the stringent *Blasius* standard in this nonelection context. The decision to change the record date was not a unilateral decision but was made in response to, among other things, this court's Opinion. It was made by a disinterested, independent Board upon the recommendation of its advisors. The decision of the outside directors was unanimous, while all three interested directors abstained. . . . And, importantly, the Board was not thwarting the will of the MONY stockholders, which at that time, *supported* the transaction.

Moreover, the judgment to set new meeting and record dates appears reasonable in the circumstances. Given the circumstances — the Opinion, the renegotiation of the merger agreement resulting in terms more favorable to shareholders, the downgrade in MONY's ratings and potential for future downgrade, the deterioration of MONY's financial performance, the turnover in MONY's shares and resulting staleness of the record date, the need to provide additional disclosure to MONY's stockholders, the fact that no other bidder had emerged — there was ample room for the Board to make a good faith and honest determination that approval of the merger, and a change in the record date in order to achieve that result, was in the best interests of the corporation.

E.    THE *UNOCAL* STANDARD AND THE CHANGE IN THE RECORD DATE

. . .

. . . Cases in which both *Blasius* and *Unocal* review are implicated involve measures by a board with the primary purpose to preclude or, at least, impede the effective exercise of the shareholder franchise *and* the board's control of the . . . corporation is at play. Here, if the merger is consummated, none of the directors will retain their positions with the surviving company. . . . Thus, the court concludes that the *Unocal* standard of review does not apply.

Nevertheless, even if the *Unocal* standard did apply, the Board's actions clearly meet that test. The *Unocal* standard, as interpreted by *Unitrin, Inc. v. American General Corporation,* . . . first requires the court to determine if a defensive measure is preclusive or coercive. If so, it will be deemed draconian, and not protected by the presumptions of the business judgment rule. If it is not draconian, the defensive measure must be within a range of reasonableness, or proportional to an identified threat.

The Board clearly identified a threat — the possibility that a merger that the Board twice reasonably deemed to be in the best interests of the Company and its stockholders, and which was supported by a majority of stockholders who had voted, would fail to win approval, in large part due to a stale record date. Its response, to change the record date, was not preclusive of a full and fair vote; if anything, it enfranchised those stockholders who were equity owners of the corporation but who could not vote. Finally, the Board's response was taken on

the advice of its proxy solicitor, and is certainly, and within a range of reasonableness.

. . .

The plaintiffs cite a number of reasons why MONY's plan to use "old" proxy
cards is either legally invalid or an inequitable manipulation of the voting process
during a proxy fight. These claims were presented for the first time in briefs filed
in conjunction with the motion for preliminary injunction because the plaintiffs
apparently did not anticipate the issue and, so, became aware of MONY's intention only after MONY filed its revised proxy materials with the SEC, which was
after the completion of discovery in this matter.

Notwithstanding the lack of a factual record about the decision-making process
behind this expression of intent, all parties have urged the court to render a
decision about the continuing validity of the "old" proxies and the propriety
of their use at the postponed meeting. . . . The purpose of doing so is to clear
the air and to avoid the possibility of a post-election review of proxies on the basis
of these claims. The court concludes that it is able, at this time, to pass on the
questions of legal validity and it will do so on a summary judgment basis as
the factual record in that regard is clear and undisputed. That discussion follows.
The court cannot, however, make any determination at this time about the equitable claims advanced by the plaintiffs, since the factual record is a blank slate.
For example, it is unclear how the decision was made to rely on "old" provides,
who made it, what factors were considered, whether it was thought to disadvan-
tage the opponents of the merger proposal, etc. In short, there is no record from
which the court could determine whether this decision is of the type normally and
routinely undertaken during the course of a proxy solicitation, in which case a
conclusion that the "old" proxies continue to be valid might end the inquiry. . . .

The arguments over legal validity turn on whether the form of proxy used by
MONY continues to confer power on the named proxy holders at the new meeting
and with respect to shares owned on the new record date. . . .

The plaintiffs argue that the proxy card is no longer valid because the agency
relationship was limited to voting shares "owned on the record date" at the time
he card was signed, *i.e.,* the old record date. The language of the proxy card,
however, is not limited to January 2, 2004, the old record date. Instead, it is more
general in nature and can be seen to extend to any record date for the special
meeting. Thus, the proxy card continues to authorize the holder thereof to vote to
the extent to which a person signing the card continues to own stock on the new
record date. . . .

The plaintiffs also argue that the revised merger agreement is not the agreement
referred to on the reverse side of the proxy card. This is a hypertechnical reading
of the language of the proxy card. Surely, to any common understanding,
the slightly amended merger agreement, whose terms are in all respects more

favorable to the stockholders than the original merger agreement, is the same agreement referred to on that card. The omission of the phrase "as it might be favorably amended" does not deprive the agent of power to vote.

The plaintiffs further argue that the proxies only extend to the February 24 meeting, or any adjournment or postponement thereof, and that the May 18 meeting is a *new,* not *postponed* meeting. Although documents in the record prepared by MONY or its agents occasionally refer to the May 18 meeting as a new meeting, it is clear the term is used to refer to a meeting scheduled after the postponement of the February 24 meeting.... The May 18 meeting is simply a postponement of the February 24 meeting.

The plaintiffs final "technical" argument is that the old proxies were obtained based on disclosures the Opinion found misleading. Although this does not limit the agency authority granted by the old proxies, it does highlight a concern that those who submitted proxies be made aware of the additional disclosures. The preliminary revised proxy statement contains the additional disclosures, but presents them in a way that does not highlight them or their existence. To comply with the Opinion, the revised proxy materials should include a statement clearly visible to stockholders directing their attention to the supplemental disclosures made in response to the Opinion. The court assumes this will be done without the need for a formal order....

## V.

The plaintiffs ... argue that the proxy materials fail to disclose that the Board's primary reason for changing the record date "was to enable them to gerrymander the vote by enabling a large number of ORAN holders and arbitrageurs to vote on the Merger." ... The factual record does not support this allegation.... As already discussed, the Board met on February 22 to discuss the circumstances affecting the merger. The record shows, as disclosed in the amended proxy materials, that at this meeting, the Board considered numerous factors in deciding 'whether to keep the original record date with a short adjournment of the special meeting or to set a new record date and postpone the meeting'.... Notably, the amended proxy materials clearly state that the status of the vote on the merger was addressed at the Board meeting and was cited as one of the reasons the Board considered in making its decision to reset the record and meeting dates....

The plaintiffs next argue that the Board failed to disclose that the ORAN holders had divergent interests from the MONY stockholders with respect to the merger. The plaintiffs argue that the primary interest of the ORAN holders is to ensure that the merger is approved because the ORANs are convertible to AXA stock if the merger is consummated, thus enabling investors who are long in the ORANs to obtain a substantial profit based upon the difference in the price paid for the ORANs and the closing price of AXA's common stock. The plaintiffs argue that the Board had the duty to disclose that the ORAN holders' financial interests differed from the interests of the MONY stockholders.

. . . Proxy statements need not disclose "facts known or reasonably available to the stockholders." . . . As noted in the plaintiffs' brief, news articles were published in mid-February that described the nature of the ORANs, the interests of the ORAN holders in the merger, and how ORAN holders and arbitrageurs were purchasing large amounts of MONY stock in order to influence n96 the outcome of the merger. . . .

The plaintiffs argue that the Board's statement in the amended proxy materials that it considered "the fact that many current MONY stockholders would not be able to vote on the merger due to the extraordinary volume of trading of MONY common stock since the original January 2, 2004 record date" is misleading because it does not distinguish the five-day period in February when trading was unusually high. This claim also lacks support in the record. . . .

The amended proxy statement discloses that one of the factors that the Board considered when making its decision to change the record date was the potential for further disenfranchisement of MONY stockholders if the meeting date was delayed and the record date maintained. The Board cited the following three reasons for its concern: (i) the Opinion required additional disclosure, (ii) such disclosure would take time to prepare and file with the SEC, and (iii) the heavy trading volume of MONY shares and the expectation that it would continue.

The plaintiffs argue that this statement is misleading because additional disclosure required by the court could have been accomplished quickly and did not require a delay of the meeting. The plaintiffs also argue that the Board did not disclose a basis for the expectation that the heavy trading would continue and that in fact the heavy trading volume did not continue after the Board announced the new record date.

This claim also lacks support in the record. At the hearing on April 6, 2004, counsel for MONY stated that the additional disclosure material filed with the SEC on March 11 had been approved only that very morning by the SEC. This suggests that it was reasonable for the Board to allow time for SEC clearance. Moreover, the Board was advised that there was insufficient time to prepare appropriate disclosures and clear the SEC if it simply adjourned the special meeting. . . . Harkins also advised the Board of the substantial turnover in MONY shares since January 2 and the negative effect that this might have on the success of the merger. . . .

Furthermore, the Board had no way of knowing at its February 22 meeting when the heightened trading activity would end. It is unreasonable for the plaintiffs to now argue that the Board's disclosure was misleading because a contemplated event did not actually happen. At the time of the Board meeting, the volume of trading was high and the Board could not have predicted that the average daily trading volume would return to normal levels after February 23. . . .

For the foregoing reasons, the plaintiffs have not established a reasonable likelihood of success on the merits of any of their claims. To the limited extent described in Section IV.F, summary judgment will be entered in favor of the defendants. . . .

## 13.8   The Takeover Arms Race Continues

## 13.8.2   Mandatory Pill Redemption Bylaws

*§13.8.2, page 576: Insert the following material at the end of the section:*

### NOTE ON *HOLLINGER INT'L, INC.*

*Hollinger Int'l, Inc. v. Black,* 844 A.2d 1022 (Del. Ch. 2004), provides an ironic contrast to the *Fleming* case and mandatory pill redemption bylaws.

Through his control of a parent company, Hollinger, Inc., Conrad M. Black was also the controlling shareholder of Hollinger International. Inc., a Delaware public company. International owned a number of important newspapers including the London *Daily Telegraph.* As it happened, Frederick and David Barclay, two wealthy English businessmen, were very interested in buying the *Telegraph,* but Black, who served as CEO of both Hollinger and International, had declined to negotiate with them, stating that the newspaper was not for sale.

About this same time several large shareholders of International accused Black of diverting to himself substantial sums of company money through various self-dealing transactions and demanded that the International board investigate the matter and take action. A Special Committee of the board was established, which conducted an investigation and concluded that the charges against Black had a basis in fact. Its counsel, Richard Breeden, former chairman of the SEC, began negotiations with Black. To attempt to settle this matter, Black formally agreed, *inter alia*, to repay certain funds to International, resign as CEO (while retaining his position as Chairman of the Board), and to lead an effort to develop a value-maximizing transaction that would benefit all of the company's shareholders ratably (such as a sale of the entire company). Shortly after making the contract, Black purported to rescind it, claiming he had been coerced.

Black then embarked on an effort to sell his interest in the holding company, Hollinger, Inc., to the Barclay brothers. When Hollinger International's board discovered Black's intention it formed a so-called Corporate Review Committee ("CRC") vested with broad powers, including the authority to adopt a shareholder rights plan that would give the board power to block Black from selling his control stake. Under the terms of the pill a change in control of a controlling shareholder (Hollinger, Inc.) was deemed to trigger the International "pill."

With this defense in place, the International board would be free to negotiate a sale of the *Telegraph* itself.

In response, Black caused his holding company to file a written consent enacting bylaw amendments that purported to dissolve the CRC and henceforth would require unanimous board approval of measures such as the rights plan that might have blocked Black's ability to sell Hollinger, Inc. or his stock in Hollinger, Inc.

These facts raise the interesting question whether a controlling shareholder may exercise its voting power in order to protect its own interest to achieve a control premium in the (indirect) sale of its interest in the subsidiary (an interest which of course the black letter law generally recognizes as valid, despite the old *Perlman v. Feldmann* case). Of course, it is one thing simply to find a buyer for a controlling interest and another to take action to prevent the subsidiary itself from finding or accepting a transaction that would benefit all of its shareholders ratably, as Mr. Black was attempting to do.

The Delaware courts have dealt only a little with versions of the question of how far can a controlling shareholder go to try to assure that it (or he) can sell his control stake for a premium by preventing the subsidiary from selling itself to the same interested buyer. See *Thorpe v. CERBCO, Inc.*, 676 A.2d 436 (Del. 1996). See also *Brown v. Halbert*, 76 Cal. Rptr. 781 (Cal. Ct. App. 1969); E. Elhauge, *The Triggering Function of the Sale of Control Doctrine*, 59 U. Chi. L. Rev. 1465 (1992)

For good or ill, Vice Chancellor Leo Strine did not need in his *Hollinger* opinion to generalize very broadly on this question, since in this case Black had signed a formal agreement with the Hollinger International board (his purported rescission was declared ineffective) and his action in enacting or purporting to enact a bylaw was deemed to be a violation of that contract and also an action taken in an attempt to thwart the board from uncovering or taking action to remedy his earlier breaches of fiduciary duty. In these circumstances, the respectable arguments that a controller might have legitimately take action to protect its claim to a control premium were simply inapposite. Thus the *Hollinger* court invalidated Black's bylaws on the grounds of Black's contractual breach and his fiduciary improprieties.

## QUESTIONS

1. As a *matter of policy,* is there any reason why a bylaw requiring unanimous board consent for major company decisions should be invalid if it is in the corporation's original bylaws (assuming there is no *Hollinger*-style contract to prevent it)? If the bylaw is a midstream amendment adopted by general shareholder vote not dominated by a single shareholder? If it is adopted midstream by a controlling shareholder through consent action pursuant to Section 228?

2. Whatever your views of sound policy, in your opinion which of the foregoing alternatives would be legally valid?

3. Recall the existence of cases holding that shareholders may vote in their narrow selfish interest. This principle when applied to controlling shareholders is in tension with the powerful fiduciary duty of the controlling shareholder that applies whenever the controller engages in self-dealing transactions. Here Black was not exercising his power to elect directors or approve a merger, but he was in a sense exercising his voting power. Should that exercise of power be subjected to a

fiduciary duty of fairness? If so, is it fair to protect his "right," so to speak, to a control premium in this way?

## FURTHER NOTE ON *HOLLINGER INTERNATIONAL*

Conrad Black also argued independently that, under the *Unocal* case, that the action of the Hollinger International board in adopting a poison pill could not stand because his selling of his interest in Hollinger, Inc. (or selling Hollinger, Inc. itself) could not be deemed a legitimate *threat* to International of any kind, since he had an acknowledged right as a controlling shareholder to sell his interest in International at a premium and not share that premium. Black argued that to do so would be no wrong to International or its minority shareholders. Thus, the board could not properly take action designed to prevent him from exercising this claimed right.

Black's argument poses an interesting question. On the one hand, it seems plausible that Black (put aside his skullduggery for the moment) has the right he claims. Compare *Thorpe v. CERBCO, supra.* Allowing a board of directors to take aim at a long-term shareholder who is simply seeking to sell his interest certainly seems inappropriate. See *Condec Corp. v. Lunkenheimer Co.*, 230 A.2d 769 (Del. Ch. 1967). Does not the board's fiduciary duty run to him as much as to other shareholders? Is it right for the board to prefer the minority to Black when Black is only trying to exercise what he claims, with support, is a recognized right?

But on the other hand, does Hollinger International itself have a practical business interest in the transaction (the sale of its asset, the *Telegraph,* to the Barclay brothers)? It is, after all, the owner of the asset. Is this interest not sufficient justification for the board to take discriminatory action authorized by *Unocal* and *Moran v. Household Industries?*

In the *Hollinger* case, this abstract question was neither presented nor answered, since the facts did not show an innocent controller simply seeking permissibly (if ungenerously) to sell his stake. Instead, it showed Conrad Black as a person who both had violated his agreement with the Board and who appeared to have engaged in elaborate and costly self-dealing transaction that might fairly be characterized as looting. The character of the controller as an apparent looter suffused the Court of Chancery's approach to the problem. Thus, in this instance the adoption of the pill was upheld as valid in the circumstances.